BUILDING
A BETTER
WORLD

BUILDING A BETTER WORLD

AN INTRODUCTION TO THE LABOUR MOVEMENT IN CANADA

THIRD EDITION

STEPHANIE ROSS, LARRY SAVAGE,
ERROL BLACK & JIM SILVER

FERNWOOD PUBLISHING
HALIFAX & WINNIPEG

Editing: Jane Butler
Cover design: John van der Woude
Printed and bound in Canada

Published by Fernwood Publishing
32 Oceanvista Lane, Black Point, Nova Scotia, B0J 1B0
and 748 Broadway Avenue, Winnipeg, Manitoba, R3G 0X3

www.fernwoodpublishing.ca

Fernwood Publishing Company Limited gratefully acknowledges the financial support of the Government of Canada through the Canada Book Fund and the Canada Council for the Arts, the Nova Scotia Department of Communities, Culture and Heritage, the Manitoba Department of Culture, Heritage and Tourism under the Manitoba Publishers Marketing Assistance Program and the Province of Manitoba, through the Book Publishing Tax Credit, for our publishing program.

Library and Archives Canada Cataloguing in Publication

Black, Errol, author
Building a better world: an introduction to the labour movement
in Canada / Stephanie Ross, Larry Savage, Errol Black and
Jim Silver. — Third edition.

Revision of: Black, Errol. Building a better world.
Includes bibliographical references and index.
ISBN 978-1-55266-787-3 (paperback)

1. Labor unions—Canada. 2. Labor movement—Canada.
I. Ross, Stephanie, 1970–, author II. Silver, Jim, 1946–, author
III. Savage, Larry, 1977–, author IV. Title.

HD6524.B52 2015   331.880971   C2015-904249-6

CONTENTS

LIST OF ACRONYMS AND INITIALISMS

ACCL	All-Canadian Congress of Labour
ACORN	Association of Community Organizations for Reform Now
AFL	American Federation of Labor
BCGEU	B.C. Government and Service Employees' Union
CAUT	Canadian Association of University Teachers
CAW	Canadian Auto Workers
CBC	Canadian Broadcasting Corporation
CCCL	Canadian and Catholic Confederation of Labour
CCF	Co-operative Commonwealth Federation
CFL	Canadian Federation of Labour
CFLR	Canadian Foundation for Labour Rights
CIC	Citizenship and Immigration Canada
CIO	Committee for Industrial Organization, renamed Congress of Industrial Organizations
CLAC	Christian Labour Association of Canada
CLC	Canadian Labour Congress
CPC	Communist Party of Canada
CSD	Centrale des syndicats démocratiques
CSN	Confédération des syndicats nationaux
CSQ	Centrale des syndicats du Québec
CTW	Change to Win Federation
CUPE	Canadian Union of Public Employees
CUPW	Canadian Union of Postal Workers
FTQ	Quebec Federation of Labour

GMM	general membership meeting
GUF	Global Union Federations
HRSDC	Human Resources and Skills Development Canada
IDIA	*Industrial Disputes Investigation Act*
IFA	International Framework Agreements
ISS	International Service Systems, a cleaning company
ITUC	International Trade Union Confederation
IWW	Industrial Workers of the World
LFS	Labour Force Survey
MAI	Multilateral Agreement on Investment
NAFTA	North American Free Trade Agreement
NAICS	North American Industry Classification System
NDP	New Democratic Party
NUPGE	National Union of Public and General Employees
OBU	One Big Union
OECD	Organisation for Economic Co-operation and Development
OPSEU	Ontario Public Service Employees Union
PQ	Parti Québécois
PSAC	Public Service Alliance of Canada
RCMP	Royal Canadian Mounted Police
RWDSU	Retail, Wholesale and Department Store Union
SEIU	Service Employees International Union
SFL	Saskatchewan Federation of Labour
SPC	Socialist Party of Canada
TFWP	Temporary Foreign Worker Program
TLC	Trades and Labour Congress
TNC	transnational corporation
UAW	United Auto Workers
UFCW	United Food and Commercial Workers
UI	Unemployment Insurance
UNITE HERE	the union serving hotel and service workers
USW	United Steelworkers
WAC	Workers' Action Centre
WIRD	Workplace Information Research Division
WTO	World Trade Organization
WUL	Workers' Unity League

LIST OF FIGURES

ACKNOWLEDGEMENTS

This third edition of *Building a Better World* marks an important transition. Jim Silver and the late Errol Black wrote the first edition back in 2001. The book quickly became a staple in university-based Labour Studies programs and union-based education courses across the country, sparking important discussions about the past, present and future of Canada's labour movement. A second edition followed in 2008.

After Errol Black passed away in 2012, Jim Silver and Fernwood's Wayne Antony approached us about spearheading a third edition that would address the teaching needs of a new generation of Labour Studies students, researchers and union and worker activists. We were honoured to be asked and excited to take on the challenge.

While the critical edge of previous editions remains, this new edition restructures the book in important ways, reorganizing chapters around a set of basic questions concerning Canada's labour movement. There is much new content, including questions for discussion at the end of each chapter.

We would like to thank David Camfield and Ingo Schmidt for their ideas on revising the book and Joe Young for his help with tables and graphs. A special thank you is reserved for Nick Ruhloff-Queiruga, whose research assistance proved invaluable.

The folks at Fernwood publishing, as always, have been incredibly accommodating. Thank you to Beverley Rach and Debbie Mathers for their production assistance, Jane Butler for copy editing and John van der Woude for the cover design. We are proud to be associated with one of the leading progressive publishers in the country.

We trust readers will appreciate the revisions in this new edition and hope the ideas, arguments and perspectives put forward will inspire lively debate and discussion in classrooms, union halls and workplaces across Canada.

— *Stephanie Ross and Larry Savage*

ABOUT THE AUTHORS

Stephanie Ross is associate professor of work and labour studies and co-director of the Global Labour Research Centre at York University. She is also president of the Canadian Association for Work and Labour Studies.

Larry Savage is director of the Centre for Labour Studies at Brock University and a former member of the executive council of the Ontario Federation of Labour.

The late **Errol Black** was a professor, community activist, author, political activist, unionist and city councillor. He was also a co-founder of the Canadian Centre for Policy Alternatives–Manitoba. Errol wrote a great deal about politics, economics and labour, including the first two editions of *Building a Better World*. Throughout his life, Errol was determined, principled, energetic and deeply intelligent in his opposition to social injustice.

Jim Silver is a professor and chair of the Department of Urban and Inner-City Studies at the University of Winnipeg. He is also a co-founder and board member of the Canadian Centre for Policy Alternatives–Manitoba.

To the memory of Errol Black,
trade unionist, labour economist, community activist

CHAPTER 1

WHAT IS A UNION?

O n March 19, 2012, Toronto's library workers, members of the Canadian Union of Public Employees (CUPE) Local 4948, set up picket lines that resulted in the temporary closure and loss of service at ninety-eight library branches across the city. The city's 2,300 library workers, three quarters of whom are women and half of whom work part-time, voted to strike after failing to reach an agreement with the city's library board on the content of a new contract.

The union didn't want to strike. Union members understood that their action would disrupt the lives of library patrons but felt they had little choice. Toronto Mayor Rob Ford had swept to power two years earlier on a right-wing anti-union platform calling for cuts to and privatization of city services. His administration sent clear signals that library services were not a priority, despite the fact that the city's library system is the most widely used in the world (Harden 2013: 138–42). Toronto librarians had been working to convert more part-time jobs to full-time to improve the living standards of library workers. This goal would prove more difficult in the face of an unsupportive mayor and escalating budget difficulties.

To resist these pressures, the workers would need to work in a united fashion. Individual workers have little power but collectively they are able to put weight behind their demands. Labour unions provide workers with a vehicle to promote their collective interests with respect to employers, amplifying their ability to influence their terms and conditions of work through a legally binding collective agreement. Without a collective agreement, workers are left to fend for themselves in the workplace, subject to arbitrary management rules and procedures, with few rights and even less power. As a rule, unions are stronger when their members exhibit greater solidarity with one another, seeing and identifying themselves as a group worthy of mutual support and pursuing collective goals and objectives. Solidarity grows even stronger when union members attract the support of community stakeholders and other groups of workers.

Toronto library workers were able to count on the solidarity of prominent authors and members of the Writers' Union of Canada, who organized a "read-in" and rally in front of the downtown Toronto Reference Library to draw attention to the labour dispute and highlight the value of properly funded libraries. Best-selling Canadian author Margaret Atwood tweeted her support for the striking workers, and at the rally library patrons took turns at a microphone praising the city's library workers and explaining why the services provided by members of Local 4948 were important to them personally. According to media reports, a "rather adorable little boy" stole the show when he asked the crowd of supportive onlookers, if libraries close, "where will the learning happen?" (Dart 2012). Galvanizing support from members of the community who rely on library services was a key part of the union's bargaining strategy. Library workers understood that without a supportive public they could not pressure the city's library board to commit to maintaining adequate library services. This idea was encapsulated on library workers' picket signs: "Libraries work because we do."

After an eleven-day strike, the library board agreed that no full-time positions would be converted to part-time and even agreed to create a limited number of new full-time positions. The board also dropped its proposal to weaken benefit provisions for members, but it did manage to win cuts in employment security provisions for library workers with less than eleven years in the system (Harden 2013: 145).

Strikes, demonstrations and battles with employers are important, but they represent only a small part of what unions do. While these defensive tactics tend to grab the greatest number of headlines, what unions do day in and day out for their members, workers in general, and the marginalized in society tends to pass unnoticed. However, the example of the Toronto library workers' successful struggle to both protect library services and improve the working lives of library workers points to several key themes about unions and the labour movement.

WORKERS NEED TO ACT COLLECTIVELY TO IMPROVE THEIR WORKING LIVES

The right to join unions and bargain collectively with employers, the eight-hour day, employment standards legislation, workers' compensation, health and safety legislation, pay equity and anti-discrimination laws were all achieved through workers' collective struggles. In unionized workplaces, unions provide a collective voice for workers through negotiation of collective agreements and legally enforceable grievance procedures designed to obtain redress and justice in response to unfair or unilateral employer conduct. The skills required to operate a union are taught to members through union-organized training and educational programs, thus reinforcing the union's strength and capacity in the workplace.

BEYOND THE WORKPLACE, UNIONS ARE A KEY VEHICLE FOR ACHIEVING A BETTER WORLD

Democracy, freedom, social justice and equality are some of the core values and principles of the labour movement. Organized labour's legacy can be found in the many reforms fought for and achieved throughout history: public healthcare and public education, lifting of restrictions on the rights of citizens to vote and run for office, employment insurance, public pension plans and anti-discrimination laws. These achievements have improved the lives of all workers regardless of union membership. Today, unions continue to advocate and act for social justice, making representations to governments and their agencies for increases in minimum wages, tougher health and safety measures in workplaces, more resources for child care, health, education and affordable housing, improvements in employment insurance and social assistance, more resources for training and education, and expanded opportunities for young people and people with disabilities. Unions also play an important role in campaigns to fight racism and other forms of discrimination and actions by corporations and governments that damage or undermine the living conditions and rights of working people and their families in Canada and abroad. Indeed, international solidarity is the key to confronting global capital and ensuring that social justice and economic equality are available to workers regardless of where in the world they reside.

UNIONS FACE IMPORTANT CHALLENGES THAT MUST BE OVERCOME FOR THE SAKE OF UNION MEMBERS AND FOR BROADER SOCIETY

There can be no doubt that the labour movement's historic gains are now in danger. Decades of employer and government assaults on union rights and freedoms have undermined the capacity of unions to enhance and defend economic and political gains for working people. This in turn has facilitated the growing income and wealth gap between the super rich and the rest of society. Corporations and governments have waged a concerted and long-term campaign to curtail workers' rights and undermine the power of unions. Employers justify this attack by arguing that labour rights and unions impede business flexibility in workplaces and impair Canada's ability to compete in international markets. Despite resistance from unions, employers have met with considerable success. The curtailment of union rights is especially evident in our political system, where changes to labour relations legislation have created greater obstacles to unionization and weakened the capacity of workers to conduct their affairs. It is also reflected in declining union density rates and in changes to some collective agreements—changes that have reduced unions' and workers' control over practices such as contracting out and allocation of opportunities (access to training or promotions, for instance) within workplaces. The labour movement's growing weakness can be directly correlated to increased levels of income inequality, thus pitting various members of the working class ("privileged" unionized workers and precarious non-union workers) against one another in what Thomas Walkom (2010) has described as a form of "reverse class resentment."

Despite these challenges, unions continue to mobilize their resources and apply pressure for greater social justice in an effort to improve conditions for workers, the homeless, the hungry, the poor and the disadvantaged. Indeed, unions are one of the few institutions in society that have the organizational and financial capacity to act as an effective counterweight against the power of employers and governments. This unique power is precisely what makes them a target.

In the chapters that follow, we pose several basic questions about labour unions intended to provide a comprehensive overview of the Canadian union movement's history, structure, purpose, goals, impacts, strategies and political orientations. Chapter 2, "Understanding Unions," looks at the unique position of workers within capitalist societies and surveys competing perspectives on unions as organizations created by workers. It details various theoretical positions on their "proper" role and evaluates their explanatory potential. The next two chapters focus on labour history. Chapter 3, "Early Union Struggles in Canada," examines workers' first attempts to defend themselves against the advance of capitalist industrialization,

FIGURE 1.1 UNION DENSITY AND INCOME INEQUALITY IN CANADA

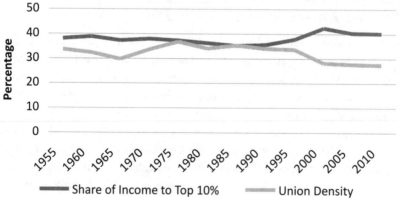

Sources: Income Data: Alvaredo et al. 2014; Union Density Data: Statistics Canada/Social Science Federation of Canada 1983; OECD 2015

looking at how these struggles shaped workers' relationships with employers, governments and specific segments of the working class and caused serious political fissures along the way. Chapter 4, "From Keynesianism to Neoliberalism: Union Breakthroughs and Challenges," documents the increased strength of the labour movement in the postwar period and its decline in more recent decades. It details the factors that stalled the forward momentum of unions, placing them on the defensive and weakening their capacity to shape the course of events in the economy and in society. These chapters provide the context for more contemporary discussions, beginning with Chapter 5, "Unions in the Workplace," which examines the core workplace functions of unions (organizing, collective bargaining, grievance handling and strikes), describing both the sources of union power in the workplace and the mechanisms through which that power is exercised. Chapter 6, "Unions and Political Action," explores some of the key political orientations in the labour movement, describing how unions engage in electoral strategies, social movement-based strategies and judicial strategies in an effort to influence the broader political, social and economic context. Chapter 7, "How Do Unions Work?," delves into the structure of the Canadian labour movement, from union locals to parent unions, and from labour councils to union centrals. It examines the question of union democracy, explaining how decisions are made within labour movement structures. Chapter 8, "What Difference Do Unions Make?," explains the various ways that unions advance equality and improve wages, benefit entitlements, employment standards, occupational health and safety standards and social programs for both union members and non-union workers. Chapter 9, "Who Belongs To Unions? Who Doesn't and Why?," provides a demographic portrait of the contemporary union movement, outlining various barriers to unionization and exploring employers' union avoidance strategies. Finally, Chapter 10, "The Future of Unions: Decline or Renewal?," evaluates the prospects for union renewal given the current hostile political and economic climate, and assesses the strengths and weaknesses of new approaches to organizing, bargaining and representation. This concluding chapter explains why it is important that unions rejuvenate and move forward while emphasizing the critical challenges (both internal and external) that must be met so that this can happen.

As the authors of this book, our aim is not just to provide a richer and deeper understanding of the role and impact of unions and the labour movement in Canada. It is also to emphasize, using evidence from past and present struggles, the crucial contribution of unionism to the shaping of a more just and equitable society and the stake that all of us have in maintaining a strong labour movement.

CHAPTER 2

UNDERSTANDING UNIONS

As organizations created by working-class people, unions have emerged wherever capitalism has. The development of capitalism as a particular kind of economic and social system has driven workers to organize themselves into unions to defend and promote their common economic and political interests. Today, unions still emerge in opposition to employers, often provide a deeper critique of capital and the state, and put forward an alternative vision of the workplace and the community.

Historically, the growth of unions in western industrial societies reflects the development and evolution of the working class—created through the transformation from an agricultural to an industrial economy. Beginning in the mid 1850s, immigration from the British Isles, France, Eastern and Southern Europe and the movement of large segments of the male population working on farms into the wage-labour sector of the economy caused the working class in Canada to grow significantly. Women further expanded the ranks of wageworkers: while many worked for wages in the early industrial era, the end of the Second World War saw increasing numbers of women seeking and remaining in paid employment, whether by choice or necessity. The postwar years also saw a significant increase in the proportion of the paid labour force of non-European descent—workers from Latin America, the Caribbean, Asia and Africa. In other words, the working class has consistently increased in its demographic diversity over the past 150 years. Recent decades have also seen significant changes in the industrial and occupational composition of waged employment. While employment in the goods-producing sector (manufacturing, construction, forestry, agriculture, fishing, mining) was more typical before the Second World War, since that time there has been significant growth in service-sector employment (retail trade, personal services, business services, health, education, social services).

Class is a complex concept. For the purposes of this book, we adopt a definition of the working class that includes more than just the people actually engaged in wage labour. Our broader definition includes those dependent on wages for survival but it excludes managers who exercise a significant degree of control over workers. That means members of a family—children or a spouse who stays at home to do unpaid domestic labour—are part of the working class if they depend on the wage of a breadwinner. That also means that people employed by others in professional occupations, like accountants or engineers, may also be considered working class, even if their autonomy and elevated salary levels are significantly higher than those we typically regard as employed in working-class jobs. Retirees and the unemployed can be working-class too, even if they aren't working. The experience of being in the working class is widely varied, ranging from that of a single parent on social assistance or working part-time for minimum wage, struggling to raise three kids, to a married couple, one a unionized autoworker and the other a unionized nurse, who are able to live a comfortable "middle-class" lifestyle. But all have in common a relationship to employers that fundamentally shapes their lives and their economic and political power.

What is it about the shared working-class experience that drives workers to create unions? Amidst the enormous variety in the kinds and conditions of work, and the types of workers themselves, the basic relationship between workers and employers remains essentially unchanged since the early days of capitalism. Workers sell their labour-power—their capacity to work—to employers in exchange for wages. Individual workers compete with each other in the labour market to be hired while employers seek to hire qualified workers at a price they prefer. As German philosopher Karl Marx aptly observed, worker and employer appear to meet as equals in the labour market and to enter freely into a bargain that establishes the rate at which workers will be paid in exchange for a given period at work. However, the appearance of equality and freedom is an illusion; because capitalist employers own the means of production—factories, warehouses, office buildings, machines, technology—and legally control access to them, workers' livelihoods are dependent upon employers agreeing to hire them. Workers' dependence is deepened all the more because normally there are more workers looking for jobs than there are jobs available. While employers depend on workers to produce their goods and services, they can defer the hiring of workers if the price is too high, an option denied to workers when the price is too low. In other words, while workers aren't "forced" to take any particular job, they can't wait outside the labour market for long and often have no option but to work for a wage they wouldn't otherwise choose.

Once workers are hired and enter the workplace, they encounter other inequalities. Their capacity to work is under the direction of employers, who again, because of their ownership of the means of production, have legal control over the labour process and how workers' capacity to work is put to use. Employers want to maximize workers' productivity—the amount of work they can get out of an individual worker in a given period and for a certain cost—because that way they can increase their profits. But that means workers are under constant pressure to work more intensely. Employers in the private sector also control the profits generated by workers' labour, further exacerbating existing gaps in wealth, and therefore power, between workers and their bosses.

The harms that come from class inequality do not merely have an impact on the workplace. Workers also experience forms of "class injury" in other aspects of their lives. For instance, working-class people, their occupations and their ways of living, are culturally devalued, often the subject of ridicule or scorn in popular culture. Moreover, workers are more often subject to the control of others at work and are, relatively speaking, powerless. As Iris Marion Young (1990: 56–57) argues, working-class people have a "social position that allows [them] little opportunity to develop and exercise skills ... have little or no work autonomy, exercise little creativity or judgment in their work, have no technical expertise or authority, express themselves awkwardly, especially in public or bureaucratic settings, and do not command respect." While the experiences of working-class people vary, in general their position in the social division of labour undermines their broader social status.

Workers' experiences of these inequities—in the labour market, in the workplace, and in the political, social and cultural realms—have long motivated them to form unions and other collective organizations. The ability to mitigate these inequities depends on union power: the collective capacity to compel employers and/or the state to make concessions that would not be attainable in the absence of unions. This power in turn depends on the activism, militancy, combativeness and solidarity of the members.

All histories of unions trace their origins to the negative experiences of the majority of the population during the transition to industrial capitalism. Unions began as an essential response to capitalism. All union theories also agree that workers form unions to give themselves greater power in their dealings with employers and the state, power that they don't have as individuals. However, there has never been a consensus over what unions can or should do to mitigate the economic, political, social and psychological harms that workers experience under capitalism. There have always been debates, amongst workers and amongst those who study workers' organizations, over what the role of unions should be in economic, political and social life. What are workers' problems and interests, and can they be met within a capitalist society? Should unions work within capitalism as it is, attempt to reform it or attempt to replace it with another system? What kinds of strategies and methods should unions use to make social change? Who should unions seek to represent? From a common starting point, accounts of unions diverge into several themes: unions as a means for workers to improve their economic circumstances within capitalist society; unions as a democratizing force in the workplace and in society more generally; unions as a source of social cohesion; and unions as a source of revolutionary class consciousness and, potentially, action that seeks to replace capitalism with different economic and social relations. Although these roles are not mutually exclusive, it is useful to distinguish them for the moment.

UNIONS AS ECONOMIC ACTORS

Most commentators agree that unions emerged to help workers improve their economic circumstances, manage their relationship with employers, and moderate the worst harms from the inequalities of the capitalist labour market and workplace (see Chapter 5 for a more detailed discussion of the techniques unions use to do this). Marx (1886), for instance, acknowledged the crucial role that economic motivations play in unionization, arguing that the earliest unions arose to address "questions of wages and time of labour." This activity, he argued, is "not only legitimate, it is necessary." However, unlike Marx and his close collaborator Friedrich Engels, some theorists who emphasize unions' economic role argue such organizations should not or need not seek deeper or more radical transformations in the basic terms of capitalist society. For them, "pure and simple" unionism, unionism focused on making immediate material improvements to workers' lives, is a sufficient response to workers' problems.

In the U.S., this view was expressed by the "Wisconsin School" of labour economists and historians who were influenced by the work of John R. Commons and were active in the first half of the twentieth century. Commons based his thinking about unions on a careful study of the shoemaking industry in the United States (Chamberlain 1965: 256–62). Unions, he said, developed as a defensive strategy after the geographical extension of markets and competition had destroyed the skills and status of craft workers. Originally, shoes were produced in small shops for the local market, with owners working alongside skilled shoemakers. The interests of shop owners and workers coincided: a good price for shoes meant a good wage for workers. With the increase in the size of markets, local establishments were forced to compete on a wider scale. This development placed pressure on the owners of shoemaking shops to reduce labour costs by holding down wages, mechanizing aspects of production and replacing skilled with less skilled workers. Eventually the geographical extension of the market promoted mass production and obliteration of the craft. According to Commons, unions were thus initially formed on a local basis to defend traditional craft-based production. They eventually grew into regional and national organizations, and as that happened, they became part of the power structure, working jointly with business and the state to establish a "web of rules" to govern the allocation of resources and opportunities in society. Within this framework, unions are simply another special interest group seeking to use their power to secure benefits for their members.

Selig Perlman, a student of Commons, also emphasized workers' economic motivations to unionize. In *A Theory of the Labor Movement* (1928), Perlman theorized it was workers' concerns about the scarcity of job opportunities and the insecurity created by competition for those jobs that motivated them to form unions. Their objective in forming unions was to alleviate these problems by gaining more control over how available work was allocated amongst workers. Unions create a "communism of opportunity," a set of rules that distribute jobs fairly amongst the group rather than according to who can compete most successfully (by working more intensively or for lower wages). These rules would prevent some workers from taking more than their rightful share of work and protect others from not having enough work to survive. This "job consciousness" required solidarity, willingness to forgo individual benefit for the good of other members of the community, and preparedness to oppose employers who would resist any constraints on their ability to exploit opportunities for greater profits.

However, Perlman argued that such control was pragmatic rather than part of workers' ambition to control production as a whole. For Perlman, workers were psychologically "risk averse" and didn't want to shoulder the burden of management. Instead, it was outside intellectuals, not workers themselves, who were dissatisfied with the workings of the capitalist system and advocated for a revolutionary approach to unionism. Perlman condemned the intrusion of intellectuals into union activities and argued instead that labour theory should be deduced from the "concrete and crude experience of the wage earners" (Perlman 1928: 1). For this reason, Perlman believed the American Federation of Labor (AFL) and its emphasis on pragmatic "business unionism"—the securing of the best possible economic deal from capitalist employers and "delivering the goods" to union members (Hoxie 1914)—was the expression of workers' "natural" orientation.

Business unionism grew out of a particular approach to unionism emphasized by Samuel Gompers, a New York City cigar maker and first president of the AFL from 1886 to 1924. For him, economic interests were central to the question of why workers unionized. For Gompers, unions' main purpose was to sell the labour of their members at the highest price possible, thereby increasing and protecting workers' wages, benefits, working conditions and job security. Although Gompers did believe that the interests of workers and employers were in conflict, and that the distribution of profits was unfair, his solution to this unfairness was to use strong workplace organization, collective bargaining and workers' militant action (if necessary) to effect redistribution (Reed 1966: 16). In other words, Gompers thought workers' welfare could be achieved within the capitalist framework by focusing on gradual economic improvements. While workers and employers were at odds over economic matters in the workplace, they could cooperate on other issues of mutual interest. In that sense, Gompers was politically pragmatic, looking for allies who could deliver to labour the best deal, electorally "rewarding friends and punishing enemies" rather than creating either an independent workers' political party or seeking to transform the capitalist system itself.

UNIONS AS A DEMOCRATIZING FORCE

Others have argued that even when unions are focusing on their economic role in the workplace, they also have democratizing effects on both capitalist workplaces and societies. Because private ownership over the means of production gives employers the legal and practical power to organize the workplace as they see fit, workers are subject to their control. U.S. political economist Harry Braverman (1974) referred to this situation as "managerial despotism," in which those in control exercise unrestrained power over workers. As individuals, most workers are unable to counter this power, as they are vulnerable to being replaced. However, collective organization gives workers an independent means to express their interests and partake in defining the rules that govern the workplace. One of the things workers gain by their participation in unions, then, is industrial citizenship: the right to participate in the decisions that determine the terms and conditions of their employment in the workplace. Linked to this is the way that unions, by insisting on fair procedures in the distribution of work, the processing of grievances, or the meting out of discipline, develop the rule of law in the workplace. Another way of saying this is that unions, and the collective agreements they negotiate, place limits on the otherwise arbitrary power of employers and therefore make the workplace more democratic than it would otherwise be. According to this line of thinking, the democratizing role of unions is good for both workers and capitalists because it improves working conditions while legitimizing the economic system.

Unions' democratizing effects also spill over into the broader political system. Workers' organizations have historically made very important contributions to political democracy, expanding both who could access citizenship rights and the content of those rights themselves. In nineteenth-century Europe, the labour movement—through the action of unions and workers' political parties—was central to the fight to expand the right to vote to non-property owners. In their advocacy for expanded public services based on citizenship rather than ability to pay, unions have also expanded the notion of citizenship itself to include social rights.

Beyond the advocacy for working-class citizenship rights, Seymour Martin Lipset (1983) argued that, as an organized interest group in society, unions (and the labour movement of which they are a part) protect political democracy by educating members/citizens and by training leaders, promoting civic engagement and preventing the domination of one group over society as a whole by articulating their alternative views of problems and solutions.

Internal union life also enhances workers' capacities for democracy. As members, individual workers have the right to participate both directly and indirectly (through their delegates) in the deliberations and debates that take place within their own unions and within the labour movement as a whole. They vote on the selection of their leaders, on whether or not to strike in support of union demands, on the priority bargaining demands and ratification of collective agreements, on the selection of delegates to union conventions and on other issues discussed at union conventions. They can seek election as shop stewards or executive members and put their names forward to serve as delegates to conventions or other labour union bodies. This offers a much more engaging experience of political participation than is typical in most other institutions in our society.

Marxists also see unions as democratizing, but they have a different understanding of democracy. For them, by participating in their own organizations and challenging their employers, workers develop capacities essential to more transformative goals and struggles. As Marx put it, workers develop "social instincts in place of egotistical ones," which are the result of "centuries of bourgeois rule." They throw off "all habits of deference," acquire "confidence in [their] own ability to organize and rule" and develop "experience in organization and in the making of political decisions" (Geras 1986: 137). As Sam Gindin (1998: 79) puts it, workers need to develop, in their own organizations, "the kind of capacities and potentials which are absolutely fundamental to one day building a different kind of society: the capacities for doing, creating, planning, executing" that are systematically underdeveloped by capitalism. For this reason, Marx placed a very high priority on the development of unions as spaces for the working class to learn how to "walk by themselves," and he condemned those leaders who substituted themselves for the workers and denied that the latter were able to liberate themselves. The democratizing potential of unions is therefore, for some, more subversive and potentially radical.

UNIONS AS CREATORS OF COMMUNITY

A number of theories emphasize the social role that unions play in creating forms of community and collective identity. Depending on how it is carried out, this role can serve either to sustain workers' oppositional culture or to integrate workers into existing capitalist social relations. U.S. labour historian Frank Tannenbaum, for example, attributed the emergence of unions to the rise of individualism and the destruction of community that accompanied the growth of capitalism and the transition from a feudal to an industrial society (Chamberlain 1965: 266–69). Unions restored community ties and brought renewed social connection to the lives of workers. But Tannenbaum feared that as unions grew in size and scope to counter the growth in the size of firms in monopoly capitalism, union leaders would become entrenched and lose contact with the social and moral needs of their members.

In class-divided societies where culture is dominated by the most powerful, the distinctiveness of workers' experiences, needs and values is made invisible (Young 1990: 58–59). Unions thus provide a space for workers to explain the world to themselves, and to express pride in their work and in their struggles for a better workplace and society. Unions organize parades to show pride in members' work and support the development of music, poetry and art that reflects workers' lives, values and struggles. These parades and a variety of other practices and rituals help create a sense of belonging and togetherness. Such cultural expressions have also solidified workers' identification with and commitment to labour organizations because they provide both an alternative to the dominant culture and the basis for developing an oppositional consciousness (Mansbridge and Morris 2001). A common identity based on shared values is important when one is involved in risky struggles: the emotional community ties strengthen and reinforce people's commitment to oppose the power of economic and political elites.

On the other hand, unions can also foster workers' incorporation into existing social relations, stabilizing their relationship to the employer and making them feel they have a stake in and influence over the system. As U.S. labour economist Richard Lester (1958: 13) argued, unions help workers feel "like they count for something, that they are not just little cogs in a large and impersonal wheel of industry." By developing rules and procedures in the workplace, unions guide workers' discontent into productive, orderly channels, help to reconcile conflicting interests and therefore, in Lester's view, contribute to constructive social change (1958: 17). The stability that comes from a union presence can even help management, in that unions (especially their elected leaders and staff) ensure the efficient administration of work rules and conflicts, restrain unauthorized activities (like wildcat strikes), and elicit "cooperation and consent of the governed" (Lester

1958: 18). U.S. sociologist C. Wright Mills (1948) called this "the management of discontent"—positioning labour leaders as equally responsible for managing workers—although he was critical of the effects that this role was having on the labour movement's ability to advocate for workers' interests.

Similarly, many religious communities have a particular understanding of the role of unions, emphasizing the essential common (rather than conflicting) interests between workers and employers. This perspective is sometimes referred to as "corporatism," the view that society, though organized into different interest groups that play different roles, is fundamentally a harmonious whole, like a body with interconnected parts, some of which are more important than others. This human body analogy is based on a conservative view of society, not only because it values cooperation above conflict, but also because it normalizes hierarchy, interdependence and the notion that everyone has a proper place.

The Catholic Church, through its popes, has long attempted to situate unions within its own moral precepts. *Rerum Novarum,* a papal encyclical issued by Pope Leo XIII in 1891, rejected the idea of class struggle, condemned socialism as a dead end for workers and insisted that the way forward for unions was through collaboration and harmony between capital and labour (Black 1984: 11–14). In *Laborems Exercens,* a papal encyclical issued a century later in 1981, Pope John Paul II set out an analysis of labour that was intended to clarify the Church's understanding of the rights of workers and the role of unions in the late twentieth century. John Paul adhered to the core ideas advanced in *Rerum Novarum*: unions are simply one organization among many established to ensure the rights of their members in capitalist society. Their struggle for social justice for their members "is not a struggle against others" (Pope John Paul II 1981: 40). On the contrary, the struggle is for social harmony with the owners and managers of capital. John Paul also rejected the notion of labour unions having a role in politics:

> Unions do not have the character of political parties struggling for power; they should not be subjected to the decision of political parties or have too close a link with them. In fact, in such a situation they easily lose contact with their specific role, which is to secure the just rights of workers within the framework of the common good of the whole of society.
> (Pope John Paul II 1981: 41)

John Paul cautioned that strikes, while a legitimate tool for workers in their struggle for rights, must not be used in a manner at odds with the interests of society and "must not be abused especially for political purposes" (Pope John Paul II 1981: 42). These ideas had a powerful influence over the development of unions in Quebec, although much of that was lost in the 1960s with that province's Quiet

Revolution, a period of rapid social and economic modernization. Although these views no longer have favour in Quebec, they continue to hold sway in marginal labour organizations like the Christian Labour Association of Canada, which promotes "Christian values of respect, dignity, and fairness for everyone in the workplace" (CLAC 2015). The organization, which is greatly out of step with the mainstream labour movement in Canada, has built a reputation for strongly opposing strikes and political action, and for developing cozy, rather than oppositional, relationships with employers.

Despite attempts to frame "Christian values" with regard to labour relations in a conservative manner, some religious ideas have taken on a more radical tone, promoting unions as a moral alternative to capitalism's degrading effect on social values other than profit-making. Religious values supported a vociferous critique of capitalism among the Knights of Labor in the late nineteenth century (Marks 1991) and among the left-wing social gospel movement in the early twentieth century (Allen 1971). More recently, in 1983, the Canadian Conference on Catholic Bishops issued *Ethical Reflections on the Economic Crisis* and in it condemned the policies adopted by employers and the federal government to deal with the recession of the early 1980s. As an alternative, the Bishops proposed "economic policies which realize that the needs of the poor have priority over the wants of the rich; that the rights of workers are more important than the maximization of profits; that the participation of marginalized groups takes precedence over the preservation of a system that excludes them." As well, the Bishops called for the protection of union rights and "a decisive and responsible role [for unions] in developing strategies for economic recovery and development." In 2013, Pope Francis criticized the "tyranny" of unfettered capitalism and the "idolatry of money" in an apostolic exhortation, widely considered the official platform for his papacy (Yakabuski 2014).

While unions can help to produce both conservative and radical sources of community, the most influential theories of the labour movement have tended to focus on the latter, and have expanded those ideas to capture labour's transformative role in the economic and political spheres.

UNIONS AS AGENTS OF REVOLUTIONARY CONSCIOUSNESS AND ACTION

For Karl Marx, workers formed unions and bargained with their employers over wages and working conditions as a means of improving their economic lot—the lot of the members of a particular union—within the capitalist system. However, Marx argued that unions on their own were ultimately doomed to fail because the best they could do under capitalism was to try to prevent wage cuts when the economy slumped and the ranks of the unemployed increased, and to extract wage gains from employers when economic times were good. Those efforts would not permanently resolve workers' problems, he reasoned, because the general tendency in capitalism was to increase the exploitation of workers and drive down wages. While workers' fights with individual employers might slow down the decline in wages, during bad times wages would nevertheless continue to decline. More importantly, Marx argued that even if workers did achieve wage gains, the nature of the employer-worker relationship made workers—the majority of the population—subordinate to capitalists. This subordination, structured into the wage-labour relationship, meant that democracy and freedom were not possible within capitalism. Unions trying for a better economic deal could never end this subordination, only blunt its worst effects.

For Marx, the solution was for workers and their unions to move beyond these never-ending battles with employers to challenge the wage-labour system in its entirety. Workers, Marx (1947: 55) said,

> ought to understand that, with all the miseries it imposes upon them, the present system simultaneously engenders the material conditions and the social forms necessary for the … reconstruction of society. Instead of the conservative motto, "A fair day's wage for a fair day's work!" they ought to inscribe on their banner the revolutionary watchword, "Abolition of the wages system!"

In that sense, even narrow, economistic unionism has a kernel of anti-capitalism in it that could generate a more critical class consciousness among workers. Even "pure and simple" unionism rejects the legitimacy of capital's appropriation of profits. As well, when workers come up against the limits of union action alone, whether because employers control the purse strings or because the state intervenes, there is a potential for them to be politicized and to ask questions about the justice of the status quo.

Marx also believed that the lessons workers learned in their formation of unions and participation in the labour movement created the conditions and capacities that would allow them to challenge the very existence of capitalism. For example, workers' early initiatives to establish unions and improve their conditions were an assertion of their rejection as human beings of the oppressive and dehumanizing conditions they faced in capitalist production. Moreover, the struggles for better wages and conditions clarified for them the limits of their potential to improve relationships with particular employers. Their inability to gain ground in isolated conflicts motivated certain workers to unite with others to build a labour movement based on collective interests and a common vision. Finally, worker involvement in the labour movement and struggles with employers and the state equipped workers with the insights, knowledge and skills required to achieve social revolution (Draper 1978: 92–98). According to Marx (1955: 149), unions were "bulwarks" or "ramparts for the workers in their struggles with the employers," "centres of resistance against the encroachments of capital" on the basis of which other class action could take place. Unions were thus the first step in the process of workers transforming themselves from a class objectively constituted by capital to one that possesses class consciousness, which acts as "a class for itself" (Marx, 1955: 149).

Socialist thinkers in Europe and North America subsequently expanded and/or modified Marx's ideas on unions. V.I. Lenin, leader of the 1917 Bolshevik Revolution in Russia, saw the spontaneous formation of unions as the first step in a process that would see workers outgrow their preoccupations with conditions in their own trade or enterprise or with sectional interests; they would move away from their immediate struggles with particular employers over quite limited objectives and forge a united force that would take aim at social revolution. Union activities, organization, collective bargaining and, in particular, strikes would provide workers with practical schooling:

> A strike teaches workers to understand what the strength of the employers and what the strength of the workers consists in; it teaches them not to think of their own employer alone and not of their own immediate workmates alone but of all the class of employers and the whole class of workers … A strike, moreover, opens the eyes of workers to the nature, not only of the capitalists, but of the government and the laws as well … Strikes, therefore, teach the workers to unite; they show them that they can struggle against the capitalists only when they are united; strikes teach the workers to think of the struggle of the whole working class against the whole class of factory owners and against the arbitrary, police government. (Lenin 1970: 63–64)

For Lenin, though, a revolutionary vanguard party was a key ingredient for concrete change. By bringing together the most militant activists in the working class, he argued, such a party would help workers discover and build their revolutionary potential and ultimately lead them to revolutionary social change.

North American refinements and modifications of Marxist ideas originated primarily with radicals who either had leadership roles in labour organizations outside the mainstream of unionism—for example, in the Industrial Workers of the World (iww)—and/or in socialist political parties (Chamberlain 1965: 263–64). In contrast to Lenin, the iww downplayed the importance of the party and emphasized instead the syndicalist view that revolution could be achieved through direct industrial action in the workplace. If workers took control of capitalist production by creating one big union and organizing a general strike to paralyze production economy-wide, control of the state would follow.

Most socialists, however, envisioned distinctive roles being played by unions and political parties. Unions had as their primary purpose the struggle for improved conditions for workers in their jobs within the existing capitalist system. But unlike the syndicalists, socialists believed that the broader aim of social revolution and the elimination of the wages system could only be achieved by means of the revolutionary socialist party. This was the approach taken up in Canada by the Communist Party. Other socialists, like those in Canada's Co-operative Commonwealth Federation (CCF), believed such revolutionary change could be achieved through parliamentary means. In the postwar period, a social democratic version of this perspective envisioned the party not as the vehicle for the revolutionary overthrow of capitalism and the wage-labour system, but rather as a means for promoting the broader political interests of labour within a reformed capitalist system. In Canada, the New Democratic Party (NDP) is now the main expression of this approach.

UNIONS AS A CONTESTED TERRAIN

Unions are contradictory organizations: they serve to both oppose as well as to adapt to capitalism. They carry out a multiplicity of roles, and some of these are in conflict with each other. Clearly, the various theories advanced to explain the role of unions under capitalism show considerable diversity. If we can draw one conclusion, it is that unions and the labour movement play multiple roles in both the lives of their members and the life of society. The question of which roles loom largest in their activities and actions at any given time seems, moreover, to be dictated by economic and social conditions and the nature of the concrete demands made by union members. The issue of what it is that unions do—the roles and/ or functions of unions—has always been and remains a contested terrain, yet the kernel of opposition to exploitation is at the heart of union activity. The history of the labour movement in Canada demonstrates that these various ideas and orientations, from simple unionism to revolutionary consciousness, contributed to its growth and development as well as its trajectory.

QUESTIONS FOR DISCUSSION
1. What do the various theories of the labour movement in this chapter have in common, and in which ways do they fundamentally diverge?
2. Which roles do you think unions are emphasizing the most today? Which roles do you think they *should* be emphasizing and why?
3. What makes unions "contradictory organizations," according to the authors?

CHAPTER 3

EARLY UNION STRUGGLES IN CANADA

Prior to and immediately after contact with Europeans, work and economic activity in what would become Canada was focused on Indigenous subsistence labour (hunting, gathering, fishing and craft-making) where people made and consumed the things they needed to survive. European settlers brought with them capitalist modes of production, which eventually dominated and displaced Indigenous labour processes and early independent commodity production. Capitalism brought with it hard work for long hours at low pay in difficult, often appalling conditions. That was the lot of most workers, especially women and children and the most recently arrived immigrants, during the first half of the nineteenth century. The vast majority of the population lived and worked on the land, moving into wage labour if needed but not completely dependent on it. Those who did not have access to land toiled at a variety of tasks: as day labourers on construction sites and on the docks; building canals; rafting logs downriver to mills; as domestic labourers; and in small workshops. Factories were rare. By 1851, even in an industrial centre like Hamilton, Ontario, only one quarter of workers were employed in a workplace that had more than ten people (Palmer 1992: 83). Among the few instances of collective labour were the large numbers of workers, predominantly Irish, who dug the St. Lawrence and Welland canals in the early decades of the 1800s. Conditions there were especially harsh, and strikes and riots were frequent (Bleasdale 1981; Patrias and Savage 2012: 8–10). But no "working class" existed as yet, in that most people were not engaged in wage labour and those who were did not see themselves as a group with common interests. Workers were fragmented and stratified along regional, occupational, and income lines, as well as on the basis of ethnicity and gender. Difficult though their working conditions were, very few would enjoy the benefits of unionization until well into the twentieth century.

PRE-INDUSTRIAL WORK, CAPITALISM AND THE RISE OF CRAFT UNIONS

Unions did emerge in the first half of the nineteenth century, though, formed by those at the top of the labour force, the craft workers—carpenters, stone masons, printers and tailors, to name a few. Craft societies brought together into one organization workers who shared an occupation and set of skills. Common to all crafts was a method of production that united knowledge and execution: a craft worker had both the knowledge to design a product and the skill to make it. At the heart of the craft labour process was the apprenticeship system. A boy was bound by contract to a master craftsperson for anywhere from three to ten years, during which time he learned the craft under the guidance of the master, eventually becoming a skilled tradesperson—first a journeyman and later, in some cases, a master. Apprenticeship was a highly personal form of education that blurred the boundaries between work and home life, but it was also an important strategy to maintain and transmit craft traditions and standards and to limit the numbers of people entering the craft (so as to manage competition). Because craft workers determined how many people learned the craft, they also had a lot of control over how they did their work, including the techniques used, the quality of the product, the pace of work, and the prices charged. These matters were determined by tradition rather than by market competition, and by social values, such as ensuring that there was enough work for everyone in the craft community without creating overwork, unemployment or poverty. Craft workers could exercise such control because their skills were not easily replaced.

Apprentices, journeymen, and masters were united in a common dedication to their respective crafts. Craft pride was expressed through rituals and celebrations, lavish banquets with speeches about the honour of the craft, and festive and colourful public parades. Craft workers were the elite of the nineteenth-century labour force, an "aristocracy of labour" whose skills were highly valued socially and in short supply and who thus could command a good living. However, craft pride was also rooted in a set of values. The importance of hard work and the dignity of labour, the significance of mutuality and community, and the value of being a "respectable" member of the community were all central elements of craft identities.

Through the nineteenth century, in the face of growing competition from Britain's industrial factories, many master craftsmen began to think of themselves and act as capitalists, focusing on increasing profits rather than on maintaining craft traditions or creating quality products. To compete with cheaper imports produced through factory methods, masters began to pressure craft workers to work faster. Class differences within craft communities therefore began to emerge. Apprentices and journeymen began to see their collective interests as distinct from their employers. Some of the craft societies evolved into unions, a handful of them early in the nineteenth century (carpenters, mechanics, tailors and printers, for example), and more by the 1840s (coopers, blacksmiths, painters, bakers, shipwrights). However, these early craft unions were only occasionally confrontational. Despite the changes afoot, the line between master and journeyman was still blurred. Attachment to craft values, including respectability, was still stronger than the emergent working-class identity. Craft workers sought to protect their trade from the increasingly dominant capitalist values of individualism, acquisitiveness and competition.

However, the pressures of industrializing capitalism continued to upend the world of craft workers. In the second half of the nineteenth century, mechanized factories began to emerge and their owners, often investors interested in maximizing profits and not in craft traditions, actively reorganized production in ways that reduced reliance on the relatively expensive craft workers and their exclusive knowledge. These processes, especially those that broke production processes down into smaller parts, meant that less skilled, less expensive and more replaceable workers could be used. These changes posed a major threat to craft workers' standard of living and standing in the community.

In the face of changes that cheapened their labour, craft unions were pressed to develop more militant forms of opposition. Craft workers worked hard to maintain their monopoly on skill by collectively regulating apprenticeships, the use of unskilled labour, the hiring of new journeymen, and the setting of wage rates, work rules and the pace of work. These craft standards were set out in union constitutions or rulebooks, and all card-carrying members of the craft had to pledge to uphold and defend them. Where employers refused to abide by these standards, craft workers would use collective direct action—strikes and/or boycotts—to enforce them (Kealey 1976).

Craft unions also sought to manage an increasingly continental labour market in their skills. Especially after the 1850s and the spread of the railway system, craft workers frequently travelled in search of work. Because they moved back and forth across the Canada–U.S. border, they sought affiliations with the similarly emerging craft unionism in the U.S. Having a union card meant a journeyman adhered to craft work methods and traditions and could be accepted into the craft local in any community across the continent. These unions with members in both Canada and the U.S. came to be called "international" unions. By 1880, Canada had at least 165 local and international unions (Palmer 1992: 94).

But these strategies also meant that those who were entering factories as semi-skilled workers were excluded from craft unions. "Craft" and "cheap" labour had a particular gendered character. The vast majority of craft workers were men, while in industries such as clothing and shoemaking, women were employed as factory labour. Most women factory workers were not only poorly paid but also subject to the patriarchal discipline of their male employers. They tended to be young and to leave their employment upon marriage. Many married women worked for wages but they were most often in the "putting out" system, doing consignment work at home, usually on a piecework basis, at even lower wages than women in the factories. Because so much importance was placed on being the family breadwinner and on earning enough that one's wife need not work for wages, women's entry into the factories was perceived as a threat to craft workers' identities as well as their wages.

There was also an ethnic character to different categories of labour. Skilled workers tended to be English, Scottish or French in origin, while semi-skilled workers were Irish, Black, Eastern or Southern European or Asian. Chinese workers, for example, were brought to British Columbia from China in the 1880s as indentured contract workers to lay the track in the last leg of the cross-country Canadian Pacific Railway. They were brutally exploited:

> Accidents were frequent, with far more Chinese than Whites as victims. Many workers died from exhaustion and rock explosions and were buried in collapsed tunnels. Their living conditions were appalling. Food and shelter were in insufficient supply, and malnutrition was widespread. There was almost no medical attention, contributing to a high fatality rate from diseases such as scurvy and smallpox. It is estimated that there were six hundred deaths in British Columbia of Chinese labourers working on the construction of the railway. (Henry et al. 2000: 73)

Once the rail line was completed, the government passed legislation to prevent further Chinese immigration: the *Chinese Immigration Act* in 1885; and the imposition of a head tax of $50 in 1888, which grew to a prohibitive $500 in 1903 (Li 1988b: 107).

If unions were less than welcoming to women in the workforce, they were downright hostile to workers of colour, and Asian workers in particular. The Canadian labour movement was among those organizations in support of these and later anti-Chinese policies. For example, "[t]he white labour movement of British Columbia proudly shared credit for the Canadian government's discriminatory $50 head tax on Chinese entering Canada, the first in an escalating series of anti-Chinese measures adopted by the provincial and dominion governments" (Iacovetta, Quinlan and Radforth 1996: 96). Chinese workers were excluded from some unions; in others, wage differentials were embedded in collective agreements, allowing for lower wages to be paid to "oriental" than to "occidental" (i.e., white) workers (Henry et al. 2000: 73). This is an early example of what has been called the split labour market, in which employers benefit from the lower wages that can be paid to workers of colour, and workers as a whole are divided along colour lines and thus weakened (Li 1988a: 43; also see Roediger 1991). Chinese workers were also barred from various occupations and institutions, which meant many ended up in the service sector, in restaurants, laundries, and domestic work, for example, because nothing else was open to them. These conditions provide an early example of how the labour force was intentionally stratified along ethnic and racial lines, to the detriment of all working people.

Journeymen reacted to these changes with growing militancy, because they struck at the heart of craft union power: their monopoly over the supply of a particular skill. Craft unions excluded semi-skilled workers and, by extension, maintained their exclusive gendered and ethnic character. As well, more craft workers created unions and engaged in strikes even though it was formally illegal to do so. Prior to the 1850s, the various provinces had all passed legislation modeled after the British Combination Acts (1799–1800), which defined unions as "conspiracies in restraint of trade" and made it illegal both to belong to a union and to engage in the typical activities of unions (meetings, wage-fixing, strikes, blacklisting employers, picketing). In practice, unions were tolerated as long as members behaved "responsibly," but employers could—and increasingly did—fire union activists. Conflict between employers and craft workers heated up in the 1870s: strikes became frequent in Canada's largest cities and especially resistant employers attempted to have union members charged under these anti-union statutes (Heron 2012: 12).

Despite exclusions, craft workers did attempt to broaden their solidarities and forms of action in other ways. One was through building links between crafts, and acting together to pressure all employers. As they faced employers' common project to increase productivity in all industries, craft workers began to realize their common interests and their need for a multi-craft and multi-city workers' movement to improve conditions in industry as a whole. A key example of building broader working-class solidarities was the Nine Hour Movement in 1872, which sought to reduce the length of the working day and week through coordinated citywide strikes (Battye 1979). Although the Nine-Hour Movement did not succeed in its immediate aims, the unrest it produced led Conservative prime minister John A. Macdonald to pass the country's first labour legislation, the Trade Unions Act of 1872. The act decriminalized unions, so no worker could be prosecuted for attempting to influence wages and conditions of work through collective means.

Craft unionists also created local trades and labour councils to make links across their occupations more permanent and to bolster their power and organizational capacity. In 1886, U.S. craft unions also formed the American Federation of Labor (AFL), headed by Samuel Gompers, and the Canadian sections of the craft unions were affiliated with this new continent-wide organization.

Craft unionists also increasingly saw the need to act politically, to influence government policy that shaped the economy and labour's place within it, which meant developing a strategy towards political parties and elections. In the nineteenth century, most unions, or at least union leaders, supported one of the two existing main political parties—the Conservatives or the Liberals—a strategy known as "partyism." For instance, Macdonald's introduction of the *Trade Unions Act* in 1872 cemented the political loyalty of many skilled craftsmen to the Conservative Party. Although party loyalties tended to be organized on ethnic and religious lines, workers did shift their votes according to which party they thought would support working-class issues and interests. This political strategy emerged independently in Canada but was consistent with Gompers' dictum: "Reward your friends, punish your enemies" (Harvey 1935: 165). Gompers believed in working within the existing party framework and opposed the creation of an independent labour party, especially a socialist one, as being too divisive of workplace solidarity. However, most unionists found that the mainstream parties—both of which were dominated by the business elite—would abandon them when workers' interests began to conflict with those of their bosses. Seeing this, some craft union leaders sought to elect independent labour candidates as early as the 1870s (Heron 1984).

However, despite craft workers' growing workplace militancy and political activism, an increasing number of workers concluded the craft model of organization could not, in the long run, address the changing nature of capitalist industry. In particular, the craft unions' refusal to organize the growing numbers of semi-skilled industrial workers seemed to some a recipe for failure. As a result, some from within the craft union tradition itself began to develop a new union model, in the form of the Knights of Labor, and to make the first serious attempt to organize these new industrial workers.

THE KNIGHTS OF LABOR AND THE ORIGINS OF INDUSTRIAL UNIONISM

Formed in Philadelphia in 1869, the Holy and Noble Order of the Knights of Labor established their first "local assembly" in Canada in 1881, in Hamilton. By 1886, the organization had exploded to one million members in Canada. Workers could join "trades" assemblies of particular crafts or "mixed" assemblies of various occupations—the first opportunity many semi-skilled men and women workers had to join a union (Kealey and Palmer 1982). The Knights were also unique in that they welcomed Irish and Black workers into their ranks, but like many segments of the North American labour movement, continued to exclude Asian workers (Goutor

2007). The Knights were the first example, albeit in a modified form, of industrial unionism, which seeks to bring all workers in an industry together in one organization regardless of their craft or job. The Knights recognized that working-class solidarity could not be forged by dividing skilled and unskilled workers, and their message resonated with a growing number of non-skilled workers. By the end of the 1880s, the Knights were playing important roles, alongside the craft unions, in most of the trades and labour councils established in cities and towns.

Like the craft unions, the Knights of Labor promoted a working-class culture that opposed the acquisitive and individualistic norms of capitalism. Workers' festivals, picnics, dinners, and dances all served to create a culture of collectivity and mutual aid. The Knights' emphasis on education—the regular promotion of lectures and various other educational events, the establishment of newspapers and reading rooms—encouraged the flowering of a working-class intellectual tradition. By the 1880s, significant numbers of working-class intellectuals furthered the development of a distinctive, solidaristic working-class culture (Kealey and Palmer 1982; Patrias and Savage 2012: 13–14).

The Knights also worked to shift labour's political strategy away from partyism. Discontented with their marginalization within party priorities but unable to completely break with them, by the mid 1880s some labour candidates were running under "Liberal-Labour" or "Labour-Conservative" banners. In some cities this movement towards labourism—the idea that workers should elect other workers, on the grounds that only workers could adequately represent the interests of labour in the legislature—was further developed as independent labour organizations like the Workingmen's Political Club of Cape Breton and the Hamilton Labour Political Association emerged. While electoral victories were few and the fledgling labour political associations short-lived, efforts to go beyond partyism to a more independent labour politics nevertheless continued to be made, and began to bear fruit in the first two decades of the twentieth century (Heron 1984).

As for the Knights, the organization declined as precipitously as it arose. By the early 1890s, the Knights were a shadow of their former powerful selves. Their decline was the result of their leaders' timidity in promoting strike action in pursuit of members' interests; their growing rivalry with the craft unions; and, most importantly, their inability to respond adequately to the dramatic changes being wrought by the end-of-the-century transition to monopoly capitalism. But they were an important nineteenth-century example of what a union might be: inclusive of all workers, irrespective of occupation, gender, race or ethnicity, and committed to building a culture of mutuality and solidarity opposed to the greed and individualism of the emerging monopoly capitalism.

In the last decade of the nineteenth century, despite the political and economic action of craft workers that did protect some, workplace transformations continued, worsening the conditions faced by most industrial workers. These conditions are most thoroughly documented by the Royal Commission on the Relations of Labour and Capital, created by John A. Macdonald's government in 1886 in response to growing union militancy in the form of strikes and the electoral efforts of labour candidates. The Royal Commission's 1889 report found that a seventy-two-hour workweek—ten to twelve hours a day, six days a week, without overtime pay—was common. Wages were below subsistence levels for most workers: whereas $9 per week was considered the minimum to support a family, most workers did not make this. While craft workers were able to earn $15 per week, non-craft workers were bringing home $7 per week. Women earned one third of men's wages, between $2 to $3 a week, while children earned one tenth of men's wages, about 70¢ a week. Child labour was widespread, as working-class families found it increasingly difficult to survive on the male breadwinner's wage alone. Children as young as eight years old worked twelve-hour days in textile mills, mines and small manufacturing enterprises, and their status as children made them especially subject to corporal punishment. Workers were subject to fines and discipline for being late or 'insolent,' refusing to work overtime, or poor workmanship, meaning that they could actually owe the employer money by the end of the week. In the absence of sufficiently strong health and safety legislation, devastating injuries like amputations or even workplace deaths were commonly assumed to be the worker's fault (Kealey 1973). Monopoly capitalism had arrived and workers would find alternate ways of organizing to confront the challenge.

MONOPOLY CAPITALISM AND INDUSTRIAL UNIONISM, 1890–1914

By the turn of the century, the relatively slow and gradual growth of the factory system had given way to the full-fledged arrival of monopoly capitalism. Giant corporations emerged in new industries such as automobile manufacturing, steel, rubber, electrical parts, oil, chemicals, and pulp and paper. Mergers were frequent; corporations grew ever larger. U.S. investment in Canada expanded rapidly, creating the branch plant structure that would characterize twentieth-century Canadian industry. Before the introduction of free trade in the late 1980s, large U.S.-based corporations frequently set up branch plants in Canada. The branch-plant economy was a product of John A. Macdonald's 1876 National Policy, which sought to protect and build up Canada's manufacturing base by imposing heavy tariffs on imported manufactured goods. These U.S.-based corporations were also deeply anti-union and responded aggressively, even brutally, to the craft unions they encountered in Canada. They used industrial spies, *agents provocateurs*, and strikebreakers, fired strike leaders and union organizers, and maintained a shared blacklist of those not to be hired.

These ever-larger corporations also had the resources to dramatically reorganize work processes using new technologies and management strategies to further fragment and speed up work. Factories were increasingly organized on the basis of "scientific management," introduced and promoted by U.S. engineer Frederick Taylor. Also known as "Taylorism," this management strategy broke up factory production processes into various tasks, assigned each small task to one worker, and then had managers use stopwatches to establish the fastest possible time in which workers could complete each task. This benchmarking allowed management to design the production process in ways that ensured "speed-up" and forced all workers to perform at the maximum rate. At its heart, scientific management separated the conception of how work was to be done from the actual execution of work tasks. Relatively unskilled workers could do work organized in this way. This deskilling strategy further eroded craft workers' traditional control over their work, placing more power in the hands of managers. Henry Ford's introduction of the moving assembly line at his Dearborn, Michigan plant in 1913 was the prototype of this new way of organizing industrial work, and the increases in productivity were immense. However, work organized in this way was rejected by all but the most desperate, and the turnover rate was extremely high. Ford thus developed another technique for controlling workers with the "five dollar day," a significantly higher wage than the going rate for similar work (Milkman 1987: 22). Higher wages increased productivity by securing a stable workforce and reducing training and turnover costs. The larger paycheques also ensured buyers for Ford's cars, the foundation of the postwar age of mass production and mass consumption.

The new demand for workers less skilled than craft workers was met in large part by a dramatic, turn-of-the-century increase in immigration from Eastern and Southern Europe. Between 1896 and the outbreak of the First World War in 1914, a massive wave of mostly non-English-speaking immigrants flooded into Canada, filling the newly opened Prairies with farmers, and the emergent factories of monopoly capitalism with semi-skilled labour.

Women also continued to be used as unskilled labour in reorganized industrial workplaces, mainly because industrial capitalism was continually degrading the male breadwinner wage. A large proportion of women worked in relatively isolated workplaces: in domestic service in the homes of the well-to-do; in the small sweatshops of sub-contractors, or at home as part of the putting-out system that was so common in the clothing and textile industries; and in small retail shops, where young women commonly worked twelve hours a day and sixteen hours on Saturday. Wages were low. By 1913, "the average female factory worker in Montreal earned $4.50 to $5.50 per week, at a time when the lowest estimate of the minimum living wage was $7.00 per week" (Frager 1983: 45). In the factories, abuse, including the imposition of fines for laughing or talking on the job and even physical beatings by employers, was common.

Because women typically left the workforce when they married, too often they "were deprived of the opportunity to build experience in collective action, to discuss and pass on knowledge of work relationships, to develop a history of action and to provide leaders with years of work and union experience" (White 1993: 13). However, there were exceptions to this rule. In the clothing industry, for example, women were enthusiastic participants in strikes, and by the 1930s were struggling to become active in their unions (Steedman 1997: 251). In most cases—the Knights of Labor being an exception—unions themselves and their mostly male memberships continued to oppose having women in the workforce, arguing that this would drive down wages. The commonly held view was that male workers ought to be paid a wage sufficient to support a family, and that women ought to be in the home.

Workers resisted the continual reorganization of work, their loss of control over the labour process, and their economic impoverishment in various ways. Craft workers persisted in militantly defending their exclusive control over key elements of the labour process, although some went into irreversible decline. Others were able to preserve a space for themselves in this reorganized capitalist workplace (Roberts 1980).

At the turn of the century, the AFL launched a dramatic organizing drive aimed at the emergent corporate giants of monopoly capitalism and their Canadian branch plants. Between 1899 and 1903, in the biggest organizing campaign since the Knights of Labor in the 1880s, thousands of Canadian workers in many industries signed up in U.S.-based unions. However, the AFL unions remained focused on the craft model of organization, dividing workers up between the various unions even when they were in the same factory. Building on their success, the U.S.-based craft unions seized control of the Canadian-based Trades and Labour Congress (TLC) at its 1902 convention, expelling the few remaining Knights of Labor assemblies and other dual unions—competing unions representing workers in industries in which U.S.-based unions operated. The bulk of the Canadian trade union movement was, to a considerable extent, now under the control of U.S.-based unions. The struggle to break away from what some saw as American domination, like the struggle to form industrial unionism, became an important theme in the history of unions in Canada in the twentieth century.

Some craft unions also tried to emulate the more centralized power and expertise of their corporate employers by adopting "business unionism." An approach developed by AFL president Samuel Gompers, the union in this case is guided by pragmatic "bread and butter" concerns, maximizing what can be gained for its members in terms of better wages, benefits and working conditions within the existing economic system. Preserving the union's financial assets, bargaining relationships and organizational stability are priorities. Business unionism also developed bureaucratic forms of control, with expert union staff able to respond to management's knowledge. Effective though this approach often was at (temporarily) protecting craft workers from the pressures of deskilling, it had a glaring flaw: it could not stop the ongoing reorganization of factory work or the rapid expansion in the ranks of unskilled factory workers.

Inspired more by the radical ideas of syndicalism, others made a concerted effort to organize unskilled workers. Still shut out of the craft unions, immigrant workers in particular were the force behind this new wave of industrial unionism. While labourism was a product of the circumstances and needs of craft workers, and therefore the dominant form of labour politics east of the Rockies prior to the First World War, syndicalism was an important political variant in B.C. and Alberta. It emerged in the much rougher working conditions faced by miners, loggers and other, often itinerant and/or immigrant, resource-based workers.

Syndicalists were explicitly anti-capitalist, believing the existing economic system should be replaced by one that was democratically run by workers themselves. They rejected political parties and legislative bodies as means for making change, believing that the state was an inherently oppressive institution that would always do the bidding of capitalists. They preferred direct action at the workplace. Syndicalists combined union organization with revolutionary goals: workers used actions like strikes and slow-downs to make immediate improvements and build their confidence, but their ultimate goal was a general strike in which all workers would participate and which would establish workers' collective control over their workplaces. Through the general strike, workers would paralyze the capitalist economy and, as Big Bill Haywood put it in 1905, "put the working class in possession of the economic power, the means of life, in control of the machinery of production and distribution, without regard to capitalist masters" (Industrial Workers of the World 1905: 1).

The most prominent syndicalist organization in North America was the Industrial Workers of the World (IWW), commonly known as the "Wobblies," established in 1905 in Chicago and led by Haywood. They were openly hostile to the TLC and the AFL—the "American Separation of Labor" to the IWW—because they failed to organize the entire working class, divided workers according to their different crafts, and replaced workers' direct action with bureaucratic structures. The Wobblies organized the itinerant, often immigrant workers—loggers, miners, railway and construction workers, and harvest hands—who were considered "the dregs of industrial society" and ignored by the craft unions. They also built multi-ethnic organizations and challenged the racialized divisions that employers used to weaken workers' collective action.

As a result of both the resistance of craft unionists and the work of radical unions like the IWW, the number of strikes increased dramatically between 1901 and 1914 (Palmer 1992: 170) In the context of this rising workplace militancy in the early twentieth century, labourism began to bear fruit. It was not a radical ideology but rather the expression of skilled craft workers seeking to institute reforms that would benefit labour. In the period before the First World War, labourism was very successful, especially at the local level. Many labour candidates were elected to school boards, municipal councils and provincial legislatures, and almost every industrial community had an Independent Labour Party—even though these organizations tended to be small and short-lived. Sometimes these local parties federated to establish provincial labour parties. This happened in Ontario and Manitoba, albeit briefly, in 1906–1907, and more broadly across the country after 1916, when Independent Labour parties were established in Nova Scotia and Ontario, Dominion Labour parties on the prairies and the Federated Labour Party in British Columbia.

Yet labourism was highly fragmented, decentralized and somewhat episodic. When industrial conflict arose, independent labour organizations would form, but when the conflict subsided, the organizations would cease to function effectively. Many of the members would drift back to the left wing of the Liberal Party, as happened, for example, with three labour candidates elected federally before the First World War.

These workplace transformations also created the conditions for the emergence of more radical political orientations in the movement. Alongside syndicalism and labourism, a Marxist-inspired, worker-based socialism emerged. Its first important expression was the Socialist Party of Canada (SPC), created by the amalgamation in 1904 of several smaller socialist parties. In its early years, the SPC promoted the "uncompromising principles of revolutionary socialism" (Palmer 1992: 183) and adopted a form of politics sometimes called "impossibilism." The SPC's official view was that it was impossible to reform capitalism to workers' benefit. The pursuit of reform through the election of labour candidates was therefore futile. Socialist education, in preparation for the workers' revolutionary overthrow of capitalism and the wages system, took precedence over the labourists' parliamentary struggle for immediate reforms and the syndicalists' direct workplace action (Campbell 1999).

The state's response to this turn-of-the-century militancy and growing radicalism was two-fold. On the one hand, between 1895 and 1914, the state used the militia to crush strikes on more than twenty occasions, thus facilitating the decline of workers' organizations like the IWW. The working class became a "community under siege" (Palmer 1992: 163). On the other hand, a more subtle and sophisticated approach to industrial relations was developed under the direction of the young William Lyon Mackenzie King, who would later become Canada's longest-serving prime minister. King oversaw the establishment of a federal Department of Labour in 1900, and the passing of the *Industrial Disputes Investigation Act* (IDIA) in 1907. The IDIA was King's attempt to have the state intervene in industrial disputes involving utilities, railways and coalmines as an "impartial umpire," ostensibly representing the interests of the community. The provisions of the IDIA included compulsory third-party conciliation and a "cooling off" period before a labour stoppage could occur.

The IDIA did not include the right to form a union, nor did it allow conciliation boards to do more than make recommendations to resolve labour-management disputes. It was primarily a means of averting strikes, and for this limited purpose it worked. From 1907 to 1911, the IDIA was used in 101 disputes, and strikes were averted in nine of ten cases. Workers grudgingly accepted this state intervention, even though the settlements could rarely be considered complete victories, in large part because they recognized that in an all-out war with capitalists, labour would be the loser. Significantly, in this new, twentieth-century form of intervention in Canada's industrial relations, the state intervened only when labour militancy, and not employers' actions, threatened industrial peace. The IDIA's purpose was to restore relative harmony between capital and labour so that profit making could proceed without undue interruption from militant workers. These interventions also affected working-class politics, drawing trade union support away from the Conservatives and towards the Liberals.

By the First World War, "international" craft-based unionism was still dominant in both Canada and the U.S., but it was experiencing real challenges. The struggle for industrial unionism had a long way to go. While increasingly militant, workers in the early twentieth century were still very much divided. The advent of world war, however, forever changed working-class ideas and organizations.

THE FIRST WORLD WAR, THE LABOUR REVOLT AND ITS AFTERMATH, 1914–1929

The First World War and the 1917 Bolshevik Revolution in Russia inspired an upsurge in labour organizing and militancy. The number of union members was exploding, from 140,000 in 1915 to 378,000 in 1919 (Heron 1998: 270). In 1917, there were 218 strikes involving more than 50,000 workers, double the numbers for 1916 and more than any year since the turn of the century. By 1919, Canada was in the middle of a countrywide labour revolt, with 150,000 workers taking part in 427 strikes.

The labour shortage created by the First World War prompted both a surge in unionization and an expansion of unionism to new groups of workers, including municipal workers, clerical workers and postal workers. In wartime industries, workplace conditions were tough as employers pushed workers for higher levels of output in support of the war effort. This intensification of work, coupled with accelerated deskilling, inflation and profiteering with wage controls meant that workers were unable to keep up with the cost of living. Employers and governments also pushed for a ban on strikes in wartime industries. The irony was rich: Canadian workers were fighting for democracy abroad, but experiencing a lack of that very democracy at home, both politically and industrially.

The revolutionary tone of the times was accentuated by the dramatic 1917 Bolshevik Revolution in Russia, which threatened for a time to spread to Western Europe (and potentially further) and had a significant impact on workers across North America. A number of local labour councils across Canada passed motions supporting the new revolutionary government. These events gave proponents of radical industrial unionism a significant boost. In March 1919, a group of over 230 workers based largely in Western Canada met at the Western Labour Conference in Calgary and established the One Big Union (OBU). Many of the OBU leaders were members of the Socialist Party of Canada, leaders of the Winnipeg General Strike, or inspired by IWW ideas. Many were also craft unionists who saw the limitations of the craft model and were committed to creating an organization that would encompass the growing numbers of unskilled industrial workers. The OBU broke away from the increasingly cautious TLC, based largely in the East, identified openly with revolutionary movements in Russia and Germany and contributed to the widespread radical tone of the times.

The 1919 Winnipeg General Strike, one of the most pivotal events in Canadian labour history, was at the heart of this revolt and illustrates the way that working-class consciousness and action were changing in the wake of war. As in the rest of the country, industrial militancy had been growing in Winnipeg over the first two decades of the century. Winnipeg was then one of Canada's fastest-growing cities, a rail and industrial centre with a North End teeming with European working-class immigrants. Economic inequalities, deep class divisions, steep wartime inflation and poor (frequently dreadful) working and living conditions were the context in which industrial unions sought recognition and the right to negotiate the conditions of their work and wages with employers. It was a mighty battle. Winnipeg industrialists were rigidly anti-union. Streetcar workers and the metal workers at Vulcan Iron Works had fought bitter strikes in 1906. In the summer of 1918, when the City of Winnipeg workers went on strike, they were joined by between 1,400 and 1,700 other Winnipeg workers. The situation was explosive: "Confrontation was in the air. Martial law and arrests were threatened from the outset. Working class solidarity with the civic workers was palpable and explosive … The machinists called for a general strike" (Mitchell and Naylor 1998: 180).

In a move towards industrial unionism, workers in the metals trades established the Winnipeg Metal Trades Council to coordinate their attempts to bargain collectively. Their employers were intransigent. E.G. Barrett, owner of Vulcan Iron Works, typified their stance: "This is a free country and ... as far as we are concerned the day will never come when we will have to take orders from any union" (Smith 1985: 42). Barrett and the other metal-shop owners simply refused to meet with any union representatives. The Metals Trades Council appealed for support to the Winnipeg Trades and Labour Council, which then called for a general strike—a large strike that spreads beyond a specific workplace or sector, either in sympathy with particular workers' struggle or with political aims. In the following week, member unions conducted a referendum. The result was overwhelming: 11,112 in favour and 524 against the call for a general strike. On May 15, 1919, some 25,000 Winnipeg workers, including many non-unionists led by 500 female telephone workers, walked off the job to start the largest general strike in Canada's history. This action prompted many sympathy strikes in cities and towns across the country (Kealey 1984).

The strike lasted six weeks. A committee met daily to coordinate strike efforts, maintain order and ensure the provision of essential services. Essential goods, such as milk, reached citizens "by authority of the Strike Committee," making it appear as if the strikers were in control of the city. Indeed, this was at least partly true.

The business and professional class responded by forming the Citizens Committee of 1,000, an extension of the Citizens Committee of 100 formed the year before during the civic workers' strike. They cast the strike as an attempt to establish a Bolshevik-style government in Canada and therefore as a fundamental threat to the social order that had to be repressed. In this view they were joined by Prime Minister Robert Borden, who reflected, "In some cities there was a deliberate attempt to overthrow the existing organization of the Government and to supersede it by crude, fantastic methods founded upon absurd conceptions of what had been accomplished in Russia. It became necessary in some communities to repress revolutionary methods with a stern hand and from this I did not shrink" (Heron 1998: 5).

When the Winnipeg police force was dismissed en masse on June 9 because its members refused to sign a no-strike pledge, the Citizens Committee organized their replacement by untrained but sympathetic "special constables," whose one-sided aggression precipitated what little violence occurred. The Canadian government rushed through changes to the *Immigration Act* to enable it to deport foreign-born strike leaders. On the night of June 16–17, police swooped down on the homes of the strike leaders, arresting them and hauling them off to Stony Mountain Penitentiary. A mass rally on Saturday, June 21—"Bloody Saturday"—led to four Royal North-West Mounted Police charges down Main Street. On the last charge, the police fired shots into the crowd, killing two strikers. Shortly after, on June 25, the Winnipeg General Strike came to an end. About 3,500 strikers lost their jobs; many were blacklisted.

On the whole, the leaders of the strike, most of them British immigrants steeped in the non-revolutionary politics of their homeland, appear simply to have been trying to achieve collective bargaining rights. They wanted union recognition and the right to collectively bargain for their working conditions and wages. To them, the General Strike was a powerful tactic to pursue union rights. But to many others, the larger context of the strike—almost twenty years of labour militancy as industrial unions, often led by socialists and promoting socialist values, struggled with aggressive employers and governments in what amounted frequently to industrial warfare—seemed to be revolutionary. As labour historian Greg Kealey (1984: 12) observed after surveying the speeches, writings and activities of local leaders of the many pan-Canadian strikes in 1919: "The message was the same across the country. The capitalist system could not be reformed; it must be transformed. Production for profit must cease; production for use must begin." Thus, while neither the intent nor the leaders of the Winnipeg General Strike were revolutionary, the business and professional class and their state supporters believed it was a revolutionary situation. In a sense they were right—the situation *was* potentially revolutionary. From their perspective, it had to be crushed, and it was. An important aspect of this was the remarkable process by which the federal government and the leaders of the Citizens Committee of 1,000, in what can only be described as a conspiracy, afterwards railroaded the strike leaders into jail (Chaboyer and Black 2006).

The revolt signaled the labour movement's powerful potential but its defeat also had consequences for the movement in the years immediately following. On the one hand, the revolt can be viewed as the culmination of the radical, worker-based, Marxist-inspired, syndicalist and socialist elements that had for two decades struggled against employers, the state and the craft-based unions to emerge as significant elements of Canada's labour politics. Other elements—labourism, and the cautious partyism of the TLC—were pushed to the side for a time. Thousands of workers in TLC unions abandoned their cautious approach and were swept up in the radical, even revolutionary, mood of the times. On the other hand, the 1919 strikes were defeated; the rising wave of militancy and revolutionary idealism was stopped in its tracks. The consequences for union organization and politics were momentous: the dramatic fall-off in union membership, the consolidation of the more conservative elements in the labour movement, the virtual elimination of both syndicalism and independent, Canadian-controlled, Marxist-inspired socialism as viable political options; and a realignment of the politics of organized labour.

Despite the massive pan-Canadian labour revolt, most industrial workers still could not join a union. By the end of 1922, union membership had dropped by 100,000 since its 1919 peak, and matters were only getting worse. By 1922, the workers' revolt in Canada was largely over, save for some vicious battles in the coalfields of Cape Breton, in which the state intervened with armed troops, up to

1925. As labour historian Irving Abella (1973: 1) put it: "for the Canadian labour movement, no period was more dismal than the 1920s. Organization was at a standstill, membership declined dramatically, and union leadership was divided and paralyzed."

The forcible defeat of the labour revolt consolidated the power of both employers and the state, and together both were able to repress "undesirable" labour activity for a time. Employers' confidence in controlling their workplaces had returned, as had their use of methods that guaranteed the open shop, like firing or blacklisting unionists, or forcing workers, as a condition of employment, to sign "yellow-dog contracts" stating they did not belong to and would not join a union. Economic conditions helped them in this task: returning veterans flooded the labour market, and a severe postwar depression between 1920 and 1925 made it very difficult for workers to challenge their employers. The federal government deported "enemy aliens" and socialists but also increased immigration rates to further flood the market with cheap labour. The government's efforts were aided by the RCMP, who spied on communists, socialists and union and student activists as part of an emerging surveillance apparatus (Kealey 1993).

The craft union movement had distanced itself from the great labour revolt and pursued a relatively narrow and apolitical path of caution and complacency. Craft unions remained unwilling and unable to respond to the challenge created by the rise of the mass-production industries and the growth in the numbers of factory workers. Its leaders opposed industrial unionism and continued to believe that only highly skilled craft workers should be organized.

Those who remained committed to industrial unionism were marginalized. Other Canadian-based union centrals were emerging alongside the craft-led TLC. The Canadian and Catholic Confederation of Labour (CCCL)—dominated by the Roman Catholic Church and concerned about the TLC's disinterest in the particular problems of French-speaking workers—emerged in Quebec in 1921. The All-Canadian Congress of Labour (ACCL)—comprising unions expelled from the TLC for their advocacy of industrial unionism and led by the Canadian Brotherhood of Railway Employees and the remnants of the OBU—was established in 1927. The ACCL kept the flame of industrial unionism alive, but the organization was not in the mainstream, and struggled to survive.

The socialist left also underwent a process of realignment. In 1921, the Communist Party of Canada (CPC) was formed, bringing together members from the Socialist Party of Canada, the Social Democratic Party of Canada and the Socialist Party of North America (formed in 1915 in Southern Ontario as a breakaway from the SPC). The CPC formed a core of militant, ideologically committed union organizers who would keep organizing on the industrial union model alive through the very difficult inter-war period. The CPC's strategies were based on a particular approach to leadership known as "vanguardism," which holds that a cadre of professional revolutionaries is needed to develop revolutionary class consciousness amongst workers. CPC members were generally well respected by local union members as effective and militant union organizers who tended to be committed to rank-and-file activism.

However, the CPC's link to the Communist Party of the Soviet Union meant that the strategies adopted were not always suited to conditions in Canada. Constant shifts in policy and strategic direction, because of Moscow's shifts, caused conflict and disunity on the left and harmed the party's credibility. This was best seen in the CPC's swing between the strategies of "entryism" and "dual unionism." Up to 1930, the CPC's policy was based on the idea that activists should enter and work within existing workers' mass organizations, and build, through engagement in debates and by taking on leadership roles, a left-wing current that would encourage a more radical and militant stance. The entryist approach led many CPC members to join the TLC craft unions. In 1930, the party did an about-face and pursued a dual union strategy, creating competing union organizations under the banner of the Workers' Unity League that would offer a radical alternative to the TLC's more conservative craft unions. After 1935, they returned to the entryist strategy. While there are pros and cons to each strategy, these contradictions must be part of any evaluation of the CPC's approach to organizing workers.

THE GREAT DEPRESSION, 1929–1939

The 1929 U.S. stock market crash that precipitated the Great Depression quickly spread to Canada. The economic impact was unprecedented. Businesses closed down due to lack of demand. By 1933, nearly one third of the labour force was out of work and one fifth was reliant on some sort of government relief (Palmer 1992: 241). These effects were uneven across the country, with those in the Prairies suffering from the dual effects of a depression and unprecedented crop failures. Out of the desperation of the Great Depression, and in response to the government's inability to undo its harmful effects, workers looked to alternative ways of organizing the economy and new political vehicles to deliver the changes needed.

As organizations of the working class, unions would play a key role in precipitating these political responses. The Communist Party generated some of the most serious unionizing efforts in the depths of the Great Depression, attempting to expand industrial unionism and organize the burgeoning ranks of the unemployed. In 1930, in its turn to dual unionism under the leadership of Tim Buck, the CPC established the Workers' Unity League (WUL), a new union central that became "a storm centre of new unionizing efforts in the darkest years of the early 1930s"

(Heron 2012: 63). In the context of rapidly decreasing craft union membership, the WUL was militant, highly creative and extremely successful, with 40,000 members at its height (Endicott 2012: 31). Most of the strikes in the first half of the 1930s were led by WUL affiliates, and many were met with brutal state repression. In Saskatchewan, in the Estevan miners' strike of 1931, a parade of four hundred miners in cars and trucks was met with gunfire from the RCMP and local police. The shots killed three miners, and the police arrested another fifty. The next day sixty RCMP constables raided the union's headquarters and conducted a house-to-house search for union members (Hanson 1974). In the furniture workers' strike in 1933 in Stratford, Ontario, the authorities sent in troops with brand new machine-gun carriers to put down the strike. In a Bloedel's lumber strike in Vancouver in 1934, police made mass arrests and evicted strikers from their homes. Perhaps because of this capacity to organize workers' resistance in the direst of circumstances, the CPC itself was banned in 1931 and its leadership arrested.

Workers' attraction to the CPC was not always the result of an ideological commitment to the tenets of communism. Keenly aware of the need for greater gender and racial equality to build stronger and more resilient workers' organizations, party organizers worked harder than most unionists to enlist the support of women and racialized workers, on whom organized labour rarely focused (Sangster 1985; Creese 1988). For instance, the WUL actively recruited Chinese workers and included them on union executives and strike committees to overcome employers' racially based divide-and-conquer tactics (Das Gupta 1998: 318–19).

The CPC was also committed to organizing the unemployed who, given their lack of a job, were abandoned by the rest of labour movement. The Great Depression left many tens of thousands of young single men unemployed by the early 1930s. Fearful that these men might be radicalized if they gathered in large urban centres, in October 1932 the federal government of R.B. Bennett passed an order-in-council setting up rural relief camps. Single unemployed men were then denied relief in towns and cities, effectively forcing them into the camps, where conditions were harsh and the pay was paltry. Strikes and other disturbances became a frequent occurrence. Out of these conditions arose the Relief Camp Workers' Union, affiliated with the WUL.

In June 1935, after spending months protesting in Vancouver, more than a thousand Relief Camp Workers' Union members began the "On-to-Ottawa Trek" to present their grievances to Prime Minister Bennett and rally support for their cause. The federal government, fearful of the Trek's political potential, decided to stop it before it reached Winnipeg, a city with a radical tradition and a large left-wing movement, and where hundreds more people were waiting to join up. Despite the Trekkers' efforts to reach a peaceful resolution, the RCMP attacked them at a mass meeting on July 1 in Regina's Market Square. By the end of the "Regina Riot," one city policeman was dead, scores of people were injured, and several Trekkers and citizens were hospitalized with gunshot wounds. The On-to-Ottawa Trek was over, but political change was brewing.

The devastation of the Great Depression sprouted competing political ideologies, including "social democracy," a broad political orientation that seeks to balance a free market economy with a commitment to economic equality and social justice through redistribution of wealth and universal social programs. In the immediate aftermath of the Winnipeg General Strike, Canada's traditional national two-party system broke down, opening the door for relatively more radical or social democratic third parties to get elected. Both labour and farmer representatives scored electoral victories, and farmer-based governments were formed in Ontario, Alberta and Manitoba between 1919 and 1922. At the national level, sixty-five members of the farmer-based Progressive Party were elected in 1921, along with two labour representatives. These developments shaped the character of the social democracy that would struggle to emerge over the next decade.

What Canadian social democracy would look like was the subject of considerable debate throughout the 1920s. A great many organizations and ideological currents were part of a complex political landscape. Some participants advocated the establishment of a British-style labour party, with formal affiliation of the unions. Others called for a farmer-labour party, bringing together the different groups being harmed by the big capitalists. The central figure navigating these complex political waters and creating a distinctive Canadian form of social democracy was J.S. Woodsworth.

Woodsworth, a former Protestant minister, was among those charged for his involvement in the 1919 Winnipeg General Strike. He was also, along with William Irvine of Alberta, one of the two labour representatives elected to the House of Commons in 1921. Irvine informed the Speaker of the House of Commons: "The honourable member for Winnipeg Centre [Woodsworth] is the leader of the labour group—and I am the group" (Avakumovic 1978: 42). In 1924, Woodsworth and Irvine were joined in the House of Commons by eleven members of the Progressive Party to form the "Ginger Group," which by 1929 had grown to twenty-one. The Ginger Group was one of the elements that would come together in 1932 to form the Co-operative Commonwealth Federation (CCF).

Woodsworth was determined that any new party would be a socialist party. It would not, however, be a socialist labour party like the British Labour Party, wherein unions affiliated with the party have dominance in party governance and agenda-setting. Woodsworth felt that, unlike in Britain, the working class in a less industrialized Canada was too small to support, on its own, an electorally viable labour party. Instead, Canada needed a people's party that included labour, farmers, the middle class and socialists. This vision was distinct from that of British Labour, the CPC and the pre-war Marxist-inspired Canadian socialist parties, all of which were almost exclusively labour parties.

Two other ideological elements contributed to shaping what would become the CCF. The first was the "social gospel," a set of ideas advanced by a radical group of Protestant ministers who, like Woodsworth, left or were pushed out of their churches and who sought to build the kingdom of heaven, of social and economic justice, here on earth. This strain of morally based, social justice-oriented socialism became an important part of Canadian social democracy. The second ideological element was Fabian Socialism, a gradualist form of socialism characterized by a strong emphasis on central planning and the role of technical experts, with roots in the British Labour Party. The League for Social Reconstruction, established in 1932 by a group of Eastern Canadian university professors, including Frank Scott, Frank Underhill, Eugene Forsey, and, although still then a student, David Lewis, was a strong proponent of Fabianism. The CCF, which Woodsworth guided to formation, included these many non-labour elements—farmers, Fabianism, the Ginger Group, the social gospel—even while seeing itself as the party of labour.

The CCF was formally established at a conference in Calgary in 1932, the result of more than a decade of hard work, with a mandate to meet in Regina in 1933 to finalize and adopt a program. The result was the 1933 Regina Manifesto, famous less for its detailed listing of fourteen immediate demands than for its ringing declaration: "No CCF government will rest content until it has eradicated capitalism and put into operation the full program of socialized planning which will lead to the establishment in Canada of the Cooperative Commonwealth." The CCF was part movement, part party, emphasizing political education as much as electioneering (Whitehorn 1992: 24).

The establishment of the CCF crystallized the political landscape of Canada's union movement, and set up the basis for serious conflict over the next twenty years. The Communist Party of Canada, acting through the WUL, had put down deep and meaningful roots in the union movement as the champion of militant industrial unionism. The CCF, a grassroots party with only minimal labour representation, was having some modest electoral success, electing seven MPs to federal parliament in 1935. The TLC remained committed to Gomperist partyism. Finally, the Liberal Party, under the leadership of Mackenzie King, was also chasing labour votes. King, the engineer of the IDIA and author of *Industry and Humanity* (King 1918), a virtual blueprint for the welfare state in Canada, was prepared to move the Liberals to the left to hold on to the labour vote. Thus the newly established CCF found itself attacked from the left by the CPC and from the right by the Liberal Party, both attempting to prevent the CCF from becoming the party of organized labour.

From the outset the CPC and the CCF saw each other as rivals for the allegiance of the Canadian working class. While the CCF enjoyed more support at the ballot box, the energetic organizing efforts of the WUL in many unionized workplaces ensured the Communists remained a viable political force. The CCF's distinctive social character as a multi-class alliance placed it at a disadvantage relative to the more purely proletarian CPC in the eyes of many workers, and it was certainly not the party of organized labour. CCF National Secretary David Lewis and others thought it imperative, therefore, for the party to establish a much closer link with the unions and win their allegiance away from the CPC. To achieve this goal, the CCF would have to squeeze out the communists. This great battle for the hearts and minds of Canadian union members, in which Lewis played a central role, raged throughout the 1930s and 1940s, particularly in the new home of industrial unionism, the Congress of Industrial Organizations (CIO).

In the U.S., pressure to organize the mass production industries was also growing. At the 1935 AFL convention, United Mine Workers leader John L. Lewis took a historic step. Reacting against the AFL's determination to divide industrial workers by organizing them on the basis of craft, Lewis announced the formation of the Committee for Industrial Organization, which would work within the AFL to organize factory workers into industrial unions. The letters "CIO" became a call to arms. Overnight, the CIO made spectacular gains in hitherto non-union U.S. industries such as steel, auto, electrical, rubber and other areas of mass production. The greatest organizing drive of the twentieth century began. The tactic at the heart of the drive was simple, powerful and unprecedented: the "sit-down" strike. Factory workers simply put down their tools and occupied a plant.

Although the U.S.-based CIO confined most of its efforts to the huge task of organizing mass production industries in the U.S., the CIO label was magic. Scores of highly skilled organizers used the CIO name in Canada, even though they received no money from the U.S. The craft unions opposed this organizing drive as a threat to their own membership base. In 1937 in the U.S., the AFL expelled the CIO, which was renamed the Congress of Industrial Organizations. In 1939, in an expression of intense opposition to industrial unionism and loyalty to their U.S. parent unions, the Trades and Labour Congress expelled the CIO unions and their more than 20,000 Canadian members. The CIO unions in Canada responded by amalgamating with the ACCL to form the new Canadian Congress of Labour (CCL) in 1940.

Many outstanding communist union organizers, whose skills had been honed in the WUL, continued to build the industrial union movement in Canada under the CIO banner after 1935. According to Abella (1973: 55), "there was a direct pipeline from the CIO offices to Communist headquarters." This created the basis for a bitter rivalry between Communists and social democrats over who would have the greatest political influence over the burgeoning industrial labour movement in Canada.

Despite widespread excitement, the CIO drive for industrial unionism developed more slowly in Canada than in the U.S. Opposition from craft unionists and employers was very strong in both countries. For example, when the CIO-inspired Steel Workers Organizing Committee attempted in 1937 to organize a foundry in Sarnia, Ontario, where Eastern Europeans made up a significant minority of the workers, enraged citizens, "united in their hatred of the foreigners, descended on the foundry with an assortment of anti-union devices—crowbars, baseball bats, bricks and steel pipes. A bloody battle ensued, and within an hour the union was broken, as were the arms, legs and heads of many of the 'sit-downers'" (Abella 1973: 7). The Sarnia police refused to intervene, and the sit-down strikers were convicted in court of trespassing. No charges were laid against the strikebreakers. It was clear whose side the state was on.

But the main difference in Canada was the lack of support from the state. In the U.S., a key element of Franklin Roosevelt's New Deal was the 1935 *National Labor Relations Act* (usually called the "Wagner Act" after the senator who initiated the legislation), which protected those trying to organize a union from the anti-labour practices of the past and compelled employers to bargain collectively with unions chosen by a majority of workers in a workplace. In contrast, Canadian governments passed no such enabling legislation; compulsory recognition of unions when they had the support of a majority of workers was still almost a decade away.

The CIO's first significant breakthrough in Canada occurred at the General Motors plant in Oshawa. In January 1937, General Motors announced its largest profit ever, $200 million, and then imposed the fifth wage cut in five years on its Oshawa workers. In April the workers struck. Ontario premier Mitchell Hepburn, vowing that the CIO would not succeed in Oshawa, described the strike as "a fight to the finish." In the end, the strike was successful, ushering in an unprecedented era of industrial union organizing. As Abella (1973: 22) puts it, the workers' victory against the combined power of big business and the state "gave the CIO the impetus it so badly needed to begin organization in the mass production industries of the country."

However, in the absence of legislation comparable to the *Wagner Act*, gains continued to be slow in coming, even after Oshawa. By October 1937, CIO organizing in Canada had ground to a halt. That fall, Hepburn won a landslide re-election in Ontario on an anti-CIO platform, while in early 1938 Quebec premier Maurice Duplessis began using his government's infamous anti-communist "Padlock Laws" to raid the homes of organizers and confiscate their union records. The law, officially titled *An Act to Protect the Province Against Communistic Propaganda*, gave the province's Attorney General the arbitrary right to effectively "padlock" any property suspected of being used in the production of communist material, and persons found guilty of participating in the production of such materials were subject to imprisonment. The law was extremely controversial because it denied the presumption of innocence, severely restricted freedom of speech, and was overly general in its interpretation of communist propaganda, targeting CIO activists and other political opponents of the Duplessis government. Faced with these difficult conditions, membership in CIO unions declined in 1938, and by 1939, only 5 percent of their jurisdiction in Canada was organized (Palmer 1992: 256). Only under wartime conditions would Canadian industrial unions finally make their big breakthrough.

THE SECOND WORLD WAR AND THE POSTWAR "COMPROMISE," 1939–1948

The Second World War was a turning point for labour in Canada. The war acted as a catalyst for union activity, much as the First World War had done during the great labour revolt twenty years earlier. Union membership doubled, from 359,000 in 1939 to 724,000 in 1944 (Godard 2011: 77), while unemployment plummeted, leading to a labour shortage in the middle of the Second World War. The cost of living rose, and so too did workers' expectations and demands, especially for the rights to unionize and to negotiate working conditions and wages. The memory of unionism's defeat after the First World War and the long hardships of the Great Depression had also stiffened workers' resolve to struggle for permanent changes to their relationship with employers and the state.

The result was a surge of labour militancy in the early 1940s comparable to that of 1917–1919. Work stoppages doubled between 1941 and 1942 and again the following year. By 1943, one in every three union members in Canada was on strike (Panitch and Swartz 2003: 12). Many of the leaders of this renewed labour militancy had honed their organizing skills in the "Dirty Thirties" and were associated with some form of radical politics.

While Communism was one of the significant ideological currents of radical politics emerging from the Great Depression, its influence within the labour movement was severely curbed in the 1940s. In September 1939, just prior to the declaration of war, Stalin and Hitler signed a non-aggression pact, as a result of which the CPC—until then strongly anti-fascist—did yet another of its Moscow-determined policy shifts and attacked Canada's war effort as merely another conflict between capitalist countries. As historian Norman Penner (1988: 164) described it, of all the party's shifts in strategy, "none were more incredible than this decision to oppose the war against fascism. In all the countries of the West, an exodus of Party members and supporters took place, in an angry and confused response to this sudden change." On June 6, 1940, the CPC was declared illegal and its leading members, including many active union organizers, were interned, thus further weakening their efforts to control the Canadian labour movement.

When Hitler invaded the Soviet Union on June 23, 1941, the CPC again reversed its stance, becoming the labour movement's most patriotic supporter of the war effort, enforcing a no-strike pledge and promoting wartime production targets. The CCF became the more militant party, refusing to accept a no-strike pledge in the absence of government-legislated labour rights like those found in the *Wagner Act*. In 1940, the CCF engineered a merger of the ACCL with the CIO to form the Canadian Congress of Labour, an alternative to the TLC.

By the mid 1940s, growing numbers of workers had become members of the Co-operative Commonwealth Federation. The CCF would become the social-democratic and non-communist branch of the divided Canadian socialist movement. Throughout 1942, the CCF attracted more and more members, especially among union workers in Ontario. This growth in CCF influence in the labour movement was reinforced when Charles Millard—a staunch CCFer appointed CIO representative for Ontario by John L. Lewis in 1939—appointed talented young CCF organizers to important positions in CIO unions. As Gad Horowitz (1968: 68) noted, "To claim that ... staffs of the new industrial unions at this time were hired solely on the basis of their political affiliations would not be an exaggeration." Millard soon had a staff of ten active CCFers at the Steel Workers Organizing Committee headquarters, which only recently had been dominated by the CPC. Thus, by the end of 1940, the CCF had dramatically improved its position in the labour movement. In 1943, its efforts were capped when the Canadian Congress of Labour passed a resolution recognizing the CCF as the "political arm of labour in Canada."

These gains were replicated at the polls: between 1941 and 1944, electoral support for the CCF boomed at the very time industrial militancy was exploding. In 1941, the CCF formed the official opposition in British Columbia, winning a plurality of votes. In February 1942, CCF candidate Joe Noseworthy defeated federal Progressive Conservative party leader Arthur Meighan in a by-election, picking up the first-ever CCF seat in Ontario. In the August 1943 Ontario provincial election, the CCF narrowly missed forming the government. Its share of the vote jumped from 5 percent to 31 percent, and the party formed the official opposition, going from zero to thirty-four seats, nineteen of them won by active unionists. A month later, in September 1943, a federal Gallup Poll showed the CCF running just ahead of the Liberals and Progressive Conservatives in Canada-wide popularity. In 1944, under the leadership of Tommy Douglas, the CCF formed the provincial government in Saskatchewan, the first-ever social-democratic government in North America. The CCF, it appeared, was on a roll.

The simultaneous rise in labour militancy and CCF electoral strength finally forced the federal government to act. As always, labour militancy induced state intervention. The Inquiry into Labour Relations and Wage Conditions in Canada, conducted by the National War Labour Board at Prime Minister Mackenzie King's request, called for a labour code similar to the U.S. *Wagner Act*, something that would prevent the increasingly bitter recognition strikes over the basic right to unionize. King feared that unless he acted, he risked losing labour's support, thus threatening the chances of a Liberal re-election. The result, almost seven years after the victory at Oshawa's General Motors plant, was Order-in-Council PC 1003, enacted in 1944 in an attempt to control labour militancy and win back labour's political support from the surging CCF. PC 1003 guaranteed the right to organize and bargain collectively, established a procedure for the certification of unions with majority support, and declared that labour practices intended to interfere with and frustrate the formation of a union were unfair and contrary to the law. It also recognized the exclusive bargaining agency principle, prevented employers and unions from engaging in a strike or lockout during the term of a collective agreement and established an administrative tribunal to enforce these rules.

King's Liberals also appropriated part of the CCF's program for economic and social reform. In 1943, King established a Committee on Reconstruction, whose research director was League for Social Reconstruction member Leonard Marsh, to plan Canada's version of the postwar welfare state, and before the 1945 federal election he introduced the family allowance. King wrote in his diary: "I think I have cut the ground in large part from under the CCF" (Horowitz 1968: 38).

These major concessions to labour worked both to control workplace militancy and shift electoral fortunes. The CCF was stopped in its tracks. In the June 1945 Ontario provincial election, the CCF's vote share dropped by 10 percent and its seats plummeted from thirty-four to eight. A week later in the federal election, the CCF almost doubled its share of the federal vote, going from 8.5 percent to 15.6 percent and electing a record twenty-eight CCF Members of Parliament. This put the party in third place, for the first time ever. But relative to its hopes, the results were disappointing: the party was unable to win a single seat in Ontario and Quebec. It was still confined to its original Western stronghold. These results were the best the CCF would ever achieve. The 1945 federal election was the beginning of the end for the party. However, the weakness of left-wing forces at the ballot box did not stunt the growth and development of unions after the Second World War. Instead, unions would manage to gain unprecedented strength in the postwar period.

QUESTIONS FOR DISCUSSION

1. What are the differences between craft unions and industrial unions, and why do these differences matter?
2. Why were certain workers excluded from unions, and what were the effects of these exclusions?
3. Why did the rise of Taylorism and Fordism produce such a strong and radicalizing reaction amongst workers?
4. Was the Winnipeg General Strike a success or a failure for workers?

5. What were the dominant political orientations amongst unionized workers during this period? How did they shift over time, and why?

6. Many of the Canadian labour movement's achievements up to 1945 were secured outside the scope of the law. What does this tell us about the relationship between labour and the law?

CHAPTER 4

FROM KEYNESIANISM TO NEOLIBERALISM: UNION BREAKTHROUGHS AND CHALLENGES

In the aftermath of the Second World War, a new "compromise" emerged in the workplace, governed by a formal labour relations framework and growing state intervention in social and economic realms. In this period, we see the rise of the welfare state and mass expansion of unionization to new segments of the working class (namely women, racialized workers and the public and private service sectors). However, this period was not without its challenges and contradictions, as union power and employers' acceptance of the new postwar regime was uneven at best. By the mid 1970s, a confluence of events would lead to economic crisis, a return of significant labour unrest and eventually the imposition of neoliberalism as a dominant political ideology. This chapter charts the union movement's trajectory through this period.

THE KEYNESIAN "GOLDEN AGE"

From the end of the Great Depression to the mid 1970s, the theories of British economist John Maynard Keynes provided the main inspiration for economic policy-makers in Canada and other capitalist democracies. The general theme of Keynes' economic analysis was that the dramatic ups and downs of the business cycle could be tamed through counter-cyclical measures initiated by government. Government would use deficit spending (through a mixture of new spending and tax cuts) to spark demand during economic downturns, and it would use economic boom periods to build a fiscal surplus through taxation to pay for the deficits incurred during the lean years.

While Keynes' theories relied heavily on state intervention, he was not a socialist. Indeed, Keynesian economics was used to undercut calls for radical change in the economic system. The ascendency of Keynesian policy played a central role in sustaining what has been called the "Golden Age" of capitalism, a period of unprecedented global economic prosperity from the end of the Second World War to the mid 1960s. Organized labour played an important role in the new consensus after depression and war, agreeing to labour peace in exchange for organizational stability and a formalized system of labour relations.

THE BENEFITS AND COSTS OF THE POSTWAR COMPROMISE

The political and economic elites' acceptance of the Keynesian compromise was the product of the sustained and militant pressure placed on them by the labour movement during and after the Second World War. As we saw in Chapter 3, the state intervenes in labour relations when workers—whether in the form of strikes, political gains by labour's representatives or both—threaten to upset the balance of power between capital and labour. In these circumstances the state makes certain concessions to labour but also exacts a price in arranging a new class compromise to promote labour and political peace. The laws that formed the basis of labour relations after the Second World War reveal these contradictions.

In PC 1003 and the provincial labour relations acts, unions won the basic right of recognition and the right to negotiate the terms of employment. The regulations legally bound employers to recognize and deal with any union that could demonstrate the support of a majority of the workers in a workplace. The postwar laws also defined and prohibited unfair labour practices, so many of which had been important tools in employers' union-busting toolboxes. The law now included a ban on firing workers who were union activists or trying to unionize the workplace, on employer agents infiltrating the union, and on company unions—that is, workers' organizations controlled or dominated by employers. The 1945 strike at the Ford Motor Company in Windsor, Ontario, and Justice Ivan Rand's settlement of that dispute, also granted unions the right to collect union dues from all those whose work they would negotiate terms and conditions for. It also required that employers automatically deduct those dues and remit them to the union if that is what the union desired. This arrangement became known as the Rand Formula. The long struggle for industrial unionism had been won; the benefits for legions of semi-skilled factory workers were immense as their unions could now negotiate legally binding collective agreements. This led to a surge in unionization as well, pushing up the union density rate.

But many of labour's gains either came at a price or were themselves also weaknesses. First, the new legislation made the preservation of labour peace its top priority. To do that, the state now defined what counted as a legal strike and, by extension, an illegal one. Workers could no longer strike to force employer recognition of their unions, since the law set out a legal procedure for that. Nor would workers be legally able to withdraw their labour for political aims (as in the fight for the nine-hour workday) or in sympathy with other workers (as in the case of the Winnipeg General Strike). The only legal strike would now be one aimed at establishing a new collective agreement and labour legislation required that a "no strikes / no lockouts" clause be included in all collective agreements.

Legal limits on the use of the strike were connected to a second important and contradictory development: the creation of grievance procedures to resolve workplace problems. On the one hand, the grievance system represented a dramatic gain for workers because it placed strict limits on management's ability to treat workers in an arbitrary manner. On the other hand, it also took away from labour's toolbox. This system replaced the traditional method of resolving workplace problems through the direct and collective actions of workers, under which management would have to resolve problems immediately or risk lost production and profits. Now, any withdrawal of labour while a collective agreement was in force would be considered a wildcat strike and illegal. Workers either had to use the new grievance mechanisms, which tended to be bureaucratic and administered by union officials, human resource managers, lawyers and arbitrators, or be subject to various punishments, including fines or disciplinary measures. If workers did make any such attempts, union officials would be expected, under the terms of the legislation, to disavow such actions as unauthorized by the union and push their

FIGURE 4.1: UNION DENSITY IN CANADA AND THE U.S., 1945–2013

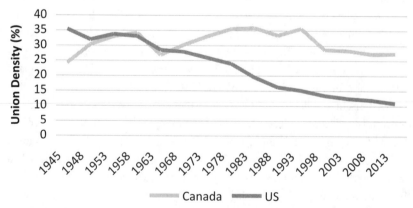

Sources: Statistics Canada/Social Science Federation of Canada 1983; Mayer 2004; OECD 2015

members back into the established mechanisms. To keep their newly won seat at the table, union representatives had to practice "responsible unionism" (Mills 1948) by ensuring their own members obeyed the collective agreement and the labour legislation. If not, they could face legal sanctions themselves. This policing role increasingly set union leaders against their own members; some were very uncomfortable with this situation (and not all of them cooperated with it) while others embraced their newfound status.

A third aspect of the postwar system was embedded in the Rand Formula's design. The provision of an automatic dues check-off, which made the employer responsible for collecting dues from workers and remitting them to the union, replaced onerous monthly dues collection by shop stewards. While this provided unions with greater economic stability, it had the side effect of creating distance between union leaders and members, leading to a breakdown in communication and the loss of one of the means by which workers kept leaders accountable and made sure the union remained relevant to their lives. Under this new regime, union officials spent a growing proportion of their time negotiating and servicing collective agreements and much less time mobilizing or organizing workers—the main preoccupation of the 1930s and 1940s. Administration and provision of services replaced mobilization and political education. As Craig Heron (2012: 89) put it, "Much union administration, collective bargaining and grievance work could be carried out in an orderly fashion from behind a desk or across a table." Member education instead became technical, focusing on learning to use the rules prescribed in legislation and collective agreements rather than on the broader dynamics and problems of capitalist societies. Union members gradually became separated from their union representatives and attempts to create and maintain a distinctive working-class culture were largely abandoned. Unions' overriding goal was now to deliver good and ever-improving collective agreements, and business unionism became the dominant union orientation.

A fourth element of the postwar compromise that had long-term effects on the labour movement was the purge of communists from union ranks. After the end of the Second World War and the removal of the unifying threat from Nazi Germany, fear and antagonism grew between the Soviet Union and the U.S. as part of a decades-long Cold War. This was characterized by severe tension but no direct military engagement between the two superpowers. In some regions, however, battles were fought between their respective allies. The advent of the Cold War promoted a generalized anti-left mentality in North American society and led to concerted efforts to drive members of the CPC out of the Canadian union movement. Between 1948 and 1950, the Canadian Congress of Labour expelled the Mine, Mill and Smelter Workers' Union, United Electrical Workers, International Leather and Fur Workers and International Woodworkers of America, in each case because of their strong Communist influence (Abella 1973). In 1949, the TLC suspended the Communist-led Canadian Seamen's Union (CSU), resulting in its replacement by the corrupt, gangster-ridden, U.S.-based International Seafarers' Union headed by Hal Banks. Most unions required that elected leaders sign an anti-communist pledge to be eligible for their positions. By the early 1950s, the Communist influence in the mainstream union movement was largely erased. Despite their problems, party organizers made enormous contributions through the WUL and then in the CIO drive in Canada. Communist-led unions were also generally democratic, relatively gender- and race-equal in policy and practice and fought effectively for the interests of their members. As a result, some of the most militant and effective unions, with the most radical critique of the capitalist economy, were marginalized.

Many in the mainstream labour movement felt the time for militant action and radical critique was over. Times were good for most union members in the 1950s, certainly much better than in the 1930s and 1940s. It was a time of unparalleled prosperity and relative labour tranquility. The postwar economic boom of the 1950s and early 1960s made higher levels of consumption possible for unionized working-class families, who were now able to take mortgages on homes in the suburbs and buy cars and a range of home appliances and even TV sets. This was the extension of Henry Ford's model to large sections of the economy, in which mass production and mass consumption reinforced each other in a so-called "virtuous cycle." The corporate media's constant message: North America was the best of all possible worlds.

Most major employers accepted unions and operated on the assumption that they would be obliged to concede wage increases and benefit improvements in each round of bargaining. Firms were also aware that failure to make such concessions could provoke a strike that would lead to lost sales and profits. In an expanding economy, employers could accommodate continued improvements in collective bargaining. As a consequence, bargaining became somewhat ritualistic and routine. Unions were able to deliver the goods, and members accepted direction from their leaders. When the union recommended ratification, the members voted to ratify. The union called for a strike vote, the members voted for a strike.

There were important exceptions to this postwar complacency, from both employers and union members. Some employers, for example, remained stubbornly anti-union, fighting every inch of pro-union labour law reform and preferring to uproot and move their businesses rather than deal with a union (Smith 2009). Some segments of the labour movement, the most important of which was in Quebec, similarly resisted the complacency of the so-called "postwar compromise." In 1945, a new leadership took over the CCCL, recruiting aggressive young organizers from Laval University and weakening the unions' link with the Catholic

Church. Manufacturing employment and union membership grew dramatically but within a very repressive legal context, as the *Padlock Law* was still in effect and Premier Duplessis saw most union activity as part of the "Communist threat." However, Quebec workers were angry over their exclusion from the benefits of the postwar era, and their struggle was symbolized by a dramatic 1949 strike at the asbestos mines in Quebec's Eastern Townships. For four months, 5,000 workers, seeking wage increases, health and safety measures and implementation of the Rand Formula, battled the U.S.-based Johns-Manville corporation and the Quebec government, which sided with the employer and offered the support of the provincial police. The company brought in strikebreakers and evicted union members from their homes (Isbester 1974: 170). Workers responded by setting up picket lines and barricades and effectively seizing control of the town of Asbestos. In response, police beat strikers and hundreds of workers were arrested. The union was defeated in June 1949. There were few immediate gains but in defeat came eventual victory. The Asbestos Strike and its embattled workers became a rallying point for Quebec nationalists and intellectuals, and fed the desire for a more profound economic and social transformation of conservative, Catholic and English-dominated Quebec society.

In English Canada, however, most union leaders focused on negotiating contracts and filing grievances and became complacent about new organizing. The major mass-production industries that had been the labour movement's main target since the early part of the twentieth century were now heavily unionized, and membership numbers grew automatically whenever employers hired new workers into the bargaining unit. Otherwise, unions most easily won new members through "raiding"—the attempt by one union to induce members of another to defect and become members of the raiding union. Of course, raiding did nothing to increase the overall number of unionized workers. By the early 1950s, raiding had become a serious problem between TLC and CCL unions. To bring this damaging practice under control, overcome the split between the TLC and the CCL and secure the postwar gains that accrued to labour in a time of prosperity, the two major Canadian labour centrals agreed to merge in 1956, creating the Canadian Labour Congress (CLC). This merger was made possible by the 1955 merger of the AFL and the CIO in the U.S. The first CLC convention was held in April 1956.

For those unions still trying to organize new members, the postwar labour relations framework made such work in the rapidly growing public service extremely difficult. Federal and provincial government workers were legally barred from joining unions (Evans 2013: 19). Saskatchewan's provincial CCF government was unique in extending collective bargaining rights to the provincial civil service. In the private service sector, it was the failure of the Retail, Wholesale and Department Store Union's (RWDSU's) hard-fought attempt to organize the T. Eaton Company's department store chain that put the limits of the new certification processes into sharp relief. The campaign, started in 1948, financed by the Steelworkers, and headed by Eileen Tallman, a first-rate experienced CIO organizer, focused on T. Eaton's 15,000 mostly female employees in Toronto. Some three years and $250,000 later, and despite a remarkable and frequently creative campaign, the union was defeated, in no small measure as a result of the atmosphere of fear created by the employer's virulent and expensive propaganda campaign (Sufrin 1982).

All of this raised questions about which workers were to benefit from the post-war labour relations framework. As Anne Forrest (1995: 139) argues, the postwar labour relations machinery was "fundamentally about the rights of working-class men." The legislation's focus on single-establishment certification and its virtual preclusion of sympathy strikes discriminated against unionizing attempts in smaller, non-industrial, service and retail establishments that were part of multi-unit operations and were more likely to employ women. Not surprisingly, women in the service and retail sectors had much greater difficulty winning union recognition and satisfactory collective agreements (Sufrin 1982; Baker 1993; McDermott 1993). Even where women were still employed in the now-unionized industrial and resources sectors, they were pushed out of well-paid skilled jobs to make way for men returning from the Second World War and relegated to low-paid "female" positions and subject to separate seniority lists. Union executives remained largely a male preserve, and women's interests were generally ignored when bargaining demands were being compiled. Traditional gender roles, with men as breadwinners and women as economic dependents, were implicit in labour law, explicit in other social policies like unemployment insurance and family allowances, and dominant within union cultures and bargaining priorities, and so women's rights to good jobs and wages were not a priority. The postwar legislative framework thus represented "a construct of workers' rights shaped by the needs of blue-collar workers and men employed in the mass-production and resources industries" (Forrest 1995: 146), and it was those workers who were most able to exercise those rights. As a result, in the following half-century, women in the private sector remained largely unorganized.

The situation was worse still for racialized women. Consider the case of the women, largely Caribbean and Filipina, who came to Canada under the Domestic Workers Program of 1955. The rates of pay and working conditions for domestic workers were sufficiently unattractive that it was very difficult to fill the positions with Canadian women, who were beginning to have more choices in the postwar labour market. In their countries of origin many of these women had been skilled workers—nurses, secretaries, teachers, for example. But as domestic workers in Canadian homes, they were easily exploited and hard to unionize, even if unions had made the attempt to do so. In a labour force stratified along gender and ethnic/

racial lines, women were particularly subject to exploitation, while racialized women—often confined to marginalized jobs such as domestic work—were even lower on the scale.

LABOUR POLITICS AND THE COLD WAR

The CCF suffered electorally in the postwar period. Its share of the national popular vote declined steadily: in 1945, it had 15.6 percent of the popular vote; in 1949, 13.4 percent; in 1953, 11.3 percent; in 1957, 10.7 percent; and in 1958, only 9.5 percent. In the 1957 federal election, CCF candidates lost their deposit in 112 of 162 ridings (69 percent), and the party elected no members in Southern Ontario or east of the Ontario–Quebec border. Following the 1958 election sweep by the Progressive Conservatives led by John Diefenbaker, the CCF was reduced to only eight seats, its worst showing since 1940. Its 9.5 percent of the popular vote was just marginally above the 8.7 percent the party had won in its first federal election campaign more than twenty years earlier. The CCF was finished.

For its part, the Communist Party, still banned, re-formed as the legally rec- ognized Labor-Progressive Party in 1943, but had very little electoral success and suffered from never-ending internal squabbling. The atmosphere of the Cold War dealt a death blow to communists inside both the electoral sphere and the labour movement.

Structurally, with communists largely removed from the major industrial unions, the ground was prepared, finally, for a merger of the industrial and craft unions. Joint meetings in 1954 and the 1955 merger in the U.S. of the AFL and CIO began the process that led to the merger, in 1956, of the industrial CCL and the crafts- based TLC, thus creating the Canadian Labour Congress (CLC). The newly created organization wasted no time in negotiating a partnership with the CCF in an effort to save the ailing party. During the CCF's period of decline, it turned increasingly to the union movement. CCF members, particularly leftists, had long been wary of the party's links to labour. They feared that labour would come to dominate the party, and would water down its left-wing policies, moving the CCF in a more moderate and pragmatic direction. But according to Horowitz (1968: 151), "By 1951 there could no longer be any doubt, even among those suspicious of 'labour domination,' that salvation could come only from the unions."

Accordingly, the 1956 Winnipeg Declaration made the party's ideology more compatible with the newly created CLC. It removed the radical rhetoric of the Regina Manifesto, making the party, as the *United Auto Worker* put it, "much more acceptable to union voters" (Horowitz 1968: 174–75). Following the CCF's resounding electoral defeat in 1958, the deliberations of the National Committee for the New Party, with ten representatives each from the CCF and the CLC, led to the 1961 founding of the New Democratic Party. The convention elected Tommy Douglas, former CCF premier of Saskatchewan, as the party's first leader.

Unlike its predecessor, the NDP had the labour movement playing a central and direct role in its very formation. The link with organized labour provided money and organizers for NDP campaigns, and the new party soon reversed the electoral decline of the CCF. By the mid 1960s, the NDP was winning 17–18 percent of the popular vote at the national level; by the late 1970s it was at 20 percent—more than double what the CCF had won in its last federal election in 1958.

THE END OF THE LONG BOOM, THE RISE OF THE PUBLIC SECTOR AND RENEWED LABOUR MILITANCY, 1965–1975

By the mid 1960s, new dynamics were shaking up the workplace, the political landscape and the labour movement. The postwar Keynesian welfare state created thousands of new jobs, many filled by women. Mass consumption fuelled expansion in private service sector jobs, also held largely by women. Women's participation in paid labour overall was on the rise, but their experience of gendered discrimination in the workplace led them to seek collective solutions, often through their unions. Public sector workers, whether postal workers, civil servants, teachers or hospital workers, all found themselves excluded from the rights granted to other workers by the postwar labour relations acts and, unable to legally bargain and strike, engaged in struggles to gain these rights. At the same time, profound social transformations were happening in Quebec that also fuelled labour militancy in general, and public sector organizing in particular. And younger workers in private sector unions found themselves discontented with many of the terms of the postwar compromise in which their own leaders were so invested, leading them to engage in an unprecedented upsurge in militancy in defiance of both employers and union leaders. The changes brought about a third wave of unionism—public sector unionism—after the emergence of craft unionism in the nineteenth century and of industrial unionism in the first half of the twentieth century.

The structure of the labour force changed dramatically in the 1960s and early 1970s because of the growing number of women entering paid employment, a process often called the "feminization of the labour market." In 1951, 23.6 percent of women over age fifteen were in the labour force; by 1976 that figure had increased to 42 percent (Statistics Canada 2000b: Table 5.1). The demographics of women in paid work also changed. As discussed previously, in the early twentieth century, most women in the labour force were young, single and tended to leave paid work after marriage. After the Second World War, despite a brief period when women were pushed out of industrial war work and back into the home, the labour force participation rates of both married women and women with children grew significantly. In short, a higher proportion of women than ever before joined and stayed in the paid labour force, even those with young children at home. This phenomenon would have major consequences for unions.

However, the effects of women's changing labour force participation were not immediately felt in the unions. In 1962, women represented only 16.4 percent of union members, even though they made up 30 percent of the total workforce (Boehm 1991: 17). As discussed previously, it was very difficult for women employed in retail, banking and finance, private services and unskilled/low-wage factory work to unionize, especially because their employers' business models relied on their ability to pay women less. This made such employers very aggressive in opposing private sector women's unionization efforts. Thus, the feminization of the labour market did not automatically translate into higher numbers of women in unions.

Some public sector workers, like municipal, hydro and school board workers, had access to unionization under the legislation that covered private sector workers, but most of the public service jobs in which women were concentrated did not. Postal workers, federal and provincial civil servants, and teachers were all explicitly excluded from these rights. In some cases, the workers themselves implicitly supported these exclusions due to an occupational consciousness that privileged loyal public service above union rights (Roberts 1994: 12–15; Savage and Smith 2013: 47).

Postal workers, for their part, were not constrained by the same occupational consciousness that dissuaded public servants from seeking collective bargaining rights. Their militant struggle against Canada Post, including an illegal strike in July 1965, precipitated passage of the *Public Service Staff Relations Act* that year, extending collective bargaining rights to federal civil servants (Evans 2013: 21). The provinces followed suit so that, between 1965 and 1975, provincial government employees in every province were granted bargaining rights of some kind. This was achieved comparatively quickly and without the long and bitter struggle that industrial workers had been forced to wage in the first half of the twentieth century.

It was only with the upsurge of public sector unionism between 1965 and 1975 that women entered the labour movement in large numbers. Even before the major growth in public sector unionism, these unions were already representing larger proportions of women than their private sector counterparts. For example, when CUPE (in 1963) and the Public Service Alliance of Canada (PSAC) (in 1967) were each formed out of the merger of pre-existing organizations, about one third of their respective memberships consisted of women. The unionization of teachers and nurses between 1965 and 1975 added still more women to the union movement. In this ten-year period, the rise of public sector unions contributed to a 144 percent increase in women's unionization (Luxton 2001: 70).

In Quebec, the Quiet Revolution—a period of intense progressive political and social upheaval—was having a profound impact on the labour movement. In 1960, after Premier Duplessis' death in office, the Liberals under Jean Lesage formed the provincial government and its state-building policies set in motion a process of rapid urbanization, modernization and secularization. These policies included adoption of a modern labour code and, in 1965, extension of collective bargaining rights to Quebec government employees (only the second province to do so, after Saskatchewan in 1944). The former Catholic trade union central became the Confédération des syndicats nationaux (CSN), and by 1960 it had dropped all of its religious connections. These processes strengthened and further radicalized the province's labour movement, which was keen on advancing the Quiet Revolution beyond its initial limits (Savage 2008a: 864–65).

By the early 1970s, all three of Quebec's union centrals had become radicalized, in part due to the rise of nationalist sentiment and opposition to the Trudeau government's decision to invoke the *War Measures Act*, which unilaterally suspended civil liberties for all Canadians. The unions were calling for fundamental changes in Quebec, including independence from Canada. The following year, each of the three major labour bodies published manifestos far more radical than anything seen in the postwar period, and all expressed their commitment to an independent, socialist Quebec. This turn of affairs represented the re-emergence of a link between militant union activism and socialist thought, which had played such an important part in the drive for industrial unionism in the first half of the century.

Unions in English Canada did not take the same radical turn, but events in the private sector certainly created conditions for renewed militancy. Generational conflict within unions added fuel to the fire, with young workers with raised expectations openly questioning the direction of the union leadership. In contrast to workers in the 1950s who were preoccupied with wages, job security and pensions, these younger workers sought shorter hours, longer vacation times and greater control over their work due to the relentless advance of automation (Palmer 2009: 221). They were also dissatisfied with "the monotony, bureaucratic regimentation and submission to authority that is imposed by the discipline" of the authoritarian workplace (Jamieson 1968: 482). While employers were prepared to bargain on rates of pay and vacation periods, they resisted all proposals that would give workers greater control over the actual labour process, including the kinds of technology to be used at work. Young workers were also impatient with their older counterparts' willingness to accept the boundaries of "responsible unionism" and chafed against their leaders' attempts to contain them.

All of these pressures led to an outburst of worker militancy in the late 1960s and early 1970s. Strikes in Canada rose consistently over the decade, from 274 in 1960 to a record 617 in 1966. From 1960 to 1965 the strikes were relatively small:

the number of workers involved averaged 241; the amount of working time lost over these five years averaged 1,381,607 days and 0.10 percent of working time. In 1966, however, strikes were bigger, involving 661 workers on average, and the time lost jumped to 5,179,993 days and 0.34 percent of working time, the highest levels since 1946. The renewed militancy continued for a decade. Of all the labour disputes after 1900, one quarter occurred in the period 1971–1975, with 1976 being the peak year (Heron 2012: 94). An increasing proportion were illegal wildcat strikes and an increasing number occurred when union members refused to ratify collective agreements, reflecting union members' growing militancy and restlessness aimed not only at employers, but also at what they saw as overly passive union leadership (Jamieson 1968: 401–403; Palmer 2009).

Public sector unions were at the forefront of this militant labour outburst across the country, especially in Quebec. In 1972, Quebec's three major labour bodies, having agreed to a "Common Front" for bargaining with the Quebec government, walked out in a dramatic general strike—the first general strike of public sector workers and up to then the largest strike in Canadian history. The Quebec government imposed back-to-work legislation, only to be defied by the three presidents of the Common Front, Marcel Pepin of the CSN, Louis Laberge of the FTQ and Yvon Charbonneau of the Centrale des enseignants du Québec. All three were jailed as a consequence. The strike spread: "In some towns complete general strikes erupted, and workers took over radio and television stations" (Heron 2012: 105). One interpretation of events is that, with the organizers lacking a clear programmatic direction and the full support of Quebec workers, the strike was defeated, and the consequences were severe: in addition to the leaders of the three major labour bodies, forty-nine local union leaders were jailed or fined or both. About one third of the CSN's members left to form a new, more conservative union central,

FIGURE 4.2: PERCENTAGE OF WORKING DAYS LOST TO STRIKES AND LOCKOUTS, 1919–1975

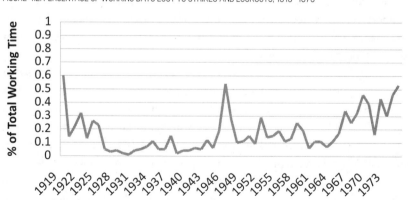

Source: Godard 2011: 77–78

the Centrale des syndicats démocratiques (CSD). Another interpretation is more positive: the three jailed union leaders were released as the result of a wave of protest strikes in the public and private sectors, and the Common Front won its demand for a minimum pay rate for the lowest-paid public sector workers, many of them women (Heron 2012: 105; Savage 2008a: 866).

By 1975, the face of the labour movement had changed significantly. Women were entering the union movement in unprecedented numbers, thanks in part to a shift towards the public sector. Women's struggle for equality in the union movement heated up during this period, an expression of the feminist demand for women's economic independence. Its effects resounded throughout the labour movement, but it also ushered in a transformation in the very nature of working-class women's activism, away from a defense of their husbands' wages and working conditions and towards a struggle to improve their own.

Working-class women from union families had long organized wives' strike support committees, sometimes as part of women's auxiliaries—voluntary organizations designed to build and sustain power for unions in male-dominated industries. Union wives often turned out to be the most militant supporters of men's strikes. Such support was key to any strike's overall success. Since homemakers bear the brunt of a strike because there is less money to run the household, any resulting pressure from union wives on their husbands to get back to work could have harmed strikers' morale and commitment. Pro-union wives thus organized to provide concrete strike support—through plant-gate leafleting and picketing, theatre performances, public speaking and press releases—and to strengthen the resolve of other wives by sharing scarce resources. Wives Supporting the Strike, a group that emerged during the 1978 Steelworkers' strike against Inco in Sudbury, was a notable example of such efforts (Luxton 1983). These tangible expressions of women's leadership ability threatened many union men, including the local union leadership, who were torn about having to rely so heavily on their wives for support. For many women, however, this work was a defining and transformative experience that cemented their support not only for union struggles but also for the fight for women's equality.

Though important, such activism still reflected the gender politics of an earlier era, which placed the male breadwinner wage at the centre of union efforts. This traditional family structure was rapidly changing in the postwar era, as more women themselves were becoming breadwinners, whether as the heads of single-parent households, as central contributors to the family wage, or as not at all dependent on a male wage. Women thus began to struggle over their own wages and working conditions rather than those of their husbands, and to insist that their unions also take on that fight. Women unionists bore the brunt of bringing women's liberation to Canada's labour movement. In meeting after meeting, women struggled to be taken seriously. In the early 1970s, for example, verbal sexual harassment was common at union meetings—as women in Manitoba found when they raised the issue of child care at a 1975 convention (Black and Silver 1991: 61–64). But women fought back: supporting each other; caucusing at conventions; networking between conventions; establishing women's committees; and demanding representation in union decision-making bodies. At conventions and in collective bargaining they insisted upon advancing gender pay equity and what had earlier been seen as personal issues—childcare, maternity leave and violence against women, for example—giving tangible expression to the slogan "the personal is political." As Bryan Palmer (1992: 333) notes, "They fought their way into the labour movement and redefined the very notion of collectivity." Although many struggles remained to be won before women could achieve equality, the impact of the feminist movement on unions, and the determined efforts of women to secure their rights within them, resulted in important gains.

The movement was also rapidly shifting towards the public sector, reflecting changes in both the labour market and in new organizing. The proportion of the labour force employed in blue-collar industrial occupations was in decline, while that of white-collar workers in the service and retail sectors as well as the public sector was growing. As the public sector grew, it unionized: between 1969 and 1973, public sector union membership surged from 430,000 to 883,000 (Rose 2007: 185). Particular occupations with workplace power and social status, like teaching and nursing, long thought to be irreplaceable professions, began to unionize. As the labour process for public sector professionals became more like that of industrial workers—deskilled, speded-up and subject to greater levels of managerial control—they came to see themselves as workers needing the protections and rights that come with unionization. These transformations were also reflected in the changing proportion of union members who were in public sector unions and symbolized by the fact that, in 1975, the Canadian Union of Public Employees surpassed the United Steelworkers as the largest union in Canada (Heron 2012: 98)

Given the recent struggles for public sector bargaining rights and the wave of wildcat strikes in the private sector, the labour movement in 1975 was more militant than it had been in two decades, with a new generation of union members introduced to the power of collective action. This renewed fighting spirit emerged just in time to respond to a renewed attack on workers' rights by both employers and governments.

THE CRISIS OF KEYNESIANISM, 1975–1984

Just as the third wave of unionization began to take hold, the long postwar economic boom came to an abrupt end. The global oil crisis of 1973—precipitated by
an embargo initiated by the Organization of Petroleum Exporting Countries that
quadrupled the price of oil—drove prices up, causing production and economic
growth in advanced capitalist countries to slow down. This led to the previously
unseen phenomenon of "stagflation"—a combination of rising inflation and rising
unemployment. The conventional wisdom was that these two economic phenomena were inversely related: when the economy slowed, unemployment would go
up, inflation would go down and demand (and hence prices) for products would
decline. When economic activity picked up, unemployment would decrease, but
with more people with money to spend, inflation would increase. When these two
began to occur together, policy-makers had to choose which one to tackle. The
consequences of this choice were not just economic: if governments chose to tackle
unemployment—which would benefit workers most—their policy tools would
increase inflation, erode the value of corporate investments and place more upward
pressure on wages. If they attacked inflation—a move that would benefit companies
most—workers would be subject to declining wages and employment. In the end,
governments chose to tackle inflation, with serious negative consequences for the
power of workers and their unions.

Corporations reacted to declining profit levels and economic stagnation with
an attack on unions' workplace power through the collective bargaining process.
Companies demanded concessions from workers and unions, meaning reversals
of previously won gains enshrined in collective agreements. Companies cited low
profits and increased competition and threatened workers with plant closure or
relocation and layoffs if they didn't yield. Concession bargaining included wage
cuts; the introduction of a two-tier system that maintained the wages of existing
workers but brought in new workers at lower wages; benefit cuts; the acceptance
of involuntary overtime; revised disciplinary procedures detrimental to workers;
and the exclusion of casual and part-time employees from bargaining units. In
non-unionized firms, employers simply imposed concessions. In unionized firms,
employers demonstrated an increased willingness either to take unions on in a
strike or lockout, or to shut down and relocate production. Fearing for their jobs,
union leaders and members alike became more reluctant to support strike action
as a means of making gains or warding off concessions, and the bargaining power
of unions was eroded.

The first round of concessions in the U.S. began in 1979, when the United Auto
Workers (UAW) accepted concessions to save Chrysler Corporation from bank-
ruptcy. They soon spread to all major unionized sectors (steel, trucking, grocery,

meatpacking, and airlines), and placed significant pressure on the Canadian employ-ees of U.S.-based companies. Companies also sought to end pattern bargaining, whereby bargaining outcomes with one company set the terms for others in the industry, and master bargaining, sector-wide agreements that covered multiple workplaces and employers, both of which created industry-wide standards for workers. Instead, companies wanted to return to plant-level bargaining to whipsaw workers, playing them off against each for jobs to get them to settle for lower wages. Many employers demanded concessions even though they admitted in a 1982 sur-vey by *Business Week* that they didn't actually need them for profitability; they just wanted to take advantage of the favourable bargaining climate (Moody 1988: 168).

Big business also pursued political strategies, creating a united public voice in the form of the Business Council on National Issues in 1976. Renamed the Canadian Council of Chief Executives in 2001, the organization represented 150 of the largest corporations in Canada, many involved in the global economy as either transnational corporations or subsidiaries. The council effectively shifted government policy to the advantage of big business and against workers and unions.

Governments responded primarily by targeting workers' wages as the cause of inflation. Pierre Trudeau's federal Liberal government took the first step in October 1975, imposing a three-year program of compulsory wage and price controls known as the Anti-Inflation Program. Labour condemned the controls because they targeted wages, not prices, which were not effectively controlled. But the controls achieved the government's purpose: the rate of increase in wages dropped from over 14 percent in 1975 and 1976 to 6.8 percent in 1978. In 1976, real wages (the value of wages adjusted for inflation) actually declined by 2.2 percent, while corporate profits increased. This outcome inspired increased anger amongst work-ers, a renewed effort to make up lost ground and more labour militancy against wage controls.

Unions responded to stagflation by seeking wage increases. Given the anti-inflation legislation, this required both militancy and some defiance of the law. Many private sector unions opted to ignore the legislation and bargained wage increases above the caps. By 1976, "The country was witnessing a full-scale rank-and-file revolt" (Heron 2012: 94), including the National Day of Action against Wage and Price Controls, which brought more than one million workers out on an illegal one-day political strike (Heron 2012: 110).

Governments responded with a renewed and multifaceted assault on workers and their unions. The federal government abandoned the idea of generalized wage controls, substituting changes in monetary policy that would drive up unemploy-ment. A cabinet document prepared by the Department of Finance in late 1980 argued that a policy of higher unemployment would reduce the bargaining power and militancy of unions and workers, driving down the rate of increase in money wages and eventually of inflation (Black 1982). In 1981, consistent with this deliberate use of monetary policy to increase unemployment, the Bank of Canada pushed interest rates to unprecedented levels, in excess of 20 percent. The result was a deep recession: unemployment jumped to 11 percent in 1982, strikes declined and real wages fell (Palmer 1992: 344–47).

The worst, for workers and their unions, was yet to come. In 1982, the federal government suspended the collective bargaining rights of public sector workers and imposed wage increases of 6 percent and 5 percent over two years, in some cases rolling back already negotiated wage increases. Most provinces adopted similar legislation, curtailing the rights of public sector workers and imposing wage settlements. This "6 and 5" policy solidified an anti-union strategy that featured the abandonment of free collective bargaining and the use of coercion in labour relations, especially in the public sector (Panitch and Swartz 2003: 104–23). With nearly half (45.8 percent) of all union members in Canada in public sector unions by 1980, CUPE and PSAC became primary targets.

The most prominent feature of this anti-union strategy was the significant increase in the use of back-to-work legislation to end strikes. Prior to 1982, governments had on occasion used legislation to end strikes (Figure 4.3). In the 1950s and 1960s, these interventions were justified as exceptions initiated in the public interest. It could be argued that they posed no threat to free collective bargaining. Beginning in the late 1960s, these exceptions became more frequent and, after 1982, began to look more like the rule.

Governments were saying, in effect, that workers have the right to strike until they actually do strike, and then governments retain the power to strip them of

FIGURE 4.3: USE OF BACK-TO-WORK LEGISLATION, 1950–2014

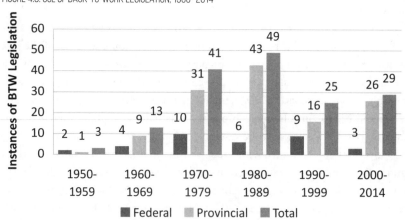

Source: Panitch and Swartz 2003; CFLR *2014*

that right. After 1982, the frequency of such legislative curtailments of free collective bargaining increased steadily, leading Leo Panitch and Donald Swartz to call this "the era of permanent exceptionalism," in which such temporary restrictions were the norm, even if the underlying labour legislation was not itself permanently changed. With the notable exception of the Manitoba NDP, every government brought in repressive labour legislation in the 1980s. The legislation was especially sweeping in Quebec, Saskatchewan, Alberta and B.C. (Panitch and Swartz 2003: 103–42). Although unions challenged the constitutionality of these laws as violating workers' rights to freedom of association, a majority at the Supreme Court of Canada disagreed, and these incursions into workers' ability to bargain and strike were legitimized.

THE ADVENT OF NEOLIBERALISM AND THE STRUGGLE OVER FREE TRADE, 1984–1993

By the mid 1980s, "neoliberalism" had displaced Keynesianism and become the dominant ideology amongst business and political elites in Canada. Neoliberal capitalism is a political and economic project that relies on competitive market forces and the profit motive to make decisions about how society is to be organized, with minimal state intervention except to support a "good business climate." Neoliberals promote the downsizing of the state through reduced expenditures to social programs, tax cuts, balanced budgets, privatization and deregulation.

Business organizations and right-wing think tanks were strong advocates for neoliberal government politics, championing anti-labour measures such as cutbacks in government expenditures on social programs, restructuring of unemployment insurance and promoting debt and deficit reduction and free trade, particularly between Canada and the U.S.

Corporate lobbyists also sought these policy changes because they would remove barriers to economic globalization—a process of capitalist expansion that facilitates transnational corporations' drive for fewer trade and investment barriers, lower wages, larger markets and cheaper raw materials to maximize their profits. Globalization was not new—international economic trade had existed for hundreds of years—but it did increase dramatically in the last quarter of the twentieth century. Free trade agreements were crucial because they significantly reduced the capacity of elected governments to interfere with the profit-seeking activities of transnational corporations. For example, companies are increasingly playing one jurisdiction off against another by relocating production to wherever labour costs are lowest and regulations are the least restrictive.

In addition to free trade, the federal Progressive Conservative government under Brian Mulroney, elected in 1984, aggressively promoted neoliberal policy measures including privatization, deregulation and government downsizing

(McBride and Shields 1997). These pro-business policy changes went hand in hand with restructuring at the workplace, both to increase profits and to subordinate workers and their unions. Some firms pursued traditional methods like speed-up, whereby workers are forced to produce more without significant changes to the organization of production or increases in pay. Others adopted just-in-time production methods, wherein large firms contract out to networks of small firms that provide materials and parts just when needed to avoid costly stockpiles. A higher proportion of jobs are outsourced, performed by outside contractors rather than by company employees. Wages and working conditions in contracted-out workplaces are inferior, and unionization rates are lower, because they are competing with each other for contracts to supply the large firms and have a strong incentive to keep costs down. Just-in-time production also replaces full-time with part-time and casual jobs designed to be more "flexible" during peak periods. (Morris 1991).

These new production methods brought a change in workplace culture, nominally emphasizing labour–management collaboration over adversarialism. But they were also designed to weaken workers' solidarity and sense of their own interests as distinct from management. Recruitment processes painstakingly weed out workers with a history of union involvement, and training is aimed at indoctrinating workers into the anti-union culture of the enterprise. This is reinforced by various worker participation schemes such as quality circles, whereby groups of workers meet regularly in the workplace, often with management assistance, to improve productivity and quality control, and team production, designed to demonstrate that workers' ideas matter to the enterprise. Firms intended the various team production schemes to promote worker and union compliance with management goals. In many plants where team production is introduced, total pay is contingent on output: team members' pay increases if the team exceeds its quota. The company penalizes teams or individual members who don't meet expectations. Team members absent from work (a woman whose child is sick, for example) may not be replaced; other team members must push harder to make the quota. As a result, team members pressure colleagues who miss shifts or cannot sustain the pace of work. Workers find themselves policing each other in the company's interests. As Michael Yates (1998: 73–74) puts it: "The dangers of the team concept are well documented, since they usually weaken the grievance procedure and eliminate hard-won work rules yet never give the union real *input* into the most fundamental management decisions."

These lean production methods—as this management system as a whole is sometimes called (Sears 1999)—were not at all new; they were merely old methods dressed up in a new participatory guise. At their core was the scientific management approach designed by Frederick Taylor a century earlier at the birth of monopoly capitalism—a management system deliberately designed to weaken the power of labour.

These changes to corporate strategies in the workplace fuelled two important shifts in the composition of the workforce in the late 1980s and early 1990s: the growth of "non-standard work," and the growth of low-wage jobs. Over half of the jobs created in the 1980s were not permanent full-time jobs. In clerical, sales and service occupations, 60 percent of workers were employed part-time and were more likely than full-time workers to be paid low wages, less likely to have access to benefits packages and much harder to unionize (Silver 2000: 5–9). Similarly, the numbers and proportion of self-employed workers grew significantly in the last quarter of the twentieth century, and was closely connected to corporate and government restructuring. From 1977 to 2004 the number of self-employed Canadians doubled, and their share of the total of employed workers grew from 12.8 to 15.4 percent (Statistics Canada 2001: Table 8). By 1995, according to Jim Stanford (1999: 131), "Self-employment exceeded total employment in the public sector of the economy for the first time in Canada's postwar history." As large corporations downsized and governments cut spending and the number of government employees, self-employment was a "solution" to higher rates of unemployment. Both part-time and self-employed workers make up the "flexible" labour force that can be pulled in or pushed out of employment according to business needs, with employers having to make no long-term commitments to the workers, nor to their pensions or benefits. In the eyes of business and government, such a labour force makes Canada more competitive in a globalized economy.

In Canada, the labour movement hotly resisted both workplace restructuring and the introduction of neoliberal policies that supported rising corporate power. In the 1980s, unions in Canada were much more willing than their U.S. counterparts to resist concession bargaining and to go on strike to do so, which led to serious conflicts between several international unions and their Canadian sections. Canadian unions in fact opted to press for wage increases, improved working conditions and additional benefits, partly because higher and still-growing unionization rates in Canada gave workers the confidence to take on these fights. The decision of Canadian autoworkers to break away from their international parent union, the U.S.-based UAW, and form their own Canadian Auto Workers union (CAW) was the highest-profile example of this dynamic (Gindin 1995: 197–227; Holmes and Rusonik 1990).

However, even when Canadian workers fought back, the pressure resulting from concessions made by unions south of the border was overwhelming. The meatpacking industry is a case in point. The United Food and Commercial Workers (UFCW) in the U.S. reversed its anti-concessions policy in the 1980s, largely because of a reluctance by members in many plants to oppose employers with strike action. A major battle at Hormel Foods in Austin, Minnesota, in 1985–1986 led to dramatic cuts in hourly wages and benefits. The cuts came despite a long and bitter strike, thus setting the stage for employers to demand concessions from Canadian meat-packing workers. In 1986, Gainer's meatpacking plant in Edmonton demanded wage rollbacks and pension concessions from its employees, but the union refused. Workers waged a bitter and protracted battle. The Gainer's strike involved the use of scab labour as well as mass arrests and a strong public reaction against both the employer and the anti-union posture and legislation of the Alberta government (Noël and Gardner 1990). The union and workers won the battle but lost the war: Maple Leaf Meats subsequently bought the plant and again demanded major con-cessions. Workers struck again in 1997 and supporters organized a very successful consumer boycott, but Maple Leaf shut down the Edmonton plant. Concessions had become pervasive in the meatpacking industry in both Canada and the U.S.

The labour movement's struggle against these trends was also political, culmi-nating in the 1988 federal election, which was essentially a referendum on free trade with the U.S. The CLC led a coalition of unions and social movements in a nation-wide public education campaign in opposition to free trade, emphasizing the negative impact it would have on Canadian jobs, standards of living and cul-ture. While labour's campaign enjoyed public support, and although a majority of Canadians voted for parties opposed to the deal, the vote split in the election worked to the benefit of the Conservatives, who were in favour of free trade.

The re-election of the Mulroney Progressive Conservative government in 1988 and the implementation of the Canada–U.S. Free Trade Agreement in early 1989 were together a major turning point for the Canadian labour movement. The removal of tariffs made it easier to gain access to the Canadian consumer market and eliminated much of the economic rationale for U.S.-based firms to locate production in Canada. This agreement set into motion a wave of plant closures and job losses in manufacturing that worsened with the arrival of an economic recession in the early 1990s.

THE CONSOLIDATION OF NEOLIBERALISM, 1993–2007

The election of NDP governments in Ontario, British Columbia, Saskatchewan and the Yukon in the early 1990s suggested that voters had had enough of neoliberal restructuring and were looking for political vehicles to undo the damage of the past decade. However, the limits of social democracy became clear rather quickly as the newly elected NDP governments seemingly could not reverse the tide. In Ontario, in fact, Bob Rae's NDP government played a central role in consolidating neoliberalism through its "Social Contract" austerity program. The NDP's anti-union incursions opened the door wide for the hyper-neoliberal politics of right-wing provincial governments across Canada. At the federal level, while voters unceremoniously dumped the federal Progressive Conservatives in the 1993 election, the incoming Chrétien Liberals immediately abandoned a campaign promise to renegotiate a new North American Free Trade Agreement (NAFTA), and instead promptly signed off on the deal. The Liberals oversaw unprecedented cuts to social programs and to the federal public service, as government focused its attention on reducing public debt. By 1997, most governments in Canada had balanced their budgets, and some provincial governments, in a throwback to the days of fiscal orthodoxy preceding the Great Depression, had established compulsory balanced-budget legislation, no matter the effects on social programs.

With all political parties embracing some version of neoliberalism, it seemed that Conservative British Prime Minister Margaret Thatcher's pronouncement that "There is No Alternative" was proving true. Certainly, an elite consensus around neoliberalism had been painstakingly built both in Canada and at the global level from the late 1970s on. However, unions and popular movements around the world mobilized en masse to contest the implementation of these policies, and the Canadian labour movement was no different. Through the 1990s, a creative and audacious anti-globalization or "global justice" movement emerged, a loose alliance of unions and popular movements opposed to corporate-driven globalization and the international agreements that facilitate it. Through mass direct actions like those opposing the World Trade Organization in Seattle in 1999, the movement's participants sought to disrupt meetings of global financial institutions that were negotiating the terms of global neoliberalism. They generated a highly successful global consciousness-raising effort about the kinds of economic arrangements that would be best for working people.

The events of September 11, 2001, interrupted this global wave of social movement organizing and for a time made it very difficult to use the tactics being developed by the global justice movement. The attacks on New York and Washington gave a pretext for intensified U.S. military aggression abroad—especially in Afghanistan and Iraq—and the restriction of civil liberties in most of the world's advanced capitalist countries, including Canada. These restrictions, and the hyper-patriotic cultural climate that emerged post-9/11, dampened militancy in general. While the rallying cry of the anti-globalization movement—"a different world is possible"—became all the more relevant, the movement for global economic justice was also seriously weakened.

Private sector employers took advantage of the pro-free trade and anti-union policy climate to restructure the employment relationship, avoid unions and introduce greater precarity to the labour market. Unions in sectors of the economy that had resisted concessionary bargaining in the 1980s and 1990s, like the auto sector, succumbed to setbacks, thus threatening the utility of pattern bargaining as a strategy for taking wages out of competition (Wells 1997). Public policy changes and global economic transformations also affected workers in different ways, shaping the tenor of their responses. In the early 2000s, there was some respite for autoworkers, teachers, oil patch workers and even federal public sector workers. Other workers, like those in steel, pulp and paper, and low-skill manufacturing, were continually pummeled by exposure to global competitive pressures. This unevenness in the experience of neoliberalism created serious strategic challenges, as different workers pursued strategies that might work for them but not for others. In the automotive sector, for example, the CAW's controversial "Framework of Fairness" agreement with Magna— in exchange for a gradual establishment of bargaining units over several years—would have eliminated the right to strike and replaced the union's standard shop steward network with management-approved employee advocates (Magna/CAW 2007: 15, 18). The agreement generated much internal dissension and external outrage from other unions, who were concerned that the CAW's deal with Magna would open the door to representation structures that would not be fully independent of management. Overall, however, neoliberalism ushered in a process of globalization and economic instability that was like a roller coaster ride in which the descents were more pronounced than the ascents. In the case of Canadian workers, each descent further consolidated the lowering of their expectations.

Even so, there is a fundamental contradiction at the heart of neoliberal economics. Early in the twenty-first century, the capitalist economy remains dependent on continued and expanding mass consumption, but the economic and political elites have pursued policies that undermine workers' wages and redistribute wealth to the top. In breaking the power of North American unions to negotiate wage increases that enabled workers to buy more of their products, capitalists had to find new ways to sustain the consumption levels needed to fuel their profits. Certainly elite forms of consumption have increased but so has consumer debt, itself promoted by the financial industry. Indeed, debt is increasingly replacing wage gains as the primary basis of sustaining and expanding mass consumption in advanced capitalist countries (Albo et al. 2010: 16–17). By the mid 2000s, a higher proportion of women than ever were engaged in paid work, in part to contribute to a sufficiently high family wage, which could no longer be earned by a single breadwinner. However, failures to improve public services like health care, child care and elder care meant that working-class people—and women in particular—had to manage the growing tensions between paid and unpaid work. The contradictions of neoliberal globalization, between capitalists' desire to elicit more consumption and their drive to lower the very wages with which workers consume, formed the basis of the financial crisis and Great Recession of 2007–2008.

THE GREAT RECESSION AND ITS AFTERMATH: CRISIS AND AUSTERITY, 2007 TO TODAY

Financial deregulation, combined with a mortgage crisis in the U.S. and the inherently casino-like qualities of capitalist economies, resulted in the financial crisis of 2007–2008. Several prominent banks collapsed, creating a global economic crisis that hit Canada particularly hard. Governments in advanced capitalist countries responded with a brief return to Keynesianism to help pull the economy out of recession, but they quickly turned to austerity. Austerity measures include reductions in public expenditures through cuts to services, public sector wage freezes and job losses, and the privatization of publicly owned assets. Governments justified this shift by arguing they needed to pay down the budget deficits resulting from expenditures to help resuscitate the economy. Unions and their allies rightly pointed out that while the state's fiscal crisis was caused by multi-billion dollar corporate bailouts, working-class people were forced to pick up the tab through major cuts to social programs and public service jobs. In Canada, these measures included taking advantage of union weakness during a period of economic crisis and are more specifically manifested in calls for right-to-work and other anti-union legislation designed to break the capacity of unions to resist austerity measures.

Emboldened by the Great Recession, many employers sought changes to the labour–management relationship that had not been possible before. Concession bargaining became more pervasive as an employer strategy. Confident that unions would be unable to resist, employers also showed a greater willingness to use lockouts or other aggressive bargaining tactics (Peters 2010). Union responses to such tactics were mixed. Increasingly, unionized workers voluntarily made concessions in bids to save their jobs. Other unions fought austerity measures through legal challenges and strikes. In the public sector, the level of militancy was uneven and the growing anti-public sector union sentiment made conditions extremely difficult (Ross and Savage 2013a).

ECONOMIC POWER AND LABOUR

By the early part of the twenty-first century, thirty years of attacks on labour had severely undermined the union movement's seemingly secure place in Canada's political economy. The massive restructuring following the economic crisis of the early 1970s had largely benefited, and been driven by, big business, with the full support of political elites who held state power. Labour was on the defensive. The Great Recession of 2007–2008 only made a bad situation worse. Although unions' forms of power in the workplace remain the same, the changing economic and policy context profoundly affects how they are able to use that power to improve conditions for members and working-class people in general.

QUESTIONS FOR DISCUSSION

1. Why do some consider the "postwar compromise" to be a double-edged sword for the labour movement?
2. What accounts for renewed labour militancy in the mid 1960s?
3. Compare Keynesianism and neoliberalism as approaches to public policy.
4. How has union power been challenged by the rise of globalization and neoliberal policies?
5. What are "lean production" methods and what impact do they have on labour relations?

CHAPTER 5

UNIONS IN
THE WORKPLACE

T he primary role of a union is to act as an agent for its members in the workplace. In part, workers form unions to achieve higher wages, improved benefits (such as pension plans and life and disability insurance), better and safer working conditions, greater security in their jobs and fair treatment. Once established, unions exert power in the workplace. In particular, collective bargaining, the process through which unions and management negotiate collective agreements, defines the terms and conditions of work and the decision-making processes for how the workplace functions. For the most part, collective agreements become the means by which unions resolve disputes including grievances, third-party arbitration and strikes. There is no doubt that unions create collective forms of power that produce better outcomes for workers overall than do individual bargains. Individually workers are relatively powerless in their dealings with employers in the workplace. Unless they have knowledge or skills vital to the enterprise and cannot easily be replaced, they are dispensable. If they confront their employers over a problematic aspect of their job, they can be and often are fired. But in forming a union, workers implicitly enter into an agreement that they will look out for and stand by one another if one or more of them become subject to unfair or arbitrary actions by employers.

FORMING UNIONS: THE ORGANIZING AND CERTIFICATION PROCESS

Today, the vast majority of workers become members of unions by virtue of the fact that they are hired into an already-unionized workplace. However, in those workplaces where unions are not yet established, workers must engage in a legal process known as union certification.

Unionization drives normally get underway in one of two ways. Many unions actively seek to organize groups of workers in specific workplaces or particular sectors of the economy that are strategically important to the union's growth and bargaining power. As organizations seeking to boost workers' collective power, most unions focus on increasing the proportion of union members—otherwise known as union density—in specific sectors of the economy rather than spreading themselves too thinly throughout many sectors. For example, in Toronto, where most large hotels are unionized, a union is likely to give priority to organizing any new large hotel, whether the workers there express initial interest or not. Unionizing new hotels in the city is strategically important because it helps defend the gains of the already organized hotel workers by further taking wages out of competition and it also builds the union's collective power in the industry. This kind of organizing is often called "strategic sectoral organizing."

In contrast, fast food restaurants in Canada's largest city have very low union density and are notoriously difficult to organize, so unions consider them a lower priority despite the substantial number of fast food workers who want, and arguably would benefit from, unionization. If disgruntled workers at a fast food outlet actively sought out a union to organize them, there is nothing to stop a union drive from getting underway. This kind of drive is sometimes referred to as "hot shop" organizing because the union is responding to a group of dissatisfied workers intent on unionizing. Organizing in this manner is sometimes a quick route to a certification victory because workers are prepared to certify without much advance work by union organizers—paid union staff who coordinate and assist with the certification process. However, while rewarding in the short term, this method of organizing often lacks strategic focus, sometimes leaving unions spread too thin across sectors and unprepared to actually carry out their bargaining and representation functions once the certification process is complete.

Whichever method they pursue (strategic sectoral organizing or hot shop organizing), unions will enlist the help of known union sympathizers and workplace leaders to convince their co-workers to sign union membership cards, thus indicating support for unionization. While the exact system of union certification differs from province to province, unions typically must demonstrate to a labour board that a substantial proportion of the proposed bargaining unit—the group of workers that will be covered by the same collective agreement—supports unionization. The bargaining unit may be very small—for example, a couple of employees in a funeral home—or very large—as in the case of General Motors, for example, which has thousands of workers in its Canadian plants.

There are three types of union certification used in Canadian jurisdictions—mandatory vote, card-based and voluntary recognition—although all three types are not available in every jurisdiction. Under the mandatory vote model, the union must get a significant number of workers in the proposed bargaining unit to sign union cards (the exact threshold is different depending on the jurisdiction) before it can serve an employer notice and file an application for certification with the labour board. In 2015, the threshold to trigger a certification vote ranged from a low of 35 percent in Quebec to a high of 45 percent in B.C. and Saskatchewan. Once the union submits an application for certification with the required percentage of cards signed to the labour board, the employer must then respond within a specified period by providing the labour board with a list of employees. In turn, the labour board reviews the list submitted by the employer to independently verify that the union has gotten the required percentage of workers to sign union cards to trigger a secret ballot election. At no point does the employer learn which workers signed union cards. If the labour board determines that the union has reached the threshold to trigger a certification election, it arranges and supervises the vote within a specified period. The union must win the secret ballot by a majority of those voting (50 percent plus one) to be certified as the exclusive bargaining agent for the workers.

The card-based method of union certification unfolds in much the same way as the mandatory vote system, with one important exception. If a legally specified supermajority of the proposed bargaining unit signs union cards that can be independently verified by the labour board, the board will certify the union as the bargaining agent for the workers without a vote. In 2015, the threshold for automatic certification ranged from a low of 50 percent plus one in Quebec and Prince Edward Island to a high of 65 percent plus one in Manitoba. This method of union certification was dominant across Canada for much of the postwar period, but since the 1980s, it has gradually been replaced by the mandatory vote method in most provinces. In 2015, Manitoba, Quebec, New Brunswick and Prince Edward Island still use card-based union certification, while all other jurisdictions use mandatory votes. Ontario has adopted a hybrid system, reserving card-based certification for the building and construction trades sector while workers outside that sector use the mandatory vote system.

Employers lobbied very hard for the move to mandatory votes because they understood that this method of union certification would make it more difficult for workers to form unions. By requiring a secret ballot after the labour board has determined the union has met the threshold for signed union cards, employers are given extra time to campaign against the union in the workplace. During such brief windows of opportunity, workers are typically bombarded with anti-union literature and an assortment of threats and promises from management designed to dissuade workers from following through with unionization. In effect, the secret ballot vote "actually inhibits workplace democracy because it provides employers with both opportunity and incentive to influence the outcome of the vote through intimidation, coercion, misinformation, or all of the above" (Patrias and Savage 2012: 151).

The last method of union certification is voluntary recognition, whereby the employer voluntarily recognizes a union as the bargaining agent for its employees without any card signing or voting. Although this was the main method of unionization before the 1940s, it is now rare in Canada and is typically found in sectors where a specific employer and union have a longstanding collective bargaining relationship. For example, a unionized grocery store chain may voluntarily agree to recognize the union for the workers at a newly opened store. In Alberta, the Real Canadian Superstore and UFCW agreed to such an arrangement in the 1980s. Voluntary recognition can also be used nefariously by employers, specifically by those who fear dealing with a specific union and therefore turn to another, offering voluntary recognition in exchange for an easy ride at the bargaining table. The Christian Labour Association of Canada is often criticized for negotiating such agreements with employers. Finally, unions can win voluntary recognition through tactics like "corporate campaigns," which uncover and expose negative things about the employer's corporate practices in an effort to convince the employer to recognize the union. This tactic is more common in the U.S., where many unions have either abandoned traditional organizing methods or supplemented them with corporate campaigns because U.S. labour laws and the National Labor Relations Board, which is tasked with enforcing them, have proven inhospitable to unions.

Card signing typically goes hand in hand with an assortment of other union drive initiatives. For example, unions may hold open meetings, take out advertising space, distribute pro-union literature to employees on their way into work, have a committee of workers organize inside the workplace on their breaks, or make house visits to workers. Different unions have different philosophies about which tactics work best. Their approaches to organizing are products of experience, both successes and failures, and can differ greatly based on a union's resource base and ideological orientation. In the end, however, the goal of every union organizing drive is the same: to get as many workers as possible to sign union cards, and in jurisdictions where representation votes are mandatory, ensure that as many pro-union workers as possible vote to certify the union.

Unions actively campaign for workers' support, but so too do employers. While there are limits in each jurisdiction as to exactly what employers can say or do when their employees are engaged in a union organizing campaign, most employers have a great deal of influence over how their employees respond to the unionization question. In many jurisdictions, employers have the right to talk to their workers about the "consequences" of unionization. Such "talks" can sometimes enter into a legal gray area, taking the form of threats—either overt or veiled—that establishing a union will result in layoffs, closure, relocation or unnecessary divisions in the workplace (see Chapter 9). Union drives are not just about money but also about workers' power and the dignity that accompanies it. Fear of losing total control over the workplace motivates some employers to go to virtually any length to avoid unionization.

The specific design of laws relating to certification clearly affects the outcome of unionization drives, as Felice Martinello's (2000) study of the Ontario Progressive Conservative government's 1995 labour law reforms demonstrated. When the Conservatives replaced the card-based system of certification (automatic certification with 55 percent of members or more signed up) with a system requiring votes in all situations, applications for certification dropped significantly. At the same time, the reforms made it easier for workers to decertify (vote to get rid of) a union, resulting in a significant increase in decertifications. However, despite these increasingly steep legal hurdles, thousands of workers in Canada make the decision to unionize each and every year. But union certification is only the first step.

COLLECTIVE BARGAINING AND WORKPLACE POWER

Once a union is established through the certification process, its primary function is to negotiate a collective agreement—a legally enforceable contract that establishes the terms and conditions of work, the rights of the union and the employer and attempts to address the concerns and interests of union members. The certification process establishes the union as the exclusive bargaining agent for a given group of workers and compels employers to bargain with them to achieve a collective agreement. Union members ideally play a central role in the bargaining process—they give guidance to their bargaining team during negotiations; they demonstrate their support for the union's bargaining position through their willingness to engage in demonstrations of solidarity or strike action (more on that later); and they ultimately approve or ratify the terms of settlement.

From the union's perspective, most collective bargaining begins with the establishment of a bargaining committee, which usually includes representatives from the local union. In some cases, collective bargaining occurs on a company-wide or sectoral basis, with a bargaining team comprised of representatives from several locals. The bargaining committee then formulates a set of bargaining priorities or positions, which specifies the demands the union will place before the employer. In many unions, the membership helps to develop the union's bargaining proposals—for example, by filling out bargaining surveys or participating in discussions on areas in the collective agreement that need improvement—and approves them at a general membership meeting.

To be achievable, a bargaining agenda must include a set of demands consistent with members' views about what is fair and possible. It must also be linked to both a long-term view of acceptable goals and the issues that members themselves think important. Unions have a number of ways of gauging and developing members' support for particular bargaining priorities, but the usual and most effective method is to do so at membership meetings, where members can debate the issues and build consensus. It is also vital that union members elected to the bargaining team and union representatives understand and are sensitive to conditions in the local—the weaknesses in existing collective agreements; the composition of the membership and how it is changing; the terms and conditions of members' employment and how they compare to what other workers are getting in the local labour market, in the industry or sector, and in similar situations in other cities and other provinces; and the nature of the relationship between union and employer.

This process is more complicated than it seems because it often involves establishing consensus among disparate segments of the workforce—for example, skilled versus unskilled workers, women versus men, and older versus younger workers. Indeed, the union's process of internal bargaining to establish unity on the issues that go to the bargaining table can sometimes be more difficult than bargaining with employers. As well, in developing a package of demands, the standard practice is to include proposals that the local can put aside during bargaining. This positional bargaining strategy leaves room to make gains on the issues that are particularly important to members. The added items are not, as a rule, "blue-sky" proposals (those the union knows the employer can never accept), but rather proposals that address the concerns of some union members. They signal, in effect, that these are matters that employers will eventually have to deal with; they could well be on the agenda in subsequent rounds of collective bargaining.

The union must also establish a strategy that will guide its efforts at the bargaining table. The objective is not simply to reach an agreement, but to reach one that is acceptable to all union members. The union must therefore set limits on its bargaining priorities as well as on the trade-offs it is willing to make to get improvements on other important issues. This task is simplified if the position is based on a principle. For example, a union may have a principle of negotiating equal absolute increases in wages for all members because this maintains internal equity within the bargaining unit. In this situation there can be no compromise; the only issue the union will bargain on is the amount of the equal absolute increase. The union must also know how it will respond in the event that the employer insists on concessions that would push the union below its bottom line.

After the Second World War, the practice in bargaining was for the union to present its proposals to the employer, which would then respond with counter-proposals. For example, on the wages issue, the union might propose an increase for everyone in the bargaining unit of 6 percent, reflecting increased productivity, increases in the cost of living, wage increases achieved by other workers in the same industry or sector, and the union's assessment of the employer's capacity to pay. The employer might counter with an offer of, say, 1 percent. This exchange establishes a bargaining range for wages, with both sides attempting to move the other side closer to its position.

Wages are inevitably a contentious issue. They determine workers' income and important elements of their quality of life. For employers, wages are the major component of labour costs. In general, the more labour-intensive the work, meaning the higher the proportion of total costs accounted for by labour costs, the more reluctant employers are to concede to union demands or to accept unionization at all. This is especially evident in fast food or garment manufacturing. Benefits and pensions are a similarly contentious issue, for the same reasons. Union proposals that are interpreted by employers as encroachments on their rights to deal unilaterally with all matters not covered by the collective agreements—such as control over production and labour processes—also generate conflict.

Since the 1980s, employers have become much more aggressive in collective bargaining, and they often bring their own demands to the table. These can include calls for union "give-backs" or concessions on previous wage and benefit gains on the grounds that the employer must cut costs to stay competitive. Or for the union to give up wording in the collective agreement that, for example, prevents the employer from contracting out to another firm work normally done by members of the bargaining unit, or that limits the employer's ability to control how workers are utilized on the job. These articles may, for example, restrict the ability of employers to transfer workers between jobs or make promotions in which a worker's seniority is not a key criteria.

Once they are together at the bargaining table, the two sides will begin by negotiating a bargaining protocol, that is, a set of procedural rules that establish the locale for bargaining (often away from the workplace in a hotel or hall). They will set out the dates for bargaining sessions and prescribe how they will construct a tentative agreement. It could be on an issue-by-issue basis or as a total package. When these preliminaries are out of the way, they will concentrate on the substantive issues each side has brought to the table.

For the union, it is also imperative that the bargaining strategy established beforehand defines roles for members of the bargaining team. Usually the union identifies a particular individual to act as the lead negotiator. Preferably this is someone who has experience in bargaining, can argue the union's position effectively and has the respect of the team and the local. Other members of the team may also be designated to speak on particular issues. Much is accomplished away from the table, when the bargaining team prepares for its sessions, scripting their arguments, planning their actions and rehearsing their roles. As much as possible, the team leaves nothing to chance; they carefully orchestrate everything, although even the best-laid plans can go awry.

Notwithstanding the skill of the negotiators, the reasonableness of their arguments and the justness of their position, collective bargaining is ultimately an exercise in power. The power of both parties lies in their respective abilities to persuade members of the other party that accepting the proposed terms of settlement would be less costly than an impasse that results in either a strike or lockout. As bargaining progresses, the parties will make concessions that reduce the cost to the other side of accepting the proposed settlement, taking proposals off the table or making trade-offs. At the same time, both parties will be seeking to change the other's mind about the costs of holding out for further concessions.

The union, for example, will seek to persuade the employer that any deal that provides less for its members than what the union is proposing will almost certainly result in a protracted labour dispute or, alternatively, harm workers' morale, quality of work and productivity within the workplace. Eventually one or both of the parties will decide that the costs of agreeing to the other party's terms are less than the costs of disagreeing, and together they will conclude a deal.

In the private sector, the employer's power in a workplace dispute derives from their ownership of the assets used in production and the extent of their ability to withstand a stoppage of production. That power is also rooted in their ability to close the workplace altogether and either transfer production to another plant or relocate production facilities to another locale. In some industries in Canada, employers' power of mobility has been strengthened by decades of technological change and free trade agreements that have eliminated barriers to capital movement across national borders.

The union's power depends primarily on the willingness of members to act in unity and to incur the costs of strike action, notably the loss of income while on strike but also the possible loss of their jobs if the establishment is closed or the strike broken. But such power is tempered by the organizational, social, economic, and political context of the bargaining. Some unions have created large strike funds to distribute strike pay, which replaces a portion of striking workers' wages by pooling the dues from many members. Other unions have fewer such resources or no strike fund at all. During an economic boom when unemployment is low, unions have a bargaining advantage, both because employers are reluctant to forego potential profits and lose market share and because striking workers have less fear of being replaced while on strike. When the economy is stagnant or slumping, the bargaining advantage shifts to employers, who are able to capitalize on workers' collective feelings of insecurity and restricted choices in the labour market.

In the public sector, the power dynamic is different since the employer is not a profit-making entity but rather taxpayer-funded. Many public sector employers, such as hospitals, universities and colleges, are not themselves in direct control of their budgets and unions must negotiate with them rather than the governments who really hold the purse strings. Therefore, the ability of a union to impose economic costs on public sector employers through a strike is complicated because, in many cases, a labour dispute would simply save the employer money. To be effective, public sector strikes therefore require strong political support from service users putting pressure on the employer to settle the strike in favour of the workers.

In both the private and public sectors, the most difficult collective agreement to negotiate is often the first one. All the terms and conditions of employment must be established from scratch in the context of a new bargaining relationship to which neither party is accustomed. Plus, employers who (unsuccessfully) opposed union certification will often seek to undermine the union at this stage, attempting to sabotage the bargaining process through delaying tactics and by refusing to compromise on key issues. Such tactics are designed to force strike action, a situation employers sometimes exploit to try to break a union, and to exhaust workers until they decide they have no hope of creating a collective agreement and then decertify the union. After recognizing these problems, most jurisdictions in Canada established legislation designed to provide an alternative method of resolving first-contract disputes, either through arbitration or imposition of a first contract by a labour board. Once a collective agreement is in place, subsequent rounds of negotiations usually focus on articles that are subject to dispute, and on wages and benefits. Collective bargaining does not necessarily become any easier, but generally there are fewer issues to address.

When a tentative agreement is reached, it goes to the union membership for ratification or approval of the proposed collective agreement. If the membership votes to approve the agreement, the deal is done. On the other hand, if the membership rejects the agreement, the parties go back to the bargaining table to try to negotiate modifications that would address the concerns that led to rejection.

If an agreement cannot be reached, then collective bargaining is at an impasse and the likelihood of a strike or lockout increases. To avoid that outcome, all jurisdictions in Canada have articles in their labour relations acts providing for conciliation and/or mediation, which normally involves government appointment of a conciliator to assist the parties in reaching an agreement, or, in the case of a mediator, a third party, voluntarily agreed upon by the parties involved, who may participate more actively and intervene to help the parties achieve a deal. In most jurisdictions, appointment of a conciliator or mediator is at the request of one or both parties or at the discretion of the minister responsible for labour relations.

STRIKES AND LOCKOUTS

Prior to the adoption of PC 1003 in 1944 (see Chapter 4), the only method workers had of collectively demonstrating mutual support and pressuring employers to address their concerns was through the use of strikes—workers' mass withdrawal of their labour—or other actions designed to disrupt production or the provision of services. Contemporary Canadian labour relations is far more regulated, and the conditions under which unions can strike legally are now much more limited.

In all Canadian jurisdictions, legal strikes may only take place once (1) a collective agreement has expired; (2) union members have authorized the strike action through a secret ballot; (3) attempts at conciliation have proven unsuccessful; and (4) the parties have waited through a statutory "cooling off" period, generally between 14 and 17 days. All four of these conditions must be met for unions to legally strike. The same legislation also defines the right of employers to "withdraw" in the form of a lockout. A lockout occurs when the employer, after failing to reach an agreement with the union, literally locks employees out of the workplace and cuts off pay, and in some cases, benefits. With the exception of the requirement to hold a vote, employers are subject to the same rules as unions to legally lock out their employees.

Strikes are designed to exert pressure on the employer to come to an agreement with the union on the terms and conditions of employment and normally take place in response to a critical impasse in negotiations. Strikes can be long, drawn-out affairs, or they can be resolved within hours. Sometimes, the real threat or possibility of a strike is enough to get the parties to reach a last-minute compromise. Strikes are typically viewed as a last resort, as evidenced by the fact that the overwhelming majority of collective agreements are renegotiated without a labour disruption.

Unions' greatest strength in collective bargaining is an informed and mobilized membership, and nowhere is this more apparent than when the union engages in a strike. Unions need to mobilize members while collective bargaining is taking place to ensure they are solidly behind the union's position, are prepared to take job action to back up their demands, and are willing to demonstrate this solidarity to the employer. As part of their preparations for collective bargaining, most unions formulate a strategy based on mobilizing member support for dealing with deadlocks in bargaining and in support of strike action. For example, union members may wear buttons or t-shirts to work or use specific hashtags on social media that display solidarity and inform the broader public of their union's bargaining priorities. These preparations can also include campaigns to gain community support, which are especially important in disputes involving public services that are financed out of taxes, such as health care or education, and disputes in certain areas of the private sector, such as transportation and communications services, that can lead to major disruptions in the economy and society.

Although, by law, unions only require a 50 percent plus one mandate from the voting membership to initiate a strike, most unions would not imagine striking unless a much higher percentage of members supported the action. A union that obtains a solid mandate for strike action—70 percent or more with a high proportion of the membership participating in the vote—will have its position strengthened in the bargaining process. A lukewarm result—60 percent or less with a low level of participation in the vote—will signal to both union and employer that in this particular round of bargaining, members are reluctant to take strike action and that more gains for the union are unlikely. In short, for unions, the success of their strikes depends on the level of solidarity amongst members.

Strikes are complicated matters involving careful preparations, not least because they involve a high level of conflict that most people are not used to. When a workplace is closed through strike action, the union typically establishes a picket line around the employer's facility to inform the public that a strike is in progress, to monitor the employer's activities, and especially to prevent the employer from operating the workplace without the striking workers. To maintain the picket line and ensure that participants comply with picket-line protocol—the rules and procedures governing picket-line behaviour and operation—the union appoints picket captains. When union members cross the picket line to continue work and/or replacement workers are recruited to maintain production, problems on the picket line can arise. No workers like to see others going into a workplace to do their jobs when they are on strike. In these circumstances, picket captains have the responsibility of preventing altercations between strikers and people crossing the picket line. Though the union wants to hold firm, it also wants to avoid any behaviour or incident (physical aggression or verbal threats) on the picket line that could lead to police intervention and criminal charges. As well, it wants to avoid any picket-line confrontations that could undermine public support for the union and striking workers.

During a strike, unions and employers alike seek to gain public support through media advertising, news stories and interviews. Both parties also seek to build the support of other organizations in the community, especially in situations where the employer is maintaining production. Employers will ask their customers for continued patronage and solicit support from other businesses in the community. Unions will call on community groups for support on the picket line and in the media.

Given the power imbalance inherent in the employment relationship, electing to withdraw one's labour is the most powerful form of leverage available to workers. It also carries with it major risks. Striking workers no longer collect an income from their employer but rather must rely on the union's strike fund to scrape by. Most unions maintain a strike fund, an amount of money created by the union and paid into by the members over time, intended to partially offset the lost wages and benefits incurred by workers when they are on strike or locked out. Strike pay helps workers meet costs of subsistence, but it is generally much less than normal pay and usually tied to participation on the picket line or other strike support activities. For example, Unifor's strike pay is set at $250 per week, far less than the typical Unifor member earns. For short strikes such payments may be sufficient to tide workers over. With longer strikes, workers may be forced to deplete their savings, cash in insurance policies or give up houses and durable goods purchased on a time-payment basis. In some cases, if the workplace is closed, they may lose their jobs permanently. Understandably then, workers are loath to take strike action unless they are certain that the potential gains (better wages, benefits and conditions on the job) will outweigh the costs they incur.

The costs of a strike can be high for both employer and union. For private sector employers, a stop in production means, as a rule, lost sales and revenues and reduced profits. Moreover, a long strike can force customers to switch to competitors to obtain their required goods or services. When the strike ends, some customers may return, but others may stick with their new suppliers, which means a loss in market share. As a strike deadline approaches, the likelihood increases of incurring undue costs, putting pressure on the employer to improve its offer to the union and avert a strike. Some employers may be able to avoid or reduce these costs in the short term by drawing down accumulated inventory, switching production to workplaces not affected by the strike, or using non-union employees or replacement workers to maintain production.

For unions, the main costs of a strike are the wages and benefits lost by members and the strike funds paid out, especially on strike pay. Another danger is a possible misreading of the situation—perhaps underestimating the employer's resolve or overestimating the employer's capacity to pay better wages and benefits—which could lead to the loss of the strike and to the workers either returning to work no better off than before or even losing their jobs. A negative outcome could damage the union's credibility and impair its efforts to organize other groups of workers and maintain existing locals.

In evaluating the potential benefits and costs of a strike, both parties must also take the long view. The current round of negotiations is immediately important, but their effect on future negotiations also comes into play. The wages established in current negotiations, for example, set the base for the next round of negotiations and any future increases. So, for the union, a strike in the short term can result in major economic improvements over a longer period. However, a particularly bitter strike or lockout can have negative long-term consequences on workplace morale and trust between the union and management. The longer the strike lasts, the more resentment builds, making an eventual return to work more difficult.

The capacity of the respective parties to impose greater costs on the other and to cope with the costs they bear in a work stoppage—their strike power—ultimately determines the outcomes of overt conflicts. Eventually one party or the other will decide that the costs of continued disagreement exceed the costs of accepting the other party's terms, and the conflict will end. Sometimes, this realization comes too late: either the company goes under or the union is broken.

Whereas strikes and lockouts in the private sector almost always result in lost revenue for the employer, labour disputes in the public sector have the potential of saving public money; the savings, however, result from non-delivery of critical public services. Public sector strikes are understandably contentious affairs and their implications stretch far beyond the workplace. When public sector union members exercise their right to strike, they are not striking a capitalist business but rather the government or school boards, and arguably, by extension, the public. In short, the public purse is used to pay for the salaries and benefit entitlements of public sector workers. As a result, when they strike, public sector unions tend to face greater "taxpayer" backlash in response to the interruption of services that members of the public depend on (Ross and Savage 2013b). Strikes by sanitation workers in Toronto and Windsor, Ontario, in 2009 resulted in high levels of taxpayer backlash; as uncollected garbage mounted, the public's support for the striking workers plummeted. This dynamic was clear during the 2015 strikes by teaching assistants at the University of Toronto and York University, who, while enjoying significant support from students and their organizations, also faced severe criticism on social media from individual students concerned about how the labour dispute would impact their ability to graduate on schedule.

Governments may put an end to a work stoppage through back-to-work legislation—a law that terminates the dispute and often refers all outstanding issues to an appointed arbitrator. As Panitch and Swartz (2003) have demonstrated, the use of back-to-work legislation has increased significantly since the 1950s, as have permanent restrictions on various workers' right to strike (see Figure 4.3 in Chapter 4). While the use of back-to-work legislation peaked in the 1980s, governments in recent years have been no less willing to use such laws to end work stoppages. Beyond the actual use of back-to-work legislation, there are many instances where the mere threat of government intervention has pre-empted a work stoppage. Indeed, the threat of government-imposed back-to-work legislation hangs over every collective bargaining table in Canada, particularly in the public sector, but increasingly in the private sector, as witnessed in the Harper Conservative government's interventions in bargaining at Air Canada in 2012 (Stevens and Nesbitt 2014). In that case, the federal government pre-empted strikes by flight attendants, pilots and machinists by declaring that it would immediately use back-to-work legislation to ensure the continuity of service.

But while these kinds of restrictions reduce the likelihood of strike action, they do not guarantee its elimination. On the contrary, in some situations conditions become so desperate that union members will strike illegally despite the threat of fines and jail sentences. This happened in Alberta in 1988, when nurses defied legislation and waged a nineteen-day strike because they had lost faith that arbitration could deliver the kinds of improvements that would allow them to provide decent patient care (Coulter 1993). In B.C. in 2005, teachers (and other workers in sympathy) walked off the job to protest a government-legislated contract (Camfield 2007). In 2012, Air Canada baggage handlers engaged in a short-lived wildcat strike to protest back-to-work legislation being held over their heads by the federal government (Stevens and Nesbitt 2014). What these last two conflicts share is a frustration with governments that intervene to suspend the rules of the collective bargaining system when workers' bargaining power is significant, thereby unfairly undermining workers' ability to improve their lives and working conditions and driving them to engage in strategies not sanctioned by the labour relations framework.

ESSENTIAL WORKERS AND ALTERNATE DISPUTE RESOLUTION

In all Canadian jurisdictions, certain public sector workers do not have a legal right to strike. These workers are typically referred to as "essential workers" and can be classified differently depending on the jurisdiction. For instance, police officers and firefighters are designated essential workers in every Canadian jurisdiction, and nurses working in hospitals are deemed essential in most (but not all) provinces. Government has decided that these workers are essential and should not have the right to strike because their involvement in labour disputes could put the public at risk. Conservative anti-union politicians have been working to broaden the definition of essential workers to include those whose work is important to the functioning of the economy and whose absence would create great public inconvenience. Occupations like teachers, transit operators and healthcare workers have been targeted on this basis and unions representing these workers have fiercely resisted removal of the right to strike. In Nova Scotia, for example, the Liberal government's Bill 37 (*Essential Health and Community Services Act*) severely curtailed the right to strike in the healthcare sector and sparked widespread union protests at the provincial legislature, a wildcat strike by nurses and a sit-in at the labour minister's office. Passed in April 2014, the law requires healthcare unions to negotiate essential services agreements with their employers to guarantee patient safety in the event of a strike. However, these essential services agreements must be approved by the employer, otherwise any strike by healthcare workers is considered illegal and the union and its members become subject to heavy financial penalties for engaging in strike activity. Critics of the law argue that Bill 37 gives employers an unfair veto that effectively eliminates the right to strike (CBC News 2014).

While some labour disputes unquestionably inconvenience the public, that fact alone should not dictate whether the legal right to strike should be withheld from certain groups of workers. As Peirce and Bentham (2007: 297) have argued:

> While most people are familiar with the dysfunctional effects of work stoppages, fewer recognize that they can serve a useful function in the labour-management relationship. The ability to impose costs upon one another through a strike or a lockout is perhaps the most compelling reason collective agreements are resolved. Often, it is the lurking threat, or perhaps the actual experience, of a work stoppage that finally motivates the parties to compromise their positions sufficiently to make a deal they both find acceptable.

In other words, the more limited the right to strike, the more likely it may be that collective bargaining comes to an impasse.

Where workers have no statutory right to strike, binding interest arbitration is the most common way to resolve disputes that arise through the collective bargaining process. There are two main forms of interest arbitration: conventional interest arbitration and final offer selection. Under conventional interest arbitration, both the union and the employer provide a third-party arbitrator with their positions on all outstanding bargaining issues. Arbitrators use this information along with their own independent research to craft a compromise settlement that is binding on both parties. Some argue that conventional interest arbitration dissuades both parties from compromising as part of the collective bargaining process, secure in the knowledge that an arbitrator will impose a settlement that "splits the difference," leading to a dependence on arbitration that some people have described as its "narcotic effect" (Kochan et al. 2009: 4). However, neither party can control the arbitrator's decision, so rolling the dice in this way, rather than securing a negotiated settlement between the parties themselves, does carry some serious risks.

Final offer selection is similar to conventional interest arbitration, but with one important twist. In final offer selection, each party puts an offer to the arbitrator that would resolve all the outstanding bargaining issues, but the arbitrator must choose either the employer's offer or the union's offer, in full, with the result being legally binding on both parties. Therefore, the arbitrator has no opportunity to construct a compromise settlement. This system is based on the idea that the threat of losing at final offer selection will induce both parties to make the most reasonable final offers possible. The "winner takes all" results, however, can also be problematic. For example, in March 2012, Air Canada and the Air Canada Pilots' Association were subjected to final offer selection arbitration as part of the *Protecting Air Service Act*, which prevented a labour dispute. In July of that year, the arbitrator sided with the employer, imposing a five-year contract that the union complained would allow the employer to impose work rules that "will cost many pilots their jobs, demoralize the rest and kick other important issues years down the road, where they will fester and undermine any effort to achieve positive culture change at our airline" (CBC News 2012).

Critics of the interest arbitration process argue that the system is so legalistic in nature that it often focuses on narrow, technical, comparative interpretations rather than on the substance of the issues being contested, thereby undermining the relative importance a union may attach to a particular workplace issue. As a result, some unions rely on direct workplace actions like work-to-rule campaigns, "sickouts," sit-ins and wildcats as alternative means of resolving workplace disputes. Work-to-rule campaigns are especially popular with workers who do not have a legal right to strike. Union members engaged in a work-to-rule campaign do not withdraw their labour completely but rather continue to perform their work duties exactly as required by the collective agreement, without any extra effort. A work-to-rule campaign could, in the case of school teachers for example, take the form of a mass refusal to work voluntary overtime or supervise extracurricular activities, or a strict adherence to complex occupational health and safety regulations or other work procedures to slow down the labour process.

Sickouts are coordinated attempts to disrupt business as usual by having workers call in sick on the same day or for the same shift, thereby causing a critical labour shortage in the workplace. While unionized workers are typically provided with rights to call in sick under their collective agreements, it is the coordinated and strategic use of this right that makes the sickout a powerful protest tool in the workplace.

Workplace actions like sickouts, which are designed to slow down service or production, in some instances, may constitute illegal strikes. Illegal strikes, typically referred to as wildcats, are spontaneous work stoppages that occur while the collective agreement is still in force. For instance, workers who learn their workplace is shutting down may launch a sit-in, a specific kind of wildcat strike wherein workers refuse to leave the workplace until their jobs have been restored.

These alternate methods of applying pressure in the workplace are widely condemned by both employers and government, and often come hand-in-hand with very stiff labour board-imposed fines and penalties for the workers and unions who take part. The fact that such workplace actions take place, however, suggests that no legal framework can fully contain the competing class interests and underlying structural conflicts inherent in the labour-management relationship.

FORMS OF UNION POWER IN THE COLLECTIVE AGREEMENT

There are a number of different forms of union power that collective agreements entrench and amplify (Godard 2011: 7–8). First, collective agreements provide unions with the opportunity to control the supply of labour by exerting collective market power over buyers of labour and therefore the price of labour. The success of such a strategy hinges somewhat on the relative irreplaceability of the workers in question. Craft unions used this strategy to full effect in the nineteenth and early twentieth centuries, but the notion of protecting "bargaining unit work" was eventually extended to all kinds of workers, both skilled and unskilled, to ensure those within the bargaining unit get first crack at any available work.

Second, unions work to take wages out of competition by replacing market mechanisms for determining the price of labour with the collective bargaining process. In short, by setting a wage on which all workers in the bargaining unit agree, collective bargaining helps to prevent workers from competing with each other for jobs by offering to work for lower wages or benefits. In other words, collective agreements stop a destructive race to the bottom. When unions spread a standard wage across many unionized workplaces in a given sector, they also remove wages from the competition that exists between employers. Employers must then find other ways besides cutting wages to increase profits and make themselves more attractive to investors or customers. One technique unions use to achieve this spreading of standards is pattern bargaining, whereby bargaining takes place initially with only one firm in the industry and the union then seeks to impose the same settlement on other firms, as is the case, for example, in the automobile industry. Another such method is multi-employer or sectoral bargaining, whereby bargaining takes place between a union and an organization representing many employers, as in some segments of the construction industry, the hospital sector and in colleges.

In setting wages, hours of work, and job classifications, unions are also negotiating the wage-effort bargain with management, namely the level of pay workers will receive for a given level of effort (Godard 2011: 54). This negotiation is always contentious and antagonistic because the employer always wants more effort for the wages paid to maximize profits or cost savings, whereas workers always want to expend less effort due to the physical and mental impact of work on one's body and life. In this sense, although the wage-effort bargain is formally defined by collective agreements, it is always being renegotiated, for example when the employer introduces initiatives to save money, reorganize work, introduce technology or increase the intensity of work. For workers and unions, the terms of this bargain are shaped by conceptions of "fairness," as captured by the labour movement slogan, "A Fair Day's Work for a Fair Day's Pay."

Third, and related to the above, unions may engage in job control unionism to exert exclusive control over a particular "job territory" or jurisdiction by negotiating detailed sets of work rules for each job. This helps to define how much effort is linked to a given wage, and it prevents employers from constantly adding more tasks to workers' jobs without compensating them. Job control unionism also typically attempts to control the movement of workers in, out of and around the workplace (whether through layoffs, promotions, transfers or shift assignments) using the seniority principle—the practice of tying access to various positive things in the workplace to one's length of service with the employer—rather than an employer-determined criteria, which is more subjective and open to favouritism. Job control unionism is most commonly associated with craft unionism because of its narrowly defined communities of solidarity, and its insistence on maintaining barriers into the craft as a way to deal with scarcity of jobs. This prevents too many people from working in a given occupation when there is not enough work to support everyone at a decent standard of living. However, industrial unions have successfully adapted job control techniques to their workplaces, for instance by ensuring that bargaining unit members are given priority over people from the outside when the employer is filling a position.

Fourth, unions provide workers with a collective voice, amplifying their otherwise individual impact on the employer's decision-making. Through their workplace advocacy and defense of members' interests, unions allow workers to express views about how the workplace should be run without fear of reprisal. This is especially important when implementing a collective agreement after it has been negotiated. Once a collective agreement is signed, the union has to ensure it is applied in the way it was intended and that members are treated fairly in its administration. If one or more union members believe the employer has violated the collective agreement in ways that harm them specifically, they can file an individual or group grievance. If the union leadership believes the employer has violated the agreement in a way that affects the entire membership, they can file a policy grievance. All collective agreements contain a grievance-arbitration article, a mechanism for resolving disputes that arise out of the interpretation, application and/or administration of the collective agreement These articles prescribe a number of steps for resolving the grievance voluntarily and stipulate time lines along which the grievance must proceed.

Union stewards (sometimes called shop stewards or departmental representatives) often play an important role in individual or group grievances. They determine the validity of the grievance, assessing whether the employer has contravened the collective agreement. They help the aggrieved member draft the grievance, making sure it is done properly, citing the articles in the collective agreement that have been violated, and specifying the redress sought—the action that management must take to resolve the grievance. They attend and participate in the meetings between the aggrieved member and management throughout all of the various steps to try to resolve the grievance. Most unions provide stewards with intensive training to ensure they handle this important function effectively. As well, union representatives will work closely with shop stewards at all stages of the process, gradually taking on a more active role as the grievance progresses to higher levels.

Grievance procedures are a particularly significant advantage of union membership. They place limitations on management's ability to act arbitrarily, and thus, to some extent, they bring the rule of law to the workplace. In the absence of a union, and the grievance procedures set out in a collective agreement, workers' rights are much more fragile; management is able to act much more arbitrarily.

To ensure the employer's compliance with the rule of law, the union must take all member grievances seriously. Unions have a legal obligation or duty of fair representation to all members of the bargaining unit. Quite apart from this legal obligation, for many members a grievance provides a personal test of the union's willingness and capacity to represent member interests. Failure to process a grievance in a timely and effective fashion could sow seeds of dissatisfaction amongst the members and weaken loyalty to the union. This is especially true of grievances involving unjust disciplinary action and dismissal, often described as the workplace equivalent of capital punishment because it could permanently damage the work and life prospects of the aggrieved member.

If the grievance is not resolved through internal negotiations, the final step is arbitration. A neutral third party or arbitrator that both parties trust is asked to make a final determination of how the collective agreement should be interpreted and how the dispute should be resolved. Agreeing to send a dispute to arbitration means that both the union and the employer choose to be legally bound by the decision, even if it isn't in their favour. In most cases, arbitrators are either lawyers or individuals with an in-depth knowledge of labour relations. In Canada, labour relations acts make it mandatory that all collective agreements include a clause stating that the union and the employer agree to send such unresolved disputes to arbitration (Sack 2010: 251).

While these procedures normally result in the resolution of disputes, they are open to a number of criticisms. First, individuals may be reluctant to file a grievance either because they fear that such action will jeopardize their future prospects with the employer or lead to reprisals, or they lack confidence in the union's commitment to see the matter through to completion. Second, the grievance arbitration process is often too lengthy, sometimes taking years to complete, and in the meantime leaving the employer to continue with the action that prompted the grievance in the first place. Third, arbitration is very costly because arbitrators themselves charge thousands of dollars a day for their services, and employers—and increasingly unions—use lawyers to represent them in hearings. The cost of arbitration can sometimes embolden employers to ignore the provisions of the agreement and to do so with impunity, knowing full well that the union does not have the resources to prosecute them successfully. Fourth, some arbitrators interpret collective agreements in a very narrow way, unduly emphasizing management rights at the expense of individual workers' interests.

These criticisms of grievance arbitration are valid, and some unions have experimented with innovative practices to overcome these defects. For example, some try to reduce costs by training their own members to represent the union in grievance arbitrations. As well, some collective agreements and labour relations acts include expedited arbitration articles designed to move important grievances (usually grievances that arise from disciplinary actions by the employer) more quickly through the process. If mediation fails, some unions have tried grievance mediation-arbitration, in which the arbitrator first attempts to negotiate a voluntary resolution of the grievance before issuing a binding decision, as a way to resolve grievances more quickly and amicably.

However, there are some deeper criticisms of the grievance procedure as a legalistic and bureaucratic process that takes power out of the hands of members and gives it to "experts" who act in their place (Camfield 2011). One of the reasons employers and governments supported the development of the grievance procedure was to prevent workers and their unions from using collective direct action, like a walkout, slow-down or sit-down, to resolve workplace disputes, as was common practice before the Second World War. The grievance procedure meant that workplace activity would continue uninterrupted while a dispute was being worked out, thus removing the financial pressure on the employer to settle quickly. Critics of the disempowering effects of grievance-arbitration propose that workers' right to strike during the life of a collective agreement be restored. For instance, Larry Haiven (1995) argues that having the right to strike over grievances would restore the initiative to unions and their members and produce quick resolutions in most circumstances because employers are ill-equipped to deal with unanticipated strikes. It would give members the incentive to police their agreements more vigilantly. It would lay the foundation for continuous as opposed to episodic member mobilization, which would in turn strengthen the position of unions in collective bargaining.

A VOICE IN THE WORKPLACE

The basic activities of unions—organizing, collective bargaining, processing grievances and conducting strikes—are complex and shaped by a dynamic economy and frequent changes in political, legal, social and ideological conditions. For the most part, members determine a union's activities in the workplace through democratic practices entrenched in constitutions, traditions and organizational structures. The members themselves ultimately decide what is negotiated in collective bargaining and sanction the outcome of the bargaining process: the collective agreement. The members have influence over which grievances get priority and which grievances are pushed to arbitration. The members decide when to take strike action and when to end a strike. In short, unions give workers tremendous voice in the workplace and, in turn, the potential to reshape or transform their working conditions and participate in decisions concerning how their workplace is run.

QUESTIONS FOR DISCUSSION

1. What are the differences between card-based and mandatory-vote certification procedures? Which is more effective at determining the will of workers and why?
2. How is collective bargaining different from negotiating individual terms of employment in a non-union workplace?
3. In what ways does a formal grievance procedure democratize the workplace, if at all?
4. How do unions take wages out of competition, and why do they seek to do this?
5. What, if any, criteria should governments use to determine which group of workers should have the right to strike?
6. What would happen in the absence of a legal right to strike? Is interest arbitration an effective substitute for being able to strike?

CHAPTER 6

UNIONS AND POLITICAL ACTION

Although unions make important gains for workers through collective bargaining and workplace representation, they cannot rely exclusively on their workplace-based power to achieve all the things that improve workers' lives. Not all problems that workers face in capitalist society are resolvable at the workplace. In fact, many of the labour movement's historical achievements, like reductions in the length of the workday and adoption of a minimum wage, were ultimately accomplished outside of the workplace through political action. So much of the labour relations framework is influenced and shaped by politics. Are unions to be outlawed or legal? Will employers be required or not required to recognize and bargain with unions that have the support of a majority of employees? Will the law make it more or less difficult to organize? to negotiate first contracts? to strike? The answers to these questions are a function of political decisions. However, these are not the only issues of direct concern for workers. Should we have comprehensive or limited social programs? Should health care and education be provided on a private, for-profit or a public, not-for-profit basis? Should taxes be higher or lower? These broader social and economic questions, and others like them, are political matters in which unions and their members have a direct interest. To effectively defend these interests, unions need to act politically.

Although most unions engage in political activities outside their immediate workplaces, the strategies and tactics used, and the purposes behind these activities, vary widely. Unions provide workers with a way of strengthening their collective voice in the political sphere through a combination of traditional electoral politics, extra-parliamentary activities, and most recently, legal activism. But which is the most promising strategy? Should unions focus on influencing existing political parties, supporting the ones that are friendly to labour and opposing the ones that are not? Should unions instead work to establish a separate political party that would represent labour's interests? Should unions abandon political parties and parliamentary politics altogether and confine their efforts to direct social movement activism? Should unions bypass traditional political action and instead concentrate on advancing their priorities through the judicial system? At various times in the past, one or another segment of Canada's labour movement has practiced each of these strategic approaches. Indeed, differences over how best to engage in politics have from the beginning helped to keep the union movement in Canada divided, and they continue to be a source of division in the labour movement. However, before exploring different strategic approaches to union engagement with politics it is useful to examine the different orientations to political engagement in the labour movement, the broad philosophies of business unionism and social unionism.

BUSINESS UNIONISM AND SOCIAL UNIONISM

As discussed in Chapter 2, business unionism and social unionism represent very broad orientations to the purpose of unions in both the workplace and society in general. Business unionism emphasizes unions' workplace economic role and therefore focuses on collective bargaining and workplace representation. This, however, does not imply that business unionists eschew political engagement altogether. Rather, they engage in the political realm primarily to increase the strength of unions and their bargaining power. This agenda includes strengthening labour legislation to favour unions, lobbying for government policies that support or expand their industry, and even mobilizing in favour of politicians and parties that commit to advocate such policies. However, they pursue these goals in non-partisan ways, meaning that they do not attach themselves permanently to a particular political party. Instead, their relationship with political parties calls to mind the maxim famously expressed by former AFL president Samuel Gompers: reward your friends and punish your enemies. In other words, business unionists will mobilize their members to support politicians with a labour-friendly record, but they will work to shift that support if those politicians do not deliver for labour (Ross 2012a: 37).

Social unionism has a more expansive vision of unions' purpose, and therefore of the role and types of political engagement appropriate in the labour movement. Social unionism is premised on the view that, because workers' interests lie both inside and outside the workplace and because those interests are as citizens and not just as wage earners, unions both should and must engage in strategies that are political (Kumar and Murray 2006: 82). For instance, publicly provided health care is very important to workers, given that in almost all cases they would otherwise be unable to afford it; however, because social programs or public services are not direct bargaining issues, workers need strategies and organizational forms that transcend the workplace to fight on such issues. Workers also have interests in particular kinds of arrangements, namely those that create more economic and social equality in their communities. In that sense, not all political parties are created equal, and social unionists tend to be more partisan in their political identifications because some parties are clearly more pro-union and pro-worker than others. Social unionism also holds that those sections of the working class that have been able to gain organizational strength should use it to support working-class people who haven't been able to do so. As Sam Gindin, former assistant to the CAW president, argues, unions act as a vehicle for members not only to address bargaining demands, but also to lead "fights over everything that affects working people in their communities" and beyond (1995: 268). J.S. Woodsworth, the first leader of the CCF, encapsulated this dimension of social unionism in his famous quote: "what we desire for ourselves, we wish for all" (McNaught 2001: 138).

UNION ELECTORAL STRATEGIES

There exists a broad spectrum of union engagement with electoral politics in Canada ranging from formal non-participation and non-partisanship to institutionalized partisan links and heavily resourced electoral interventions at the federal, provincial/territorial and local levels. Some unions provide educational programs or promotional materials designed to make members aware of the benefits or disadvantages of government actions and policies, and to encourage them to be politically active, mobilizing them around elections and lobbying activities. Many unions also promote support for the New Democratic Party and commit resources, both personnel and financial, to the party's electoral efforts where permitted by campaign finance law.

Unions engage with electoral politics to help shape the legislative agenda in a way that will benefit workers. The Mouseland fable—made famous by former Saskatchewan Premier and the federal New Democratic Party's first leader, Tommy Douglas—is the key to understanding why working men and women, including many union activists, came together to form their "own" political party, the NDP, for exactly that purpose. The political message behind Mouseland is that Liberal and Conservative parties exist only to serve the interests of "fat cats" in the business community, at the expense of working-class people. The fable promotes the idea that average voters—the mice—in Canada's political system face an empty choice between two competing parties made up of cats—the Liberal and Conservative parties respectively—who are distinguished only by their colour. After electing successive governments made up of cats, who clearly were not working in the interest of mice, one mouse wonders aloud why the mice do not get together and elect a party of their own. The mouse is immediately imprisoned for proposing such a revolutionary idea and the fable concludes with the famous line: "you can lock up a mouse or a man, but you can't lock up an idea."

The idea that working people should create their own political party helped to drive the creation of the NDP in 1961 as a partnership between the CLC and the CCF, the precursor to the NDP. The NDP's institutional link with union affiliates made it unique among political parties in Canada (Archer and Whitehorn 1993: 3–4). Founders of the NDP had hoped the presence of a social democratic labour party in Canadian politics would challenge the longstanding electoral dominance of the Liberal and Conservative parties by realigning Canadian politics on a left-right basis, as had occurred in the U.K. after the creation of the British Labour Party (Smith 1967: 190). While the NDP showed early signs of electoral success in provincial politics, particularly in Western Canada, it took another half century, until May 2011, to displace one of the major federal parties and form the Official Opposition. However, the realignment of the party system at the federal level is far from permanent. While the NDP's breakthrough in 2011 represented an electoral high mark for the party, the NDP has struggled historically to compete with the Liberal and Conservative parties in federal politics.

Whether responsibility for the federal NDP's overall electoral performance rests primarily with organized labour, with the party or with the lack of class consciousness among voters is a topic that has been hotly contested (Archer and Whitehorn 1997; Brodie and Jenson 1988; Bradford 1989). What we do know for certain is that, in the Canadian context, the institutional party-union link has always been weak. Although the NDP was modeled after the British Labour Party, it never achieved the strong union affiliation realized by social democratic parties in most European countries. Union affiliation with the federal NDP reached its peak (15 percent of union members) shortly after the party's founding convention in 1961 and has been in decline ever since (Archer and Whitehorn 1997: 49–51). Low rates of affiliation are reflected in the relatively low proportion of union members who have actually voted for the federal party historically. Although union affiliates continue to be represented within the federal party's central decision-making bodies, their relative influence over the party has also declined in recent years, in part due to a legislative ban on union donations at the federal level (Savage 2010).

Does the labour movement's relationship with the NDP actually translate into more votes for the party at election time? The answer is complex. First, union membership does apparently influence individual voting behaviour. Studies of the 1965, 1968, 1974 and 1979 federal elections (Archer 1985: 357) show union members were *twice* as likely as non-union members to vote NDP. Members of unions affiliated with the NDP were *three* times as likely to vote NDP. Still, even though union membership increased the likelihood of an NDP vote, more union members continued to vote Liberal than NDP in federal elections, and this was the case even for unions affiliated to the NDP. Therefore, while being a member of a union increases the likelihood of voting NDP, Canadian unions, despite their linkage to the party, have not been very effective at delivering their memberships' vote to the party, at least at the federal level.

At the provincial level, the party has proven more successful, having formed government in six provinces (Saskatchewan, Manitoba, B.C., Ontario, Nova Scotia and Alberta) and one territory (Yukon). The party's experience in provincial and territorial politics demonstrates both the possibilities and limits of social democratic labour parties as vehicles of workers' political interests.

The 1970s-era NDP governments in Manitoba, Saskatchewan and B.C. introduced relatively strong labour legislation, including significant gains in both health and safety and social legislation, and it would be reasonable to argue that these governments served Canada's unions relatively well, thus justifying union support for the NDP. However, the party could not resist the pull of neoliberalism in the 1990s, as the political climate shifted to the right and dragged NDP governments along with it. The decade initially brought new hope and optimism for workers. NDP governments were elected in Saskatchewan and B.C. in 1991, in Yukon in 1992, and, most important by far, in Ontario in September 1990. The unexpected election of Bob Rae's NDP government in Ontario seemed to represent the pinnacle of NDP success and promise. Finally, a provincial NDP government had been elected in Canada's industrial and commercial heartland, the largest province in Canada. In the early 1990s, more than half of Canada's population was now governed by the NDP. This was a genuinely exciting prospect.

But despite introducing some pro-labour legislation, all of the NDP governments in the 1990s alienated the labour movement to some degree. Rather than challenging capitalism in the interests of working people, they accommodated their policies to its demands, practicing restraint and implementing cutbacks that made provincial NDP governments little different, in practice, from governments led by other parties.

By all accounts, the Saskatchewan NDP's most recent stretch in office (from 1991 to 2007), characterized by aggressive deficit reduction, corporate tax cuts and hospital closures, had more in common with neoliberal than social democratic ideology (Stanford, 2001: 95; Warnock, 2005: 89–91). In the area of workers' rights, the Saskatchewan NDP government raised the ire of the labour movement in 1999 by ending strikes by nurses and power utility workers with back-to-work legislation (Warnock, 2005: 95). In private, the union leadership was furious, but in public, most of the labour movement was careful not to criticize the party (Byers, 2002: 75). Despite its increasingly neoliberal orientation, the union leadership remains firmly committed to supporting the Saskatchewan NDP at election time. Labour support for the party endures because the union leadership is "trapped, choosing always to support the NDP as the lesser of the evils. With labour in its back pocket, the NDP leadership has concluded that it has to do very little to retain labour's support" (Warnock, 2005: 95).

A similar dynamic exists in the province of Manitoba, where the NDP has formed governments from 1969 to 1977, 1981 to 1988, and again from 1999. Known for its pragmatic left-wing policy innovation in the 1970s, Premier Gary Doer's NDP administration (1999–2009) strayed very far from its democratic socialist roots. Wesley (2005: 11) argues that the Manitoba NDP "severed its ties to Keynesian social democracy, as applied under [former NDP premiers] Schreyer and Pawley. In their place, New Democrats now follow the 'Third Way' approach to politics, openly pursuing partnerships with the private and voluntary sectors, balancing budgets, and remaining at least somewhat open to the 'integration of the North American economies.'" However, as in Saskatchewan, Manitoba's unions have taken the position that the NDP, despite its flaws, must be supported to prevent the ascendance of an even more right-wing party.

Donne Flanagan (2003), who was a senior policy advisor to Premier Gary Doer, clearly laid out the Manitoba NDP's strategy for making policy decisions in an era of neoliberalism. According to Flanagan, NDP policy-makers "inoculate" themselves by giving their traditional enemies at least a bit of what they demand, much as we inoculate ourselves against a disease by injecting into our bodies a bit of the disease. In recent years, the business community and their various associations—Chambers of Commerce, the Canadian Taxpayers Federation, the Canadian Federation of Independent Business and corporate-funded think tanks like the Fraser Institute—have aggressively demanded tax cuts. Their purpose is to reduce the role of government and turn more powers over to the private sector. NDP governments in Manitoba and Saskatchewan have acquiesced to these demands. That is, they give the business community at least some of what it wants—tax cuts—to dampen the opposition and thus increase their chances of re-election. To date this approach has worked, at least electorally.

The problem is that NDP governments end up defining their governing strategy through the demands of their traditional enemies. They do not want to offend the business community. Thus their improvements to labour and social legislation are meek, making them increasingly indistinguishable from other parties. For example, NDP governments in Manitoba and Saskatchewan have steadfastly refused to implement anti-scab laws similar to the ones that exist in B.C. and Quebec, despite repeated requests from the labour movement. As the NDP moves to the ideological centre, it runs the risk of losing many of its traditional supporters—those who do the work in election campaigns, who knock on doors and get out the vote.

The fiscal problems faced by all provincial NDP governments in the 1990s also highlighted the crisis of social democracy and the unraveling of the traditional party–union relationship. Nowhere was this more apparent than in Ontario. The Rae government did amend labour relations legislation to the advantage of labour, including passage of an anti-scab law restricting the ability of employers to maintain production during a strike or lockout, pro-union improvements to certification procedures and introduction of employment equity legislation. However, for some unions, these gains paled into insignificance when weighed against the 1993 imposition on public sector unions of the now infamous *Social Contract Act*, which effectively removed the right to free collective bargaining for public sector workers. It did this by forcing the reopening of existing public sector collective agreements and imposing unpaid days off—"Rae days"—to cut costs. Although it is widely accepted that poor economic conditions narrowed the NDP's room to manoeuvre politically, the Ontario NDP government's decision to implement the *Social Contract Act* was pursued without considering more progressive alternatives, like raising corporate income taxes, to make up for budget shortfalls (Walkom 1994: 139–40).

The unions that fought the proposal suffered deeper cuts than the ones that acquiesced. Union members, feeling betrayed by their political ally, were outraged. The *Social Contract Act* also had a destructive effect on party–union relations and resulted in the Ontario Federation of Labour's decision not to endorse the party's re-election bid in 1995 (Walkom 1994: 121). Panitch and Swartz (2003: 178) have argued that the act "shattered the confidence of trade unions in their central political strategy: electing NDP governments ... the contradictions between the unions and the party it so brutally revealed took a tremendous emotional toll."

In the 1995 Ontario provincial election—in which the Rae government ran a campaign virtually devoid of social-democratic content or vision—most unions offered only tepid support to the NDP, while others refused to support the party in any way. But the result of this withdrawal of support was the election of a particularly regressive, pro-corporate, anti-labour government: the Progressive Conservatives led by Mike Harris. Harris immediately introduced a range of legislative attacks on labour, the public sector and the poor. These events most vividly illustrated the quandary with which the labour movement continues to grapple. Should labour refuse to support the NDP when that party's governments let them down, on the grounds that nothing is to be gained from supporting a party that does not defend labour's interests? Or should labour continue to support the NDP, even when the party lets labour down, on the grounds that even a weak NDP is better than the alternative as represented by the likes of the Harris government?

NDP governments argue to their traditional supporters that they are better than the right-wing alternatives that would replace them if they were to be defeated. And this is true: they *are* better for working people than their right-wing alternatives. But the logic of such a strategy is that, as time passes, the amount by which they are better diminishes, until many former supporters argue there is no difference, or that the difference is so minimal that it is not worth working for or even supporting. Such governments spend so much time and money placating their electoral enemies that they have little left for building what, for their supporters, would be a better world. At what point do people stop supporting a party that is increasingly indistinguishable from the parties that have historically been anti-labour? Is it always the case that for labour a middle-of-the-road NDP is better than any alternative?

The NDP's uneven record on labour issues has regenerated an essential debate in the union movement about how organized labour ought to do politics. This debate goes back to the 1870s and earlier. Since then unionists have advanced and promoted a variety of political strategies, including partyism, labourism, syndicalism, socialism, communism, social democracy and establishing a labour party. The debate appeared, for a while, to be settled with the 1961 establishment of the NDP. But the failure of that party, and social democracy more generally, to respond adequately to changing economic circumstances has once again thrown open the issue open to debate, and has once again split the labour movement.

Disappointment with NDP provincial governments throughout the 1990s prompted some segments of the labour movement to build political alliances with social movements outside the electoral arena. A good example of this movement-based strategy was the Ontario Days of Action, a series of rotating city-based general strikes held between 1995 and 1998. The strikes were organized by local union-community coalitions and were designed to cause economic disruption and highlight the widespread damage being done by the Harris Conservative government. However, for most unions, this experiment could not withstand the tyranny of the electoral cycle as unions drifted back to the familiar territory of electoral politics.

The Ontario Federation of Labour's controversial decision before the 1999 provincial election to jettison the Days of Action strategy in favour of reconciliation with the NDP alienated several unions that were not prepared to forgive the NDP for its past sins. While most industrial unions and CUPE Ontario backed the NDP, another group of unions came together with community organizations to form the Ontario Election Network in an effort to promote "strategic voting" as a method of blocking the Progressive Conservative party from winning re-election (Tanguay 2002: 145–64). In effect, strategic voting meant casting a ballot for the candidate (Liberal or New Democrat) best positioned to defeat Conservative candidates in each local riding. Teachers' unions, autoworkers, building trades unions and nurses' unions were key proponents of this strategy (Savage 2012: 78).

Despite the failure of strategic voting to defeat the Conservatives in the 1999 provincial election, the CAW decided to take the strategy national in 2006 in an unsuccessful effort to prevent the election of Stephen Harper's Conservative Party. At the time, then CAW President Buzz Hargrove explained the union's reasoning to a group of university students this way: "If we simply go to our members today and tell them—as we did for decades—'We recommend the NDP, and if they get elected, everything will be OK,' they will laugh at us ... we've learned the hard way that electing the NDP does not solve all our problems" (Hargrove 2006: 23). Instead, Hargrove argued in favour of an "active, demanding, independent labour movement to push the envelope and hold government accountable—whatever party is in power" (Hargrove 2006: 23). Whether it works or not, strategic voting has become a key electoral tactic practiced by a growing number of unions, reflecting both unions' growing disenchantment with the NDP and their increasingly defensive political strategies in relation to employers and the state (Savage 2010, 2012).

In practice, however, many of the unions promoting strategic voting have simply cultivated deeper pragmatic or Gomperist relationships to the Liberal Party, both federally and in provinces where Liberal Parties are considered electorally viable. Therefore the question persists: Should union members and working-class people generally support a Liberal Party that seems more likely to defeat a hardline Conservative government? Or should they vote NDP on the grounds that in the long run working people need a healthy pro-labour party in the political arena?

In provinces like B.C., Saskatchewan and Manitoba, the provincial NDP sections themselves benefit from strategic voting in provincial elections, having successfully realigned provincial politics in each respective province along a right-left axis. In many ways, the more polarized party systems in each of the three provinces allow the NDP to take union support for granted, whereas in other provinces the NDP must compete with the Liberals for official labour support.

Quebec is a special case. All major union federations in Quebec are officially committed to operating with complete political independence in the realm of electoral politics. After amending its constitution to sever its official ties to the NDP in 1971, the Quebec Federation of Labour (FTQ) has chosen to endorse parties in elections on a case-by-case basis. This policy has brought the FTQ closer in line with the CSN, which have jealously guarded their independence from political parties. Since 1988, the FTQ has required a special convention resolution to endorse a political party in a provincial election campaign. The FTQ endorsed the sovereignist Parti Québécois in the provincial elections of 1989, 1994, and 2007, but chose not to endorse a party in 1999, 2003, 2008, 2012 and 2014.

In Quebec, where the province's future within Canada represents an important political cleavage, unions traditionally bypassed the NDP in favour of sovereignist parties (Quebec's labour movement has officially supported various forms of independence for Quebec since the 1980s) (Savage 2010: 21–23). Union support for Quebec sovereignty or independence is historically rooted in workplace struggles revolving around issues of language, specifically protection and promotion of French as the primary language of work in the province (Tremblay 1972; Cyr and Roy 1981). For instance, Quebec workers resented that many of their collective agreements were written in English only, at the insistence of some anglophone employers, and that many opportunities for advancement in the workplace were reserved for unilingual anglophones.

The Parti Québécois (PQ), launched in 1968, was eventually able to secure the support of Quebec's French-speaking working class by tapping into a growing nationalist sentiment that manifested itself in labour disputes that took on linguistic dimensions. For example, in June 1976, a group of English-speaking pilots engaged in a nine-day work stoppage to protest the federal government's decision to gradually extend the use of French at airports. Anglophone pilots and air traffic controllers argued that because English was the language of the skies, the implementation of bilingualism in the day-to-day work operations of airports was potentially unsafe. In response, the federal government agreed to set up a commission of inquiry, which, in effect, delayed the implementation of bilingualism in airports and ignited a political firestorm in Quebec. Public opinion in the province was solidly behind a group of francophone pilots and air traffic controllers fighting for the right to communicate in French at work. In English Canada, the public backed English-speaking pilots and air traffic controllers as overwhelmingly as Quebecers supported the French-speaking workers. The air traffic control confrontation had a disproportionate impact on the political relationship between French and English in Quebec and across Canada (Borins 1983). The politics of language had collided with the politics of labour in a way that raised the collective national consciousness of Quebecers like never before, setting the stage for a majority PQ government in the November 1976 Quebec provincial election.

The PQ managed to form government from 1976 to 1985 and again from 1994 to 2003. In each instance, the government's main priority was to hold a referendum on Quebec independence. The party was careful not to alienate labour in the run-up to the referendum campaigns in an effort to secure union support for the nationalist movement that contained many non-working-class people. However, as Tanguay (2002: 153) has correctly noted, "PQ leaders were certainly not above exploiting the workers' favourable prejudice towards their nationalist project." In fact, in the aftermath of referendum losses in both 1980 and 1995, labour was tested by the decidedly anti-union austerity policies of PQ governments, which featured privatization, back-to-work legislation, limits on the right to strike, hospital closures and deep cuts in social spending (Savage 2008a). Although party–union relations were strained as a result of the PQ's legislative actions, the labour movement's support for Quebec's independence remained firm.

The Quebec labour movement's pro-sovereignty position has made it difficult for unions to collaborate electorally with the federalist NDP, which strongly opposes Quebec separatism while supporting Quebec's right to choose its own constitutional destiny. Even during the "Orange Wave" election of 2011, wherein the federal NDP, under the leadership of Jack Layton, unexpectedly swept 59 of Quebec's 75 seats, most unions officially backed the sovereignist Bloc Québécois. The future of party–union relations in Quebec is now uncertain given the realignment of Canadian politics in recent years. However, one can expect that the question of Quebec's constitutional future, along with its unique linguistic and cultural concerns, will continue to shape party–union relationships in the province (Graefe 2012).

Overall, the labour movement in Canada has no uniform electoral strategy. Various strategies can be employed simultaneously, and sometimes at cross-purposes, even within a single province. These divisions are both regionally and ideologically based. In short, it is very difficult to achieve a firm political basis for party–union solidarity in a country as regionally and linguistically polarized as Canada, which leads some unions to engage in political action outside the familiar parliamentary framework.

MOVEMENT-BASED STRATEGIES

Extra-parliamentary or movement-based union strategies are designed to challenge and influence government policies and actions, independent of electoral politics. This typically involves organizing and participating in public demonstrations, public awareness campaigns, pressure or lobbying campaigns and union–community coalitions. The aim is to show that a significant group of people support a cause or dislike a particular government action. Such tactics can be focused on trying to make reasoned or impassioned arguments for why power-holders should change their minds on an issue. However, they can also be designed to disrupt "business as usual" for governments or for the general public, whom protesters hope will be motivated to learn more about an issue or take sides in a conflict that has interrupted their regular lives in some way.

What explains the return of social movement activity in the labour movement? In part, unions have always used such efforts to supplement attempts to elect labour-friendly representatives to government, since there is always a need to make sure those politicians deliver on their commitments between elections. However, such social movement strategies and tactics are often characterized as the "repertoire of the excluded": those relatively less powerful groups in society must mobilize outside the established political system to press their concerns. In the last several decades, there has been a growing sense that electoral politics does not produce enough influence over the policy process, especially by and for those who are not wealthy. More people in general feel that elected governments do not listen to the public or to groups representing the less powerful in society. In recent decades, federal and provincial governments have not only adopted policies favouring big (and small) business over workers (see Chapter 4), but also pushed the union movement in Canada off to the sidelines. By doing so, they have failed to give serious consideration to the interests and priorities of working-class people. In other words, unions in general have again been made into political outsiders. In response, the CLC, provincial federations and other union organizations have developed campaigns and coalitions to counter this "corporate agenda." Such campaigns often involve working with various social movements or community organizations towards a common goal. Over the years, various unions have created partnerships with student organizations, anti-war groups, the women's movement, environmental organizations, Indigenous rights movements and queer rights groups.

Since the free trade fights of the late 1980s (see Chapter 3), the Canadian labour movement has been involved in the global justice movement. Sometimes called the "anti-globalization movement," this coalition brought together unions, community organizations and non-governmental advocacy organizations to oppose the economic policies being developed by governments and international institutions, like the World Trade Organization (WTO), to deepen neoliberal globalization and entrench the rights of capitalists and corporations over those of workers and citizens. Global in character, and rooted in longstanding international solidarity efforts with countries of the Global South, which had long been feeling the negative effects of globalization in their societies, the movement used a variety of extra-parliamentary and direct action tactics in an attempt to hamper corporate and political elites seeking to negotiate further trade and investment agreements.

The North American wing of the global justice movement peaked between 1998 and 2001, demonstrated in a series of successes, starting with the derailing of the Multilateral Agreement on Investment (MAI). Proposed by the Organisation for Economic Co-operation and Development (OECD), the MAI would have standardized and liberalized foreign investment rules internationally, preventing governments from regulating investment through restrictions on the level of foreign ownership of key strategic industries or public assets. However, the MAI was abandoned in 1998 due to mass internet-based activism that allowed anti-free trade activists from around the world to coordinate their message and lobbying efforts with their respective governments. Canadians, including Maude Barlow of the Council of Canadians and activists with Operation SalAMI in Montreal, were prominent participants in these efforts (Drohan 1998; Deibert 2000).

A year later, in November–December 1999, a broad coalition including labour and environmentalists emerged to demonstrate against the Seattle meetings of the World Trade Organization (WTO), the multilateral organization that defines and enforces international rules of trade. Again, activists opposed to the entrenchment of free trade by the WTO used direct action to physically prevent WTO delegates from gaining access to the convention centre. The Seattle police responded with violence, tear gas and mass arrests. Soon after, in April 2001, hundreds of thousands of demonstrators flooded into Quebec City to protest the Summit of the Americas and its attempt to negotiate the Free Trade Area of the Americas, which would have extended NAFTA-like arrangements to the rest of South America. The meetings were taking place in the Old Quebec neighbourhood, behind a massive newly erected fence that literally and symbolically excluded the public from crucial decisions over their future. Protesters sought to tear down the fence, and a confrontation similar to the one in Seattle between protesters and police ensued. The negative effects of free trade were suddenly being debated all across the country, with information about the agreements and the demonstrations spreading like wildfire via the Internet and the alternative media.

Labour was present in large numbers at both the Seattle and Quebec City demonstrations. These events were dramatic forms of political protest—tens of thousands of demonstrators marching, using various forms of creative political theatre and engaging in civil disobedience—that revealed and rekindled a remarkable anti-capitalist sentiment. Many union activists were significantly energized by these events and began contemplating whether direct action rather than electoral activism might be a more effective way to change government policy. However, as noted in Chapter 4, the events of September 11, 2001, slowed the use of this direct action repertoire by unions, at least for a time.

Direct action strategies have resurfaced since the 2007–2008 global financial crisis. In 2011–2012, various union organizations, including the Ontario Federation of Labour, the CAW and the Ontario Public Service Employees Union, provided financial resources and support to the Occupy Movement, which carried out sit-ins and occupations of key public spaces in cities around the world to highlight the growing problem of income inequality in capitalist countries and the inability of the current economic system to address the problem. Various provincial federations of labour in Canada officially endorsed Occupy activities. For example, in announcing his organization's support for an Occupy rally in Vancouver, British Columbia Federation of Labour President Jim Sinclair stated that the Occupy movement "expresses an underlying desire for fairness and equality in the economy and our society." He pledged the federation's solidarity and called on both the provincial and federal governments "to act swiftly and decisively to narrow the gap" (Hospital Employees' Union 2011).

In 2012–2013 many unions, including CUPE and PSAC, extended support to Idle No More, a protest movement created by Indigenous communities to fight back against the Harper government's perceived disregard for Indigenous communities and Aboriginal treaty rights in Canada. In particular, Indigenous groups opposed the federal government's omnibus budget bill that eroded environmental regulation and facilitated resource extraction that could be harmful to Indigenous communities. Coordinated Idle No More protests included disruptive blockades of important transportation corridors and a high-profile hunger strike by Attawapiskat Chief Theresa Spence, which eventually prompted Prime Minister Harper to meet with a delegation of Indigenous leaders in January 2013 to hear their concerns (Harden 2013: 70–83).

Alongside this, more traditional campaigning strategies have also persisted. In Ontario, unions worked with community organizations as part of the Campaign to Raise the Minimum Wage, designed to pressure the provincial Liberal government to boost the minimum wage to $14 per hour. In addition to distributing background research, posters and petitions for campaign participants to use, the coalition organized community demonstrations in cities across the province on the fourteenth day of every month, made extensive use of social media and organized supporters to lobby politicians and write letters to local newspapers (Campaign to Raise the Minimum Wage 2015). The coalition scored a partial victory when the Wynne government, in advance of the 2014 provincial election, agreed to increase the minimum wage from $10.25 to $11 per hour on June 1, 2014, and tie future increases to Ontario's Consumer Price Index (Monsebraaten 2014).

Movement-based strategies have the potential to reduce labour's isolation and raise the public profile of the issues championed by unions and their allies, from specific workplace-based concerns to wider issues confronting working-class people more generally. Disruptive tactics also place direct pressure on decision-makers, who may fear threats to their re-election or the ire of a public either inconvenienced or angered by their inaction (Piven and Cloward 1977). In particular, the development of partnerships and coalitions with other social justice organizations helps to increase the collective power of each organization in the coalition.

Nonetheless, movement-based strategies also have real limitations and involve risks. Direct actions like street protests, blockades or sit-ins may unduly inconvenience the very public who is being courted for support, thus potentially undermining the effectiveness of the strategy. Many people, including union members, are reluctant to engage in demonstrations for fear of how they will be perceived or because they have little concern for the specific issue prompting the action. For their part, union-community coalitions, while sometimes successful, are not without their problems. For starters, unions tend to be unequal partners insofar as they typically bring the lion's share of financial resources to the coalition table. This financial capacity tends to give unions the expectation that they will have greater decision-making authority in such coalitions, creating tensions with social movement activists who resent the idea that labour should get to call the shots.

Finally, despite their significant achievements, social movements do not seek to exercise state power as such. The exercise of state power, and the use of such power to shift social and economic relationships to the advantage of unions and working-class people generally, requires a political party. Many social movements do eventually evolve into political parties, or engage with sympathetic political parties to have their interests and priorities enacted in legislation, but some are deeply suspicious of government power, not least because of the dangers of being "captured" by those powerful economic groups—capitalist employers and their political representatives—who have so much influence over government policy. The limitations of electoral politics and movement-based politics have steered some unions into exploring judicially based strategies.

JUDICIALLY BASED STRATEGIES

Despite unions' best efforts to affect political decisions through electoral or social movement-based activity, they are often faced with unfavourable outcomes, in some cases even at the hands of their political allies. Given this climate, unions have increasingly turned to the courts to defend and in some cases assert their rights. Judicial strategies can be effective if they result in anti-union legislation being overturned. However, legal tactics are very expensive and involve lengthy processes. Most importantly, they do not always produce favourable results for workers and their unions.

According to the Supreme Court of Canada, the *Charter of Rights and Freedoms* guarantees workers the right to organize into unions, to bargain collectively and to strike. Adopted in 1982, the Charter is a bill of rights embedded in the Canadian Constitution—the highest law of Canada. The Charter created constitutional protections for individual rights and freedoms, which apply to laws passed by all governments in Canada, and gives Canadians the ability to challenge in court laws that restrict their rights. The Supreme Court is ultimately responsible for interpreting the Charter and ruling on Charter challenges.

Unions were suspicious of the Charter when it was first introduced, unsure of how it would affect the Canadian labour relations regime. After all, courts had not been kind to workers' organizations historically, having sided almost exclusively with employers when they sought injunctions to prevent workers from effectively pressuring employers. However, when governments began to escalate their use of back-to-work and other forms of restrictive legislation in the 1980s, the labour movement tested these suspicions. Unions launched court actions challenging several of these government actions. Section 2 of the *Charter of Rights and Freedoms* in the 1982 *Constitution Act* identified "freedom of association" as a fundamental right. Labour argued that to have meaning, this freedom must encompass the right to bargain collectively and to strike. After judgments in the lower courts produced contradictory rulings, the issue went to the Supreme Court for resolution in April 1987. In a landmark group of cases known as the Labour Trilogy (*Alberta Reference* (1991); PSAC v. *Canada 1987*; and RWDSU v. *Saskatchewan 1987*), a majority judgment ruled that workers were not guaranteed those rights under the Constitution. More than a century of struggling for the right to bargain collectively and to strike had come to naught. These rights were still not guaranteed.

After this series of anti-union Charter decisions declared there was no constitutionally protected right to either collectively bargain or strike, unions were again reluctant to appeal to the courts for fear that the Charter would be used by individual employers and anti-union workers to further dismantle hard-fought collective union rights and freedoms. However, at the turn of the twenty-first century, a shift in the Supreme Court's interpretation of the Charter's guarantees of freedom of association and expression gave unions hope that the Constitution could indeed be an instrument to defend and even enhance unions' economic and political power.

The first wave of pro-union decisions began with *United Food and Commercial Workers Local 1518 v. KMart Canada Ltd.* (1999), in which the Supreme Court ruled that a union had freedom of expression rights to distribute information outside businesses not directly involved in an ongoing strike. In *Retail, Wholesale Department Store Union Local 558 v. Pepsi-Cola Canada Beverages (West) Ltd.* (2002), the Supreme Court took an additional step, overturning rules outlawing secondary picketing. In an Ontario dispute, the Supreme Court ruled in 2001 that the exclusion of agricultural workers from the province's labour relations regime violated their collective right to organize (*Dunmore v. Ontario (Attorney General),* 2001). That same year, the Court upheld Quebec's longstanding mandatory unionization system in the construction industry (*R. v. Advance Cutting & Coring Ltd.,* 2001). In 2007, the Supreme Court partially overturned the Labour Trilogy decisions by declaring the Charter did indeed include a right to collective bargaining (*BC Health Services,* 2007).

This string of Charter victories encouraged some unions to more explicitly use the language of "human rights" to frame their claims for increased constitutional protection of workers' rights (Savage 2009). Proponents of the "labour rights as human rights" approach to advancing labour's interests argue that the normative weight associated with human rights discourse helps to boost the rights-based claims of workers and their unions, not only in the courtroom but also in the political arena and society more broadly. Moreover, given the increasingly hostile political climate in which unions operate, champions of labour rights as human rights argue that courts offer the most promising route to promoting and defending union rights against anti-union legislation (Adams 2003). Pro-union critics of this approach argue that workers' legal rights flow from working-class power, and not the other way around. According to them, a human rights-based approach to understanding workers' rights threatens to depoliticize and ultimately undermine traditional collective and class-based strategies for advancing labour rights, such as strikes and political action. While critics understand the judicial system as a terrain of struggle where workers can legitimately challenge the power of employers and governments, they point to an unresolved tension between judicially enforced individual rights of association and expression and organized labour's pursuit of collective worker power (Savage 2009).

The outcomes of the labour movement's human rights-based legal strategies have been mixed. In *Plourde v. Wal-Mart Canada Corp.* (2009), the Supreme Court fell back on a traditional interpretation of rights in a capitalist society, placing the "individual" rights of Wal-Mart above the collective rights of workers who organized the retail giant's store in Jonquière, Quebec, only to see Wal-Mart shut down the store in retaliation. In *Ontario (Attorney General) v. Fraser* (2011), the Supreme Court reined in labour's expectations about the Charter's constitutional protection of collective bargaining by watering down its previous decision in *BC Health Services*. The Court clarified that the BC case was not designed to constitutionalize a specific labour relations regime but simply to guarantee the parties' procedural right to "meet and engage in meaningful dialogue," with no expectation of outcomes or formal procedures under labour relations acts.

However, in January 2015, the Supreme Court shocked the judicial establishment with a pair of important pro-union decisions. In *Mounted Police Association of Ontario (MPAO) v. Canada (Attorney General)*, the Court struck down legislation prohibiting members of the RCMP from unionizing. One week later, the Court moved to constitutionalize the right to strike as part of its decision in *Saskatchewan Federation of Labour (SFL) v. Saskatchewan*, fully reversing the Labour Trilogy decisions made in the 1980s. In a 5–2 decision, the court struck down the Saskatchewan government's anti-union labour law reform, which had effectively removed the right to strike for any of the thousands of public sector workers the state deemed essential. Writing for the majority, Justice Rosalie Abella explained:

> Through a strike, workers come together to participate directly in the process of determining their wages, working conditions and the rules that will govern their working lives. The ability to strike thereby allows workers, through collective action, to refuse to work under imposed terms and conditions. This collective action at the moment of impasse is an

affirmation of the dignity and autonomy of employees in their working lives. (*Saskatchewan Federation of Labour* (SFL) *v. Saskatchewan, Para 54*)

The decision to extend constitutional protection to strike activity represented a major legal victory for the labour movement (Brown 2015). The ruling "levels the playing field for workers by placing checks on the power of governments, as employers, to legislate unfair essential services arrangements that tip the scales in management's favour," declared CLC President Hassan Yussuff (CLC 2015).

While directing union resources to legal challenges can help overturn or stop anti-union laws, there are no guaranteed outcomes in the courtroom. Legal challenges are also very costly and time-consuming, and take the struggle out of the workplace, away from the workers, and place it instead in the hands of judges and lawyers (Savage 2009; Smith 2012).

SHOULD UNIONS ENGAGE IN POLITICS?

Regardless of which strategy for engaging in political change the labour movement chooses, there are those, even from within the ranks of organized labour, who believe it is inappropriate for unions to spend members' dues on political activity of any kind. When members of the St. Catharines and District Labour Council were debating whether or not to support the creation of the NDP back in 1960, some members expressed the view that unions ought not tell their members how to vote in elections. Labour Council president John Ideson scoffed at the suggestion, arguing, "organized labor is losing more members through unemployment, automation, plant shutdowns and senseless government policies than it will ever lose through taking political action" (Patrias and Savage 2012: 173). Ideson's blunt response effectively captures how the debate over union involvement in electoral politics has been framed within the labour movement itself. While some union members entirely reject the legitimacy of union political activity, a more expansive view of the labour movement's political role emphasizes that unions have a responsibility to engage on questions of social justice and equality.

Even the more narrow vision of business unionism acknowledges the need for unions to engage in politics, if not on the basis of partisan loyalties. At root, political decisions determine the rules that shape unions' strength and capacities. In a democracy, unions must have some influence over those rules. Likewise, business owners and their advocacy organizations would not accept being subject to government rules without having a say.

Nevertheless, some union members, unhappy with the labour movement's political activity, have gone so far as to challenge its legitimacy using the *Charter of Rights and Freedoms*. In *Lavigne v. OPSEU* (1991) community college instructor Merv Lavigne argued that his union's support for the NDP and other left-wing political activities violated his freedom *not* to associate, stating that his own political views did not align with those of his union and that he should not be compelled to pay dues to an organization pursuing political causes he himself did not espouse. In the end, the Supreme Court ruled against Lavigne. Justice LaForest explained:

> The integrity and status of unions as democracies would be jeopardized if the government's policy was, in effect, that unions can spend their funds as they choose according to majority vote provided the majority chooses to make expenditures the government thinks are in the interest of the union's membership. It is, therefore, for the union itself to decide, by majority vote, which causes or organizations it will support in the interests of favourably influencing the political, social, and economic environment in which particular instances of collective bargaining and labour-management dispute resolution will take place. (*Lavigne v. OPSEU* 1991: 637)

Even though the 1991 Supreme Court decision seemed to be the final word on union political spending, right-wing activists have continued to organize around the issue. To some extent, they are inspired by U.S. laws that constrain unions' capacity to use dues to fund political activity. In the U.S., many states have adopted what proponents term "paycheque protection acts," which require unions to allow their members to opt out of the portion of their dues that would be used for political activity. In 2011, Conservative Canadian politicians began proposing laws with similar intent in an effort to undermine the political capacity of unions to oppose the policies of right-wing political parties (Ferguson 2011). In effect, such laws restrict the democratic capacity of unions to decide how to most effectively use their resources. They assume a false separation between the economic and political realms in capitalist societies, as though a union's political activities can be completely and neatly separated from its economic functions. In reality however, the two are very much linked since the political context directly shapes and influences the economic and legal context in which unions operate. For most union activists, the question is not whether unions should engage in politics, but rather how and with what goals, and further, how such decisions about political strategy get made.

UNIONS MUST BE POLITICAL

Unions engage with the political system in a myriad of ways. Some prefer electoral engagement, others prefer movement-based strategies, and still others favour a judicially based approach. All of these strategies have strengths and weaknesses and none are mutually exclusive. In fact, many are interconnected and unions pursue them simultaneously. For example, in 2012, when the Ontario government passed Bill 115, which curbed the collective bargaining rights of education workers, teachers' unions and their allies responded with widespread demonstrations and petitions, a coordinated and successful effort to defeat the governing Liberals in a crucial by-election in Kitchener–Waterloo, and the launching of several judicial challenges to the legislation. The Ontario government backed down, repealing the legislation in 2013.

Despite the multi-faceted approaches of some, many unions remain committed to one of the three political strategies. They must contend with a constant barrage of external pressures and internal demands that force the leadership to opt for one path over another. In addition, the weight of past strategic choices and habits, themselves reinforced by union structures (the kinds of staff, training, etc.), should not be underestimated. However, in the context of a growing anti-union sentiment amongst political elites, unions must self-consciously integrate these various strategies, leveraging the power that flows from each strategy.

QUESTIONS FOR DISCUSSION

1. What are the main differences between business unionism and social unionism?
2. Do unions need their own party, or should they try to influence all the existing parties?
3. Should unions be able to use their members' dues for political purposes?
4. Which do you think is more effective for labour—electoral, movement-based, or judicial strategies—and why?
5. Larry Brown of the Saskatchewan Government Employees Union once argued, "working people have made their progress in the streets and on picket lines, in meetings and demonstrations, in struggle and confrontation … not in the halls of justice." Do you agree or disagree, and why?

CHAPTER 7

HOW DO
UNIONS WORK?

The internal and external structures and dynamics of unions shape and influence how unions interact with employers, their members, the broader labour movement and the general public. These structures are complex. They include the union local led by elected members and a professional paid staff, where many collective agreements are negotiated and administered. But most locals are part of a larger structure, a parent union that provides locals with various kinds of support and organizes political action. Finally, many union locals are connected through municipal, provincial and national federations of unions, the labour centrals within which the decisions about the labour movement's overall political direction are made. Unions strive to make these decisions about priorities, strategies and actions in a democratic fashion. How and how well the labour movement makes its decisions has a huge impact on the lives of workers, and on society in general.

LOCAL UNIONS

The labour movement is built on local unions, which represent workers in a particular workplace or location. Individual workers first become involved in union activity at the local level. Sometimes they are directly involved through an organizing drive that results in the certification of a local at their workplace. More often they find employment at workplaces that are already unionized, and automatically become members of the union. In 2013, 4,735,367 workers in Canada—30.0 percent of non-agricultural paid workers—belonged to 14,147 locals in 771 unions (Labour Program 2014). Between 2006 and 2013, the number of union members increased by 7 percent, though the number of unions declined (from 827 to 771) as did the number of union locals (from 15,479 to 14,147). This change was reflected in increases in the average number of members per union (from 5,370 to 6,142) and per union local (from 287 to 335) and is part of a larger trend wherein parent unions become fewer, and local unions become larger.

FIGURE 7.1: UNION MEMBERSHIP IN LOCAL AND PARENT UNIONS, 1998–2013

YEAR	UNION MEMBERS (PERCENT)	LOCALS (PERCENT CHANGE)	UNIONS (PERCENT CHANGE	AVERAGE MEMBERS/UNION	AVERAGE MEMBERS/LOCAL
1998	3,937,790 (32.9 PERCENT)	16,631	1,031	3,819	237
2006	4,441,000 (30.8 PERCENT)	15,479 (-7 PERCENT)	827 (-20 PERCENT)	5,370 (+41 PERCENT)	287 (+21 PERCENT)
2013	4,735,367 (30.0 PERCENT)	14,147 (-9 PERCENT)	771 (-6 PERCENT)	6,14 (+14 PERCENT)	335 (+17 PERCENT)

Source: Labour Program, Workplace Information and Research Division 2014

Normally, local unions are established at a particular workplace to represent one bargaining unit and have their own elected executives and governing structures. But there are locals with much more complicated structures. Some include several bargaining units at a given workplace (each with their own collective agreement), which nonetheless share a union executive and other decision-making structures, as is common in the university sector. Others have broader regional locals that bring together workers in many workplaces under a centralized executive, as part of what is referred to as a composite local. The United Food and Commercial Workers (UFCW) and the Service Employees International Union (SEIU) are examples of unions that have large locals covering workers in the same industry or occupation within a province. The UFCW's Local 401 represents grocery store and meatpacking workers in Alberta, with five regional offices and province-wide collective agreements with major grocery chains. The SEIU's Local 2 represents janitors and security guards (amongst other workers) across the whole of Canada. The Canadian Union of Public Employees (CUPE), on the other hand, is much more decentralized, with thousands of locals across the country, and sometimes with multiple locals in the same workplace. The most common workplace to have multiple locals of the same union is the university. Most Canadian universities have separate locals for teaching assistants and contract professors, administrative staff, and custodial and maintenance staff respectively, even when these employee groups are all members of CUPE.

Whatever the precise nature of the local, membership provides opportunities for workers to gain a voice in the workplace and in their union. Members have the right to attend meetings, voice their opinions and participate in votes on union matters, volunteer for union committees, take part in union education programs and attend union-organized social functions. They can participate both as candidates and voters in elections for union stewards (who administer and defend the collective agreement on behalf of union members and carry forward complaints and grievances from members) and for the union executive (which manages the day-to-day affairs of the local).

In most cases, a local's general membership meeting (GMM) is the highest authority in the union and has the exclusive right to make many important decisions. The GMM is responsible for the election of officers, committee members and delegates to external bodies, and the discussion and ratification of the local's policies and positions, including bargaining demands and tentative collective agreements. Since every local union member is eligible to participate in and vote at a GMM, the meeting is a form of mass direct or participatory democracy. Most unions use formal rules of order to make decisions and to make and pass motions—proposals that, if supported, direct the union to do something.

Union activities are funded through union dues, the regular contribution that bargaining unit members make to the union's coffers. Since the Rand Formula became part of provincial and federal labour law, all union dues are deducted from members' paycheques by their employer and sent directly to the union. While some locals continue to have a set dues fee that is the same for everyone regardless of their income, the majority of unions have moved to a percentage dues structure—while everyone pays the same percentage of their wage, those making higher wages pay more in absolute dollars to the union. One of the GMM's major democratic responsibilities is to set the level of union dues, approve the annual union budget and plan for spending, and exercise oversight of the local's financial affairs.

Even though members have the right to participate in the union's decision-making bodies, not all of them become active in their union locals. A common complaint from those active in local unions is that most of the membership do not participate and the turnout at meetings is low—as low as 5 or 10 percent (Craig and Solomon 1993: 102). The exceptions are meetings at which issues that affect everyone, such as the progress of collective bargaining, the potential for a strike vote, the possibility of an increase in union dues, or employer initiatives that will alter conditions in the workplace, are on the agenda. Member participation in union activities also increases in crisis situations involving layoffs and plant closures or widespread dissatisfaction with the conduct of either the local or the parent union.

Yet low attendance at union meetings and low participation in union-organized functions does not necessarily indicate apathy or a lack of support for the union.

Members can keep abreast of union activities by checking with union activists to find out what happens at meetings. They can also relay their concerns to union stewards and others in the union who do attend meetings on a regular basis. As well, many local unions produce regular newsletters or have websites that keep members informed of key developments, and an increasing number rely on social media to engage with members.

The conduct of local unions is prescribed by a union constitution and bylaws that set out the rights and responsibilities of members, define the roles of elected officials in the locals, and set the rules for making decisions. All locals have an elected executive. The key positions on the executive are the table officers—usually a president, a treasurer and a recording secretary—but there can be other officers with specific roles, like equity, communications, and member education, or representing different segments of the membership. The local union president is responsible for administering the affairs of the local, including chairing local meetings, ensuring the local's decisions are carried out, keeping members informed of activities in the broader union and labour movement, and representing the local in the community. The treasurer is responsible for managing the local's funds and maintaining complete and accurate records of all financial transactions. The recording secretary compiles meeting minutes—a written record of the proceedings and formal decisions—and handles the local's correspondence. Together, the local executive's role is to execute decisions made at general membership meetings, make decisions between GMMs and report regularly to the membership on these actions, and make recommendations for action to the members. Depending on the local's size, complexity and financial resources, some local officers have full-time duties—they go on union leave and are paid a salary to replace the wages from their job. Others serve only part-time—carrying out their union leadership role while continuing to work at their regular job—and are usually paid either an honorarium or for the work time spent doing union business. In addition, some well-resourced locals may hire their own paid staff, sometimes referred to as business agents.

Most locals also have union stewards, who are elected by their co-workers and are responsible for representing workers in particular occupations or departments. Stewards play a key role in local unions: they are responsible for ensuring that the employer complies with the collective agreement; they do the initial processing of member grievances (writing up the grievance and attempting to get it resolved); they raise members' concerns at union meetings and inform them of events and issues within both the local and the parent union; and they help to mobilize members in support of union initiatives at the bargaining table and in strike action. Union stewards (along with members of the local executive) may also assist members in the filing of employment insurance, workers' compensation, disability insurance and other claims. In recognition of the vital role played by union stewards—in most cases on a voluntary basis—steward training is an important component of union education activities.

In addition, many unions have created other voluntary positions within locals that deal with specific issues or problems. A number of unions have established union counsellor positions, for example. These people identify and provide advice and guidance to members who are having problems with alcohol or drugs or personal problems that are undermining their performance on the job. Many Unifor locals, for example, have women's advocates, workplace representatives who support members experiencing workplace sexual harassment and domestic violence and help them access union and community resources. As well, unions that actively engage in political activities encourage local members to run political action campaigns aimed at persuading members to support labour-friendly political candidates in national, provincial and municipal elections.

PARENT UNIONS

Almost all local unions are affiliated with a parent union, a national or international union that brings together many locals, sometimes in the same industry or sector and therefore subject to the constitution and bylaws of these larger organizations. Some parent unions are very large. In 2013 in Canada, eight unions (three international and five national) had memberships of over 100,000, which taken together accounted for 42.7 percent of total union membership. Another seventeen unions (five international and twelve national) had memberships of between 50,000 and 99,999, accounting for another 22.9 percent of total membership. Of

FIGURE 7.2: THE TEN LARGEST UNIONS IN CANADA, 2013

UNION	MEMBERSHIP
CANADIAN UNION OF PUBLIC EMPLOYEES (CUPE)	630,050
NATIONAL UNION OF PUBLIC AND GENERAL EMPLOYEES (NUPGE)	340,000
UNIFOR	308,000
UNITED FOOD AND COMMERCIAL WORKERS CANADA (UFCW)	245,327
UNITED STEELWORKERS (USW)	230,700
PUBLIC SERVICE ALLIANCE OF CANADA (PSAC)	187,587
FÉDÉRATION DE LA SANTÉ ET DES SERVICES SOCIAUX (CSN)	129,032
SERVICE EMPLOYEES INTERNATIONAL UNION (SEIU)	118,191
TEAMSTERS CANADA	93,351
ALBERTA UNION OF PROVINCIAL EMPLOYEES	80,107

Source: Labour Program 2014

the eight unions with 100,000 or more members, four are public sector unions, with a combined membership of 1,286,669. The other four predominantly private sector unions have a combined membership of 903,018. Still, of the 771 national and international unions active in Canada, 421 (54 percent) had memberships of less than 10,000 (Labour Program 2014).

In most cases, local unions pay a significant portion of their local dues to the parent union, usually called a "per capita" or "per head" charge because these payments are often linked to how many members a local union has. In exchange for these dues, the parent union provides locals with various kinds of support: the expertise necessary to negotiate collective agreements, legal assistance, and educational programs that develop the capacities of both local executives and members. In most unions, the parent union maintains a strike fund that members can draw on when they are on strike or locked out, a very important motivator for locals to join a parent union. The parent union's support of its locals is provided by union staff, paid union employees who are responsible for providing services to the locals. Some staff, referred to as either union representatives or business agents, are assigned to particular locals and are responsible for providing them with ongoing support and advice, especially during collective bargaining, and are often recruited from the union's membership. Most parent unions also have full-time organizers whose job it is to organize new locals in the non-unionized workplaces in the sectors in which the union operates. As well, large unions either employ or retain lawyers, economists and researchers, journalists, educators and others with specialized expertise that they provide to the membership on an as-needed basis.

The parent union also lobbies governments for legislation favourable to the interests of its membership, which meets in convention, typically every few years, to chart the union's course. Conventions are the main policy-making body for unions, bringing together democratically elected delegates or workplace-based representatives to discuss, debate and vote on the union's strategic priorities and policy positions.

UNION CENTRALS

From the earliest days of the labour movement in Canada, parent unions have recognized the need to create organizations that advance the common goals and interests shared by workers regardless of their particular workplace, occupation or sector. They also recognized that there were important functions that they could not carry out effectively on their own. As a result, parent unions have formed federations of unions, also known as union centrals.

Since 1956, when the Trades and Labour Congress and the Canadian Congress of Labour merged (see Chapter 4), the Canadian Labour Congress (CLC) has been the dominant union central in Canada. As of 2013, 69.2 percent of all unionized workers belonged to unions affiliated with the CLC (Labour Program, WIRD 2014: 9). It is not, however, the only union central in Canada.

Quebec has three union centrals. The Confédération des syndicats nationaux (CSN), formed in 1960 as the successor to the Canadian and Catholic Confederation of Labour, is the second largest union central behind the CLC. The Centrale des syndicats démocratiques (CSD), a much smaller organization, was formed in 1972 following a split in the CSN. And the Centrale des syndicats du Québec (CSQ) originated as a teachers' organization but since the 1970s has extended its coverage to other workers in the education system. As well, the Quebec Federation of Labour (FTQ), while a provincial affiliate of the CLC, since 1994 has enjoyed semi-autonomous status and carries out many of the functions in Quebec that are the responsibility of the CLC in the rest of Canada (Boivin and Deom 1995: 462–68; Savage 2008b). Taken together, the three Quebec union centrals other than the FTQ make up 9.6 percent of the total union membership in Canada but represent a significantly higher share of union members in the province of Quebec (Canada Labour Program, WIRD 2014: 9).

Quite apart from the Quebec situation, rivals to the CLC have been established from time to time as a consequence of internal conflict over the CLC's direction and policies. In 1969, in response to discontent over the amount of influence that

FIGURE 7.3: UNION CENTRALS IN CANADA, 2013

ORGANIZATION	CONGRESS AFFILIATION 2006		CONGRESS AFFILIATION 2013	
	MEMBERS	PERCENT	MEMBERS	PERCENT
CANADIAN LABOUR CONGRESS	3,197,600*	72.0	3,277,251*	69.2
CONFEDERATION OF CANADIAN UNIONS**	9,390	0.2	7,958	0.2
AFL–CIO	74,650	1.7	36,040	0.8
CSN	284,280	6.4	329,586	7
CSD	59,160	1.3	75,400	1.6
CSQ	123,510	2.8	126,486	2.7
UNAFFILIATED UNIONS	691,955	15.6	882,646	18.6
TOTAL	4,178,445	100.0	4,735,367	100

* INCLUDES 1,145,753 CANADIAN MEMBERS OF INTERNATIONAL UNIONS ALSO AFFILIATED WITH THE AMERICAN FEDERATION OF LABOR/CONGRESS OF INDUSTRIAL ORGANIZATIONS.
** FORMERLY THE COUNCIL OF CANADIAN UNIONS.

Sources: Human Resources and Social Development Canada 2006; Labour Canada 2014

U.S.-based parent unions were wielding in the CLC, the Council of Canadian Unions was formed for the explicit purpose of creating a purely Canadian union movement (see Chapter 4). The council established a handful of locals but its appeal eroded with the growth in national unions, especially in the public sector and in key areas of the private sector like the auto, pulp and paper and communications industries. In 1962, 72 percent of union members in Canada were in international unions. By 1978 that proportion had declined to 50 percent. In 2013, it was down to 25 percent (Labour Program, WIRD 2014: 9). As well, throughout the 1970s and 1980s international unions ceded greater autonomy to their Canadian branches, and some major unions—the Canadian Auto Workers in 1985, for example—broke outright all formal ties with international unions. Therefore, in 2013, the Council of Canadian Unions represented only 0.2 percent of union members in Canada (Labour Program, WIRD 2014: 9).

Another split that created a new union central occurred in 1981, when the CLC suspended fourteen international building and construction trades affiliates for not paying their dues. A number of issues were involved in the conflict, including the political activities of the CLC, the involvement of the Quebec Federation of Labour in organizing construction workers and the method of selecting delegates to CLC conventions. The building and construction trades unions argued that the formula for delegate selection—one delegate per local up to one thousand members and an additional delegate for each additional thousand members—favoured public sector unions at their expense (Rose 1983). In 1982, ten of the building and construction trades unions formed the Canadian Federation of Labour (CFL) as a rival organization (Craig and Solomon 1993: 85–87). The CFL opposed most of the CLC's positions and policies, supporting, for example, the Canada–U.S. Free Trade Agreement and calling for greater cooperation with employers, but it never did expand beyond its initial base and did not gain much influence. Faced with declining membership in the 1990s, the CFL disbanded in 1997 and most of its affiliates rejoined the CLC (Gereluk 2001: 22).

Some unions are not affiliated to any labour central. For example, the Ontario Provincial Police Association, the Alberta Union of Public Employees and many university faculty associations remain independent from the structures of the broader labour movement. In some cases, a union's decision to remain independent reflects the importance of an occupational identity over and above a sense of solidarity with other workers. In other cases, ideological and political differences with the labour central keep independent unions from affiliating. In recent years, however, many unions of professional workers that have traditionally kept their distance from the labour movement, like the Professional Institute of the Public Service of Canada, the National Union of the Canadian Association of University Teachers, and the Society of Energy Professionals, have joined the CLC in response to "deteriorating working conditions, encroachments on professional autonomy and a seemingly never-ending cycle of government austerity" (Savage and Webber 2013: 124). These unions have concluded that affiliation will lend them greater power and support in their dealings with employers.

The CLC (and other union centrals) perform three main functions for affiliated unions. First, the CLC represents the political interests of workers and their affiliated unions in a range of ways, including attempting to influence government policies that will have an impact on workers. It does this both by monitoring and making representations on legislation and policies, and by promoting legislation and policies beneficial to its members and to working people in general. The CLC also organizes campaigns either in support of or in opposition to government initiatives.

For the past thirty years, the CLC has organized campaigns against an onslaught of policies detrimental to the interests of working people, including wage controls; restrictions on collective bargaining and the imposition of back-to-work legislation, primarily in the public sector, ordering striking workers to end strikes and return to work; free trade agreements; cuts to social programs; negative changes to the unemployment insurance program; budgetary measures (tax and expenditures changes) that provide disproportionate benefits to corporations and the wealthy; and the use of monetary policy to maintain high unemployment. The CLC has also launched advocacy campaigns to pressure governments into expanding the Canada Pension Plan, raising the minimum wage and introducing universal child-care—all aimed at improving the lot of working-class people in general, not just union members. In many of these campaigns, the CLC participates in coalitions with other social justice organizations, including feminist groups, environmental organizations and anti-poverty groups.

The CLC supports its campaigns on these issues through its own research. In addition, along with some of its affiliated unions, the CLC has been a prime supporter of the Canadian Centre for Policy Alternatives, an Ottawa-based social justice research centre established in 1980, now with regional offices across the country. The centre works with academics, unions and community organizations to produce rigorous, high-quality research on economic and social issues that counters the growing influence of right-wing think tanks funded by corporations.

A second CLC role is to regulate relations between member organizations. This involves mediating and resolving conflicts that arise either when two or more unions are seeking to organize the same group of workers or when one union engages in raiding, an attempt to take over the membership of another union. These sorts of conflicts can create serious problems for the CLC if they become protracted and divisive, diverting the leadership's energies away from other tasks and undermining both internal solidarity and the public face of organized labour. A justification process, in which union members wishing to change their parent union can appeal to the

CLC for a decision, was established in 1987 when the UFCW objected to the CAW's attempt to gain representation rights for fishers in Newfoundland and Labrador (Chaison 1996: 62–65). Another major conflict erupted in 2000 when members of eight locals of the SEIU in Ontario bolted to the CAW. The SEIU filed a complaint with the CLC accusing the CAW of raiding. In April 2000 the CLC found in favour of the SEIU and imposed sanctions on the CAW that effectively brought about the union's expulsion. Elected CAW representatives were removed from the executive bodies of the CLC, provincial federations of labour and local labour councils, and its members were officially barred from participating in CLC activities. Then-CAW president Buzz Hargrove responded by threatening to take the CAW out of the CLC and establish a new union central. Eventually, the situation was resolved through mediation and negotiation and the CAW returned to the CLC by the end of 2001. Although mediating such conflicts between unions is a very important role, the number of locals using the justification process is quite low.

A third CLC role is to provide support for member unions in organizing drives, collective bargaining and strikes or lockouts. Such support is particularly important for small unions, which sometimes lack the resources and expertise required to deal effectively with employers. But larger unions also benefit from the moral support and tangible demonstrations of wider solidarity (solidarity pickets, promotion of boycotts, publicity campaigns and government lobbying) when they are involved in confrontations with employers and/or governments.

Provincial/territorial federations of labour and local labour councils are affiliated with the CLC and perform similar functions. Provincial federations of labour are important because provincial labour laws cover the vast majority of workers, making the provincial level an especially active terrain for union struggles. Currently, there are ten provincial federations of labour, as well as equivalent organizations in the Yukon, Northwest Territories and Nunavut. The country also has 111 regionally based local labour councils (CLC 2014).

Unions affiliated with the CLC are also entitled to affiliate with and participate in the activities of provincial federations and local labour councils; however, such affiliation is voluntary. A majority of the larger parent unions affiliate with and actively participate in provincial federations. Rates of affiliation and participation tend to be much lower at the local level. This is especially true of participation, as many of the locals contributing dues neglect to elect delegates to represent them at local labour council meetings.

This lack of involvement at the local level is unfortunate because most union activity—organizing, collective bargaining, strikes, political action, coalition-building—occurs at this level, and the bulk of the support that local unions receive during periods of crisis comes from other union members in their own geographic areas. Moreover, local labour councils and members of local unions must ultimately put into action all campaigns launched by the CLC and provincial federations of labour. For example, the CLC's Municipalities Matter campaign, which revolves around identifying and endorsing labour-friendly candidates in municipal elections, is almost entirely locally driven. Similarly, the CLC's lobbying efforts rely on local union activists to contact and meet with politicians in their local communities.

From the local to the global, it is also important to note that many central labour organizations around the world, like the CLC, are themselves affiliates of international labour organizations that represent workers' interests globally. The largest is the International Trade Union Confederation (ITUC), which in 2014 had over 176 million members through its 325 national affiliates, drawn from 161 countries. Formed in 2006, the ITUC advocates for workers' rights and economic justice at major global institutions like the International Labour Organization, the World Bank and International Monetary Fund, and the World Trade Organization; develops and conducts global campaigns on issues such as child labour, domestic workers, global poverty, and decent work; and promotes cooperation and connections between unions from different countries (ITUC 2015).

UNION DEMOCRACY

Questions of union organization and structure are directly tied to questions of union democracy and decision-making. When workers form or join unions, they do so with the expectation that their participation will give them some control over decisions that affect their lives. Indeed, one of the union movement's promises to workers is: join the union and you will have a meaningful voice in the union, in the workplace and in your community.

The local union is the starting point for workers gaining and exercising power. How it structures, nurtures and promotes participation and engagement by its members is fundamental to the character and capacity of the wider labour movement. As mentioned above, all unions are formally democratic, with constitutions and bylaws that define member rights and establish procedures for participation. All members have the right to vote on union matters such as approval or rejection of collective agreements and strike action. They also have the right to seek office in the union and to represent their local union as a delegate to union conventions and other affiliated bodies, such as labour councils. It is the way in which these formal rules are put into practice, however, that makes all the difference.

A critical but often neglected or obscured point of discussion is that these local unions and their members ultimately determine the character of the labour movement. How they operate, however, is influenced to a large extent by the policies and practices of parent unions. If the parent unions see their primary role as that of delivering services to their members, sometimes called the service model of unionism, there is a greater likelihood that members will become passive. Many will see themselves as merely the consumers of union-provided services—the benefits they get from collective agreements and the processing of grievances. As a result, members in such unions are likely to perceive the union as something separate from them—a supplier of services in exchange for dues payments. Without pressure from an informed and active membership, inertia sets in and the union membership becomes disengaged.

An alternative approach by parent unions starts from a basic assumption: that a union derives its vigour and creativity from an active and involved local membership. The objective of such unions is to nurture the growth of local "cultures of solidarity" (Fantasia 1988) by articulating a vision that links the struggles of local memberships to a broader struggle involving all members of the union, other unions in the labour movement and workers in general. To this end, the union encourages its members to become involved in and contribute their efforts and ideas to building the organization. Members are not treated as passive recipients of services but as active agents playing a role in constructing both the union and the larger labour movement. Members are mobilized to take job action not just to get a better deal for themselves (more wages in their pockets, a better pension plan, shorter hours)—although that is part of it—but also because a victory will provide an impetus for similar gains by other locals in the union and by members of other unions. They are encouraged as well to get involved in political struggles and to align themselves with other progressive organizations in the community. The feedback effects generated by this dynamic relationship (pressure from the members, positive responses from the leadership, more pressure from the members) create a virtuous cycle that drives the union forward and enhances prospects for growth and improved outcomes in collective bargaining.

In most conventional interpretations, unions exist to serve their members' interests. As Neil Chamberlain (1965: 92) noted, however, "Once a union comes into existence, it becomes an ongoing institution which of necessity develops its own organizational interests and requirements, and these in some respects might differ from the interests and objectives of its members." For instance, parent unions with an interest in preserving a healthy strike fund may be reluctant to authorize a strike by a union local that could result in heavy demands on the fund, particularly if they doubt the strike can be won. The local, on the other hand, may feel strongly that a strike is needed and that their claim on strike fund resources is justified. Although Chamberlain's assertion has a certain validity, the extent to which the institutional needs of the union collide and conflict with the needs of members depends on how member interests are defined and in what ways members are engaged in their unions. Unions must be disciplined to advance collective objectives, and this discipline may require strong leadership. At the same time, they are democratic organizations and union leaders are elected to their positions. They must therefore recognize that actions by the union that go against the wishes of members could not just undermine their positions in the union but also compromise the union's very future. The impact of outright conflict on the local and parent unions will depend on the mechanisms that exist to mediate and resolve them.

Labour organizations vary considerably in terms of how, and to what extent, the union considers members' diverse voices and concerns. One school of thought is that unions must strive to be as inclusive as possible to ensure that the diversity of their membership is represented in their bargaining and political priorities. This can be difficult to achieve, however, mostly because a union's desire to promote equity and inclusiveness can sometimes bump up against other issues that represent the democratic will of the majority of the membership.

We sometimes see this dynamic in unions where a minority of members have a direct stake in the equity issue being promoted; employment or pay equity are good examples. While these are no doubt important issues, they are sometimes put aside to address issues that more broadly impact union members (like wages, pensions or benefit entitlements). A repeated pattern of pushing equity issues to the backburner sparked calls in some unions to create equity committees that would give a stronger voice and organizational capacity to workers fighting for equity-based improvements (women, Indigenous peoples, racialized, disabled or queer workers). Similarly, some unions have created youth committees or sector-specific committees to ensure that minority voices within the union are heard and have also carved out elected positions on their respective executives to give these groups greater say in the operation of the union. In some unions, where elected positions exist for members of equity-seeking groups, equity-based caucuses meet and elect their own representatives. The proliferation of equity caucuses in the labour movement has arguably improved unions' ability to address a much broader scope of member issues. It has also helped to preserve the democratic integrity of unions as representative institutions of workers.

Unions must also wrestle with the relationship between the leadership and the membership, and with how that relationship affects workers' power and the conditions that allow for members' meaningful democratic control. One school of thought holds that decentralized membership control from below is more democratic and more effective at representing workers' interests and advancing labour's cause than top-down, leadership-driven unions. Camfield (2011), for example, decries the "union officialdom," a term he uses to describe the layer of union leaders and staff members who control and direct the labour movement's agenda. According to Camfield, the labour officialdom's penchant for contract unionism—in which the negotiation and defense of the collective agreement becomes the central focus of the union's activity—weakens rather than strengthens union democracy and discourages the types of fightback strategies needed to effectively confront anti-union employers and governments. Implicit in Camfield's analysis is the idea that union leaders act as a force to constrain or even extinguish the potential militancy and radicalism of union members. Others argue that the dichotomy between strategies "from above" and "from below" represents an over-simplification of the relationship between the union leadership and the membership. They assert that strategies "from below" will not necessarily lead to either a more militant or a more radical political approach for labour (Ross 2012b). For example, when the leadership of the Ontario Division of CUPE threatened an illegal political strike to demand changes to the governance structure of the Ontario Municipal Employees Retirement System pension plan in 2006, many CUPE activists resisted, creating internal divisions that ultimately forced the President of CUPE Ontario to back down from the radical and militant action he had proposed. The same union leadership's effort to demonstrate solidarity with human rights struggles in Palestine by vocally supporting a campaign of boycott and divestment against Israel also prompted a backlash within CUPE's membership. Although delegates to CUPE Ontario's 2006 convention endorsed the boycott campaign, the union leadership's decision to actively promote the campaign prompted several locals to cut ties with CUPE Ontario (Savage 2011).

None of this is to suggest that, conversely, top-down, leadership-driven strategies are always more effective. Admittedly, in the short run, a union may find it advantageous to have a passive or quiescent membership. Collective bargaining and the handling of grievances are less problematic and less of a strain on union resources when members are resigned to having decisions imposed from on high, either because they trust the union leadership or because they feel they can't do much to influence it. In the long run, however, local unions and the union movement as a whole will suffer from a passive, disengaged and disempowered membership. Dissatisfied union members will turn against their union and against unions in general. They will become more susceptible to criticisms of unions levelled by employers and governments. They will be less likely to support the leadership's calls for strike action and more likely, if a strike vote goes against their wishes, to cross picket lines. Moreover, when union members have bad experiences in one place of work, they will be less likely to support a union in another.

Building and sustaining vigorous and engaged memberships in local unions is a difficult task. The challenges are particularly great once workplaces are already unionized and new workers become members more or less by default—not because they have been part of a union organization drive but simply because the union is there. For a parent union, however, the creation of a vigorous and involved membership constitutes a wise investment of effort and resources. Local unions with active memberships are less dependent on the parent union because they can draw on their own resources—their active members—to provide leadership. This frees up the resources of the parent union to do more of the other things required to support a growing and robust union movement—organizing the unorganized, negotiating improvements in wages and benefits and the terms and conditions of employment, and challenging government policies and actions that hurt workers.

The differences in union democratic practices can have sharp, and contrasting, practical consequences. Take, for instance, Union A; the local's agenda for collective bargaining is established by union representatives in consultation with the president and perhaps other members of the local union executive. In many cases, the agenda reflects a common core of issues that the international union is pushing in comparable bargaining situations. The leaders in the parent union have no formal consultations with the members, although members of the local executive may consult with them informally, at coffee breaks and lunch breaks, perhaps. The members are, in short, all but excluded from the bargaining process. The union representative from parent or regional headquarters is the union's chief bargainer. The local president and perhaps another member of the executive are also on the team. Union members may be advised when bargaining sessions occur, but they are not provided with details.

Then an impasse arises in bargaining because the employer refuses to concede improvements in wages and conditions requested by the union. The union has a couple of options: it can decide to accept the employer's position and recommend it to the membership on the grounds that this is the best they can do; or it can ask the members to take a strike vote. But because local members have not been directly involved in the sequence of events leading to the impasse, they must accept at face value the recommendations of the union representative and the bargaining team. They lack the detailed knowledge to make an informed decision. Whatever the outcome, the experience is likely to generate discontent and dissension within the local, alienate some of the members and weaken support for the union.

In another union—Union B—members at the local level have been involved in matters from the beginning. The local holds formal meetings to discuss the bargaining agenda and establish priorities. A parent union representative attends these meetings to provide information and statistics and otherwise facilitate deliberations. The agenda reflects the members' views. The bargaining may be structured in the same way as it was for Union A, but local representatives have greater scope for participation in the give and take of the process. As well, local representatives are responsible for keeping members informed of the progress in bargaining. If an impasse develops, and members must choose between accepting the employer's offer and taking strike action, they are in a position to make an informed decision—to evaluate the pros and cons of one course of action over the other. Whatever the outcome, local members will be able to accept it as *their* decision and abide by it. This does not mean that no friction resulting from the vote occurs within the local. The difference is that discontent and dissension are more likely to be reflected in internal debate over what members should be trying to achieve as a union, rather than being directed at the union itself.

Employers and governments frequently attack unions for being undemocratic, citing unionization drives, strikes and union political contributions. The arguments today are the same as they have always been: decisions to unionize and strike are either dictated by outside agitators and "union bosses" or they are rigged and manipulated. The critics only make this claim, however, when workers vote to join a union, take strike action, or endorse political action, never when they vote to move in the opposite direction. Employers and governments detest union democracy because it conflicts with authoritarian rule in the workplace and the economy.

Union leaderships and staffs are, in most unions, committed to the principles of union democracy. They recognize that, without an active membership, the capacity of unions to sustain themselves and grow is diminished. They also recognize that no silver bullets exist to create and entrench union democracy once and for all. As Sam Gindin (1995: 276) puts it:

> Democracy is not supplied by a constitution. Nor can it be reduced to a mechanism for keeping leaders in line (as relevant as that need is). Union democracy is primarily about workers making changes: changing themselves, changing their immediate world, and laying the basis for eventually changing the larger world. Union democracy is built by workers in their struggles to build the union, which acts as their line of defence and base for progress. Democracy is therefore not separate from struggles, nor is it static; it must constantly be redefined, recreated, and reinvented.

QUESTIONS FOR DISCUSSION

1. What is the difference between a union and the labour movement?
2. If you had to build a union from scratch, how would it be structured and why?
3. What are the strengths and weaknesses of unions' internal decision-making practices? Are unions more democratic than employers?
4. Are unions democratic enough? What are some of the barriers to democratic participation in the labour movement and how might they be overcome?
5. What are union equity committees and what role do they play in the labour movement?

CHAPTER 8

WHAT DIFFERENCE DO UNIONS MAKE?

W hat exactly have unions and the labour movement achieved in their roughly 150 years of existence in Canada? What have they done for their members? What have they done for workers in general? And what have they done for society? Today, much rhetoric casts unions as protectors of the "special interests" of their own members, which are seen to be in conflict with other social interests. In contrast, conventional wisdom tells us that enlightened leaders—the great men and, on the rare occasion, women of history—realized on their own that it was good and right to improve the economic and social conditions of the most oppressed. In fact, both of these claims are wrong. First, from its very origins, the labour movement has used both its economic and political power to improve the welfare of working-class people. While this doesn't mean the interests that unions defend don't come into conflict with those of others (even within the working class itself), the labour movement has always had the betterment of society for the vast majority at the core of its priorities and actions. Second, the idea that "enlightened" elites make political and social change denies those elites' sustained opposition to workers' rights and ignores the difficult and heroic struggles that the labour movement waged to force such power holders to change. As the U.S. slavery abolitionist Frederick Douglass once said, "Power concedes nothing without a demand." The history of the labour movement, and of the economic, political and social progress it has made and that this chapter explores, shows this to be true.

EMPLOYMENT STANDARDS

One of the labour movement's earliest achievements in Canada was to force governments to regulate working conditions in the growing industrial economy. As discussed in Chapter 3, workers of all kinds experienced constant downward pressure on their wages and working conditions as employers sought to increase both the pace of production and the profits to be derived. Craft unions responded through collective bargaining but also by seeking legislation that would either cover all workers (whether unionized or not) or protect particular categories of vulnerable workers from the most exploitative practices and conditions.

The first of these practices to be challenged was the use of child labour. According to Lorna Hurl, craft workers opposed the use of child labour as early as the 1830s, particularly when children were used as workers to compete with adults rather than as apprentices learning their trade. From the early 1880s, both the Knights of Labor and the TLC opposed the use of children under the age of fourteen as factory workers. By the late 1890s, the TLC called for the abolition of all child labour under fourteen, no matter the setting. Through lobbying and the introduction of private members' bills by sympathetic legislators, unions sought to have legislation passed at both the national and provincial levels (Hurl 1988: 93). Although hotly opposed by the Canadian Manufacturers' Association, who wanted to maintain access to this source of cheap and easily disciplined labour, unions eventually won provisions in provincial factories acts that both prohibited children under a certain age from working and regulated the maximum hours of work for those who were permitted to do so. Ontario's first *Factories Act* was passed in 1884. By the early twentieth century, all provinces had legislation that combined restrictions on child labour and compulsory school attendance.

Another central labour movement victory was in the realm of working time, specifically the reduction of the length of the working day and week, and the establishment of overtime pay and statutory holidays. In the 1870s, industrial employers sought to extract as much time out of workers as possible, but the labour movement's priority was to reduce the length of the working day to less than the usual twelve hours. Not only were they opposed to the terrible physical toll that the relentless intensification of work was taking on workers, they also believed that workers both needed and deserved time off, for leisure, community activities, education and self-improvement. The labour movement also fought for more time away from work so that workers could become better, more politically engaged citizens. As labour leader James Ryan said at the time, "We want to better our physical constitutions, and increase our mental power ... We want not more money, but more brains, not richer serfs, but better men" (quoted in Heron 2012: 14). Unions attempted to use collective bargaining to reduce the length of the working day at their particular workplaces, but employers resisted strenuously because they did not want to be less competitive than other employers who still had longer working days. This made it necessary to fight for legislation that covered all workplaces.

To achieve this goal, the Nine-Hour Movement came together in Hamilton in January 1872, at a standing-room-only meeting of carpenters, machinists, blacksmiths, and engineers at the Mechanics Institute. They established a Nine-Hour League to unify their fight against all their employers, and this spread to Montreal and many Ontario towns. The movement organized large coordinated strikes across multiple employers to demand a nine-hour day and six-day workweek (Battye 1979). Although the Nine-Hour Movement was not immediately successful in reducing the length of the working day, commitment to the cause was deep. Unions and labour federations all made the fifty-four-hour workweek a central principle from this time on, which by the twentieth century became a struggle for the eight-hour day and forty-hour workweek. Well into the 1950s, many strikes were fought with shorter working time as a central demand.

Governments responded to this militancy by gradually enacting minimum standards legislation that applied to increasingly larger segments of the workforce. In 1884, the Ontario *Factories Act* set the maximum for women, girls aged 14–18 and boys aged 12–14 at ten hours per day and 60 hours per week (Thomas 2004: 56). By the mid 1930s, federal employees had won the eight-hour day, as had Ontario provincial employees (Thomas 2004: 60). A decade later, in 1944, Ontario passed the *Hours of Work and Vacations with Pay Act*, which established the eight-hour day, 48-hour week for both men and women workers regardless of what sector they worked in, and mandated one week of paid vacation per year. In 1968, when the Ontario *Employment Standards Act* replaced all the various pieces of workplace regulation with one law, work over 48 hours a week was to be paid at time and a half, and a series of paid public holidays were established. In 1974, the overtime threshold was brought down to 44 hours per week, where it remains.

The labour movement also successfully sought minimum wage laws, particularly in response to the increasing numbers of single women working in industry at the beginning of the twentieth century and the desire to protect them from the extremes of exploitation. Labour movement pressure resulted in the spread of protective legislation, such that a minimum wage for women workers was established in seven Canadian provinces between 1918 and 1920. Minimum wage legislation applying to women workers was first passed in 1918 in B.C. and Manitoba. By 1920, Nova Scotia, Ontario, Quebec and Saskatchewan had also passed similar minimum wage laws (Strong-Boag 1979). Men were assumed able to negotiate decent wages for themselves through collective bargaining, but by the late 1920s and early 1930s, this was no longer certain and provinces set minimum wages for male workers as well (first championed in the federal parliament by J.S. Woodsworth). Minimum wage laws for men were passed in B.C. (1925), Manitoba and Saskatchewan (1934), Alberta (1936), Ontario and Quebec (1937). Prince Edward Island was the last to do so in 1960 (Labour Program 2005).

Minimum wages were deeply gendered, requiring significant struggle to overcome. The provincial boards that set the minimum wage also applied a narrow, gender stereotyped classification to the question of which women needed to work and why, assuming the majority could rely on a male breadwinner. Women's presumed economic dependence on men was used to set low legal minimum wages. Therefore, when minimum wages for men were established, they were set higher than those for women because it was assumed they needed higher wages to be the family's breadwinner. While the labour movement initially accepted the logic behind gender-based minimum wage differences, beginning in the 1960s unions fought for the principle of equal pay in minimum wages (as elsewhere), and by 1974 gender differences in legislated minimum wages were gone (Labour Branch, HRSDC 2005).

OCCUPATIONAL HEALTH AND SAFETY

Another crucial and longstanding issue for the labour movement is workplace health and safety. As discussed in Chapter 3, the capitalist industrial economy ushered in a powerful set of conditions that led to a major spike in worker injury and death: the relentless pressure to increase productivity and profit and the introduction of machines in the production process. The combination of these two factors meant some workers faced the most horrifying of situations at work. Machines with few safeguards inevitably led to the crushing or amputation of fingers, arms and legs. Many workers, like those in the textile and garment industries, faced debilitating respiratory diseases due to the lack of ventilation or protective equipment. Death at work was an ever-present threat that haunted working-class communities, especially in coal mining, where a mine collapse or explosion would kill or maim many workers at once and leave few families unaffected. For example, an explosion at the Springhill Mine in the small community of Springhill, Nova Scotia, in February 1891 killed 125 miners. In 1914, a similar disaster occurred at the Hillcrest Mine in Hillcrest, Alberta, killing 189 workers—half of the mine's workforce and one fifth of the town's population—making it the worst coal mining disaster in Canadian history. Slower deaths by occupational illness or disease, caused, for example, by prolonged exposure to asbestos fibers, also sapped workers' energies and diminished their capacity to enjoy what remained of their lives outside of work.

Although employers benefited from workers literally giving their lives and limbs to industrial production, they were rarely held legally responsible for either prevention or compensation for injury or death. Workers were presumed to have consented to the risks when they agreed to work and to be responsible for their own "unsafe" behaviour at work. According to the common law tradition, workers had to show in court that an employer had been negligent or failed to "exercise due care" to win compensation. This standard was difficult to meet because employers could argue that workers themselves either contributed to or knew the risks (Barnetson 2010: 21).

The labour movement's fight for state regulation of the industrial economy also included demands for health and safety protection, factory inspections and fines for employers who did not comply. Ontario's *Factories Acts* were the first to establish legal health and safety regulation of industrial workplaces, including a system of inspection—although with only three inspectors for the entire province, there was much to be done to improve the system.

Canadian governments also adopted forms of compulsory workers' compensation that employers had to pay into, to prevent workers or their survivors from falling into poverty due to workplace injury or death. Quebec (in 1909) and Ontario (in 1914) were the first provinces to introduce such a system, which took the matter out of the courts and replaced it with a system of no-fault insurance. In exchange for giving up the right to sue their employers in court, workers could receive compensation for workplace injuries, medical treatment or rehabilitation without having to prove their employer's negligence (Barnetson 2010: 36).

Although these improvements did help workers, there were still fundamental flaws in this system. Both the inspection and compensation systems masked the way that the very structure of work and the unequal power relationship between workers and employers continued to drive workplace injury and death. Workers themselves began to organize anew around the issue of occupational health and safety in the late 1960s and early 1970s (Storey 2005). The Saskatchewan NDP's 1972 *Occupational Health and Safety Act* led the new approach to health and safety pressed for by the workers' health and safety movement. The legislation enshrined three workers' rights that have now become pervasive in similar legislation across the country: the right to know about workplace hazards, the right to participate in health and safety issues through joint health and safety committees that include workers and managers, and the right to refuse unsafe work without fear of punishment.

SOCIAL POLICY AND THE SOCIAL WAGE

Organized labour has played a key role historically in shaping social policy in the interests of working-class people and in strengthening the "social wage"—public services or benefits that people receive in supplement of their wages earned from work and paid for by redistributing wealth through the tax system. For instance, during the Great Depression, unions campaigned hard for, and achieved in 1940, a national unemployment insurance scheme to provide all workers with temporary financial assistance in the case of layoffs, and later worked to add maternity and parental leaves to this system. Working politically through direct action, elections and lobbying, unions also helped to secure a national public pension plan in the form of the Canada Pension Plan and Old Age Security. Finally, in alliance with the CCF, unions played a central role in the fight for universal public healthcare for all Canadians and for affordable social and cooperative housing.

In short, unions not only help to advance social welfare but also to extend its reach beyond union members themselves, to the entire working class, and in the case of universal social programs, to all of society. Unions undertake this work because it helps to collectively increase workers' standard of living while ensuring that a greater proportion of the profits that workers generate for their employers is distributed for the purposes of social welfare and advancement. A strong social wage helps to address issues of income inequality but without strong unions to defend, let alone extend the social wage, capitalist interests and their political allies have plenty of opportunities to undermine and revoke such social gains in the name of private profit.

UNIONS AND THE STRUGGLE FOR HUMAN RIGHTS AND EQUITY

As we discuss in Chapters 3 and 4, the labour movement has struggled with the gap between its egalitarian values and its concrete discriminatory attitudes and policies towards particular groups of workers. However, throughout its history, there have always been leaders and activists within the labour movement committed to the elimination of gender, racial and other forms of discrimination. These pioneers succeeded in turning the labour movement into a powerful force in the struggle for human rights legislation.

Elements of the Canadian labour movement, particularly left-wing, Jewish and Black unionists, led the fight to establish anti-discrimination laws that would guarantee equality in employment, services and housing in Canada after the Second World War (Patrias 2011). Up until then, it had been accepted by the courts that private owners had the right to do with their property what they wished, including discriminate against people due to their race or religion. This norm was expressed in 1940 in the case of *Christie v. York*, in which the Court decided against Fred Christie, a Black man who had been denied service at a tavern in Montreal because of his race. Organizations like the Canadian Jewish Labour Committee were part of a larger network of human rights activists in the CCF, the United Steelworkers (USW), UAW, Canadian Brotherhood of Railway Employees, and Packinghouse

Workers Union (which later became UFCW), illustrating that the new industrial unions were more active and insistent on issues of racial equality than their craft union counterparts. These activists established city-based labour committees against racial intolerance in Toronto, Winnipeg and Montreal, and allied with the Association for Civil Liberties and the National Unity Association, an organization of African Canadians formed in 1948 to fight the Ontario government's failure to intervene in cases where a business owner refused to serve a Black customer or a landlord turned away a Black renter (Lamberston 2001).

Over the course of fifteen years, this coalition successfully shifted the default assumption that discrimination was the right of private property owners and forced the Ontario government to issue a series of laws and amendments that gradually outlawed such acts. In 1944, the *Racial Discrimination Act* blocked the posting of discriminatory signs (like "Whites Only"). In 1950, the *Ontario Labour Relations Act* was amended to prohibit the legal recognition of any collective agreement that contained racially or religiously based forms of discrimination (such as separate wage rates or job categories). In 1951, the *Fair Employment Practices Act* declared that, in line with the United Nations' 1948 *Universal Declaration of Human Rights*, it was now "contrary to public policy" to discriminate in hiring, employment or union membership "on the basis of race, creed, colour, nationality, ancestry or place of origin" (Lambertson 2001: 68). By the end of the 1950s, this human rights activism had also spread through the labour movement itself, such that seven labour councils in Nova Scotia, Ontario, Quebec, Manitoba and B.C., as well as the provincial labour federations in four of those provinces, had human rights committees (Clement 2009: 51).

However, the fight against discrimination by labour activists was not "complete" by the beginning of the 1960s. Instead, the focus shifted to gender inequalities at work. Feminists within the unions took on the task of extending the human rights legislation to cover sex- and gender-based discrimination as well. The official position of the Canadian labour movement after the Second World War was to support "equal pay for equal work"—the principle that where men and women do the same jobs, they should be paid the same wage. Beginning in the late 1940s, the Steelworkers union began working with the CCF Opposition to pressure the Frost Conservative government to introduce legislation that would protect women against discrimination in pay (Tillotson 1991). Their efforts paid off when in 1951 the Ontario government passed equal pay legislation in the form of the *Female Employees Fair Remuneration Act*, followed by the federal government with its 1956 *Female Employees Equal Pay Act*. This kind of legislation helped those who were in male-dominated job categories, and it prevented some of the most blatant forms of gender wage discrimination. However, it did little to increase most women's wages relative to those of men, since they remained excluded from higher-paid, male-dominated work and the skills associated with female-dominated work remained undervalued. This exclusion was reinforced by the "marriage bar" and the "pregnancy bar," the formal rule or informal practice that required women to quit their jobs once they either married or became pregnant, as well as by the explicit gender stereotyping of jobs.

Beginning in the late 1960s, feminist activists in the unions began to challenge the basis of the gender pay gap on two main fronts: to gain women access to better-paid jobs and to fight the undervaluation of women's jobs and skills. The Women's Committee from UAW Local 222 at General Motors in Oshawa successfully challenged the *Ontario Human Rights Code*'s exclusion of gender from its protected grounds, which then made sex-typed jobs and separate seniority lists for men and women illegal in union contracts (Sugiman 1992: 21–22).

Union women and their feminist allies also shifted towards a fight for pay equity legislation—which mandates that, where they do different jobs but with same level of skill, men and women must be paid the same. Such a system would analyze the job content of male- and female-dominated jobs and remedy pay inequalities between jobs of equal value. Although it took until 1984 before the CLC officially supported the more expansive system of pay equity, the labour movement has since been one of the main advocates for establishing pay equity legislation and defending the system when it has come under attack. For instance, in Ontario, the main impetus for pay equity legislation in the 1980s came from union women who, through their organizing efforts, turned their unions into pay equity supporters. Coalescing in the form of the Equal Pay Coalition, Ontario feminists received notable support from Cliff Pilkey, then-president of the Ontario Federation of Labour, in their sustained efforts to lobby both the Liberal Party and the NDP to make pay equity a priority. When these two parties formed a coalition government in 1985, pay equity was a top legislative priority for both. Likewise, pay equity was at the heart of the formal accord signed by the two parties in 1985, and the Ontario *Pay Equity Act* came into effect in 1988. The labour movement was also there to defend pay equity when in 1996 the Harris Conservative government repealed the section of the Ontario *Pay Equity Act* that allowed for women without comparable male-dominated jobs in their own workplace to use a proxy from another similar workplace to determine if and how much they were underpaid. In 1997, the Service Employees International Union successfully challenged the constitutionality of this move as a violation of women's equality rights under the *Charter of Rights and Freedoms*, which restored this aspect of the *Pay Equity Act* as though it had never been repealed. Beginning in 1977 and spreading through the 1980s, pay equity legislation is now established federally and in six provinces, although in some places it only applies to the public sector and in others it requires a complaint to launch the pay equity evaluation process.

The labour movement was also central in the fight for legislation designed to eliminate another key underlying basis of unequal pay between men and women—occupational segregation—and promote access to desirable jobs for women, racialized minorities, Indigenous peoples and persons with disabilities. While human rights codes prohibited individual and overt forms of discrimination in hiring and allowed individuals to file complaints if they encountered such treatment, they did little to identify and take apart the systemic forms of discrimination embedded in the design of jobs, workplaces, occupational qualifications, hiring and promotion practices. For example, before the Supreme Court's 1999 landmark decision *British Columbia (Public Service Employee Relations Commission) v. BCGSEU* (1999) that mandated workplace standards that do not discriminate, non-bona fide fitness qualifications had the effect of unfairly excluding the vast majority of women from meeting the standards for, and therefore being granted, jobs as firefighters (Hatfield 2005).

Beginning in the early 1980s, the notion of "employment equity" began to take shape, stemming from the federal Commission on Employment Equity led by Justice Rosalie Abella. In her 1984 report, Abella argued for a broad and flexible definition of equality that included both equal treatment regardless of difference and differential treatment where warranted to produce equal outcomes. The federal government issued its employment equity legislation soon after, in 1986, with Quebec following in 1987 and Ontario in 1993, although the latter was repealed in 1995 due to strong employer backlash and the election of a Progressive Conservative government. Though there have been and remain important conflicts within and between unions over this concept, since employment equity legislation was established, some unions have been amongst its strongest defenders, challenging governments and employers who sought to reverse or ignore it. For instance, when the Harris Conservatives repealed the NDP's employment equity legislation with their 1995 *Job Quotas Repeal Act*, the Ontario Federation of Labour supported the Alliance for Employment Equity's (unsuccessful) legal challenge (Bakan and Kobayashi 2007).

The establishment and expansion of paid maternity leave funded by the unemployment insurance system (UI) was in part a labour movement victory linked to the struggle to do away with the marriage and pregnancy bar. In the 1950s and 1960s, women who lost their jobs as a result of pregnancy were sometimes helped by their local unions in their attempts to get UI benefits (Porter 2003: 90). Increasing pressure to provide both paid maternity leave and a right to return to work afterwards led the federal government in 1971 to establish 15 weeks of paid maternity leave at 66 percent of a mother's previous salary (although many aspects of the UI rules led many women to be disqualified). Once this was established, unions used collective bargaining—and sometimes militancy—to further extend maternity benefits. In 1979, Quebec's Common Front, representing government, education and health workers together at a central bargaining table, negotiated 20 weeks of fully paid maternity leave. In 1981, with substantial support from the National Action Committee on the Status of Women and many other feminist organizations, the Canadian Union of Postal Workers went on a 42-day nationwide strike for longer, fully paid maternity leave, with the employer paying the difference between the worker's wage and the UI benefit (Nichols 2012: 62). The union won 17 weeks of leave at 93 percent coverage and set the tone for future reforms (Nichols 2012: 64). By 2014, maternity leave had reached 50 weeks for all eligible workers in Canada (albeit at 55 percent of salary).

More recently, the Canadian labour movement has been at the forefront of the struggle to establish equality based on sexual orientation, and it has put significant resources into establishing the constitutional right to same-sex marriage and benefits for all Canadians. Centred primarily in the public sector unions, queer activists used a variety of means to challenge the heteronormative definitions of relationships at the heart of the benefits available in most collective agreements, including spousal benefits, survivor pensions and bereavement leave. They also sought to protect union members from being fired or otherwise subjected to harassment and discrimination at work due to their sexual orientation.

However, both collective agreements and legislation had to be changed. Some unions began negotiating to include sexual orientation in their collective agreements' "no discrimination" clauses, which allowed members to file grievances and pursue arbitrations against their employers when they were denied access to various benefits. In cases where these grievances were denied, however, queer activists and their unions could not go to their Human Rights Commissions to counter their employers because, as of 1977, only Quebec had added sexual orientation to its provincial human rights code as a prohibited ground for discrimination. Supported by the labour movement, queer activists also lobbied to have sexual orientation added to the human rights codes, succeeding in Ontario, Manitoba and Yukon in 1986–1987 (Petersen 2009: 38–39). At the same time, the CLC and other unions financially supported a series of successful legal challenges in the 1990s to both federal and provincial human rights codes that did not ban discrimination on the basis of sexual orientation, arguing that this violated the 1982 Canadian *Charter of Rights and Freedoms*. When one track failed to produce a victory, focus shifted to another. The main battle was over the legal definition of "spouse," and whether, by referring only to a relationship between opposite-sex individuals, it was discriminatory and contrary to the equality rights in the Charter (even though there is no mention of sexual orientation in that document). After another decade of litigation funded by the labour movement, same-sex spousal benefits had become normalized in both collective agreements and legislation by the end of the 1990s. As well, sexual orientation was a protected ground in all human rights codes by 2002 and same-sex marriage was legal throughout the country by 2005.

THE UNION ADVANTAGE

Although the labour movement has spent much energy seeking reforms that benefit all workers regardless of union status, there is undoubtedly a clear economic advantage to being unionized. Indeed, all unionized workers from all demographics maintain an advantage over non-unionized workers in hourly wages and benefits. Many factors besides union status contribute to wage differentials, including time on the job, firm size, education and age. However, after controlling for the impact of these factors, the union wage premium—the component of the wage differential attributable to unionization alone—accounts for about 25 percent of the overall differential (Jackson and Robinson 2000: 99–100). In 2014, the average union wage premium in Canada was $5.17/hour (CLC 2014). The evidence also suggests that the union wage premium tends to increase when the economy is in a slump and unemployment is increasing, and to shrink when the economy is growing and the unemployment coming down.

The union advantage is also greater for workers in historically marginalized groups. For instance, in 2014, for women workers it was $6.89 per hour (CLC 2014). These results are evidence of two important realities: first, that employers continue to discriminate against certain groups of workers by paying them at a discount, and second, that unions significantly reduce the economic impact of that discrimination.

Unions generally create greater income equality in the workplace, reducing the wage spread between the highest-paid and lowest-paid workers within their

FIGURE 8.1: THE UNION ADVANTAGE: COMPARING AVERAGE HOURLY WAGES, 2014

Source: Canadian Labour Congress 2014

bargaining units. Historically, unions have sought to reduce wage inequalities by raising the wages of the lowest-paid workers relative to the highest paid. As a result, the incidence of union members in low-paid jobs (jobs that pay two thirds of the economy-wide median wage) is much lower than it is for non-union members. In 2000, only 9 percent of unionized women were in low-wage jobs, as compared to 47 percent of non-unionized women. The comparable figures for men are 6 percent and 32 percent respectively (Jackson and Robinson 2000). Another measure of workplace income inequality is the ratio of earnings between the top and bottom 10 percent of workers. In 1995, the top 10 percent highest-paid unionized women made 2.5 times what the 10 percent lowest-paid unionized women made. In contrast, the top 10 percent income earners among non-union women made 3.3 times what their lowest-paid counterparts made. The situation is similar for men: while the highest-paid unionized men made 2.45 times what their lowest-paid counterparts made, the highest-income non-unionized men made 3.64 times what their lowest-paid counterparts made (Jackson and Robinson 2000: 103).

But wages are only part of the story. Union members are much more likely to have employer-paid pensions, dental and vision care plans, and extended medical benefits than are workers who are not in unions, as demonstrated by Statistics Canada in the early 2000s (Akyeampong 2002). Collective agreements also provide union members with a broad range of other benefits that are not usually available to non-unionized workers—except those workers whose skills are essential to the employer and/or workers of privilege within enterprises. These benefits may include job security, longer paid vacations, more paid days off, voluntary overtime and compensation rates for overtime in excess of what is mandated under employment standards legislation, equitable procedures for determining promotion, layoff and recall, access to training opportunities and more rigorous health and safety standards.

FIGURE 8.2: AVERAGE NEGOTIATED WAGE SETTLEMENTS AND INFLATION (PERCENT), 1980–2014

	1980–1984	1985–1989	1990–1994	1995–1999	2000–2004	2005–2009	2010–2014
PUBLIC SECTOR	8.6	4.1	2.3	1.2	2.6	2.9	1.1
PRIVATE SECTOR	8.5	4.1	2.9	1.9	2.3	2.7	2.3
BOTH SECTORS	8.5	4.1	2.5	1.4	2.6	2.8	1.7
AVERAGE CHANGE IN CONSUMER PRICE INDEX	8.7	4.3	2.8	1.6	2.4	1.8	1.8

Sources: Labour Program, Strategic Policy, Analysis, and Workplace Information Directorate, Employment and Social Development Canada 2015; Akyeampong 1998; Statistics Canada 2006

Although the union advantage in wages and benefits persists, there is evidence that unions have become less effective at their economic role. For one thing, during the twenty-year period ending in 1999, negotiated increases in base wage rates of large bargaining units (500 or more employees) failed to keep pace with inflation. Since 1999, however, the situation has improved marginally.

The incidence of strikes, the number of workers involved, the person-days not worked, and the time lost due to strikes have also all declined. These declines in strike activity reflect the suspension of bargaining rights and the de facto curtailment of the right to strike in many jurisdictions for public sector workers, as well as the high rates of unemployment that effectively regulate private sector workers' bargaining demands and propensity to strike. But the decline of strikes is also an indication that the labour movement's ability both to generate gains for their members and to exert sufficient economic and political power to transform legislation and social policy in ways that help all workers is in jeopardy.

FIGURE 8.3: STRIKES AND LOCKOUTS, 1980–2014

	1980–1984	1985–1989	1990–1994	1995–1999	2000–2004	2005–2009	2009–2014
NUMBER OF STRIKES	823	648	440	347	324	820	718
WORKERS INVOLVED (000)	355	377	172	217	175	416	548
AVERAGE NUMBER OF WORKERS PER STRIKE	431	582	391	625	540	507	763

Sources: Labour Program 2015; Statistics Canada 2015

FIGURE 8.4: PERSON DAYS NOT WORKED DUE TO WORK STOPPAGES, 1974–2014

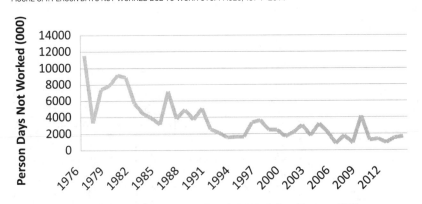

Sources: McQuarrie 2011: 389–90; Statistics Canada 2005; Labour Program 2015

UNIONS, INCOME EQUALITY AND ECONOMIC PERFORMANCE

One could argue that the union advantage demonstrates that unions merely serve their own members and widen the gap between union and non-union workers. However, unions have positive economic effects for the broader society as well. First, in what is called the "spillover effect," unions with a significant presence in a local labour market or economic sector can have the effect of raising wages in surrounding non-union workplaces. Negotiated increases in the unionized sector can sometimes have the effect of forcing non-union employers to adjust wages to remain competitive in labour markets and to avoid unionization of their firms (Godard 1994: 370–71).

Recent research has also shown that unions are connected to a more equal distribution of income at a society-wide level. Looking at how income distribution in Canada's provinces has changed since 1980, there is a clear correlation between income equality and union density: a declining rate of unionization produces more income inequality, increasing the share of income going to the wealthiest (Sran et al. 2014: 25–27). This correlation is also evident at the international level— the Organisation for Economic Co-operation and Development's (2011) own research shows that countries with higher rates of unionization are more equal in economic terms and have lower rates of poverty. These effects are due both to the way that collective bargaining reduces the number of low-income workers and the gap between the highest- and lowest-paid workers and also to the role that a strong labour movement plays in winning public policies that ensure income is distributed more fairly. However, what is crucial in both of these dynamics is the extent of union presence in the economy. The higher the rates of unionization, the greater are the effects on non-union workplaces and on the overall distribution of income and wealth in a society.

Unions have often been criticized for undermining economic productivity and profitability. Employers and their organizations, right-of-centre governments, and employer-funded research bodies such as the Fraser Institute blame unions for generating unemployment and inflation, reducing productivity, and making gains at the expense of non-unionized workers. For example, in a Fraser Institute report by Karabegovic, Gabler and Veldhuis (2012: 39), the authors contend, "unionization has been demonstrated to impede the flexibility of labour markets, a key factor necessary for good labour market performance." Right-wing think tanks and anti-union employers make those accusations in attempts to discredit unions, to make it more difficult to organize and achieve gains in collective bargaining, and to marginalize unions' influence in society. More often than not, governments scapegoat unions to deflect public attention from both their own ineptitude and the more fundamental causes of economic and social problems.

These critics muster little evidence in support of their positions, and what they do put forward is often counterintuitive and spurious (see Freeman and Medoff 1984). This is especially true of accusations that single out unions as the main cause of either unemployment or inflation—complex phenomena that defy easy explanation. In the inflationary era of the 1970s and 1980s, for example, critics cited unions as a major contributor to escalating prices. But in-depth studies revealed a variety of forces at work, including the actions of monopoly firms and increases in commodity prices, notably oil prices engineered by the Organization of Petroleum Exporting Countries. Wages followed other prices as unions responded to rising inflation by doing what they are supposed to do: seeking to protect the real wages of their members. Similarly, the high rates of unemployment in the 1980s and 1990s had little to do with unions. They were a result, rather, of deliberate government policies instituted to keep unemployment at a high level as a means of disciplining labour and controlling wages—especially negotiated wages, but also wages administered by employers (see Godard 1994; Gordon 1996; Stanford 1998, 1999).

More recently, research on productivity—the amount of economic output for a given amount of economic input—shows that unions have either a neutral or positive effect. Contrary to the stereotype of lazy union workers who sit around all day, a wide range of studies—including one from the World Bank—show that unionized workplaces are in fact more productive per unit of labour than their non-unionized counterparts (Fletcher 2012: 17–18). This is an important counter to the claim that unions reduce profits. In fact, unionized workers not only produce more through their labour but also ensure that profits are more fairly distributed, both within workplaces and in the economy as a whole.

UNIONS AND WORKERS' VOICE

At their very roots, collective agreements extend the rule of law to the workplace. They afford to workers certain rights and place limits on the arbitrary power of employers. They specifically include grievance-arbitration articles that give members rights in the workplace—rights to due process and fair treatment—not available to other workers except through the courts. The value of rights entrenched in collective agreements cannot be converted readily into dollar terms. The value to individuals of having some control over workplace conditions and of having protection against arbitrary (and in disciplinary matters in particular, often harsh) treatment by employers is incalculable. There can be no doubt, however, that union members recognize the importance of these rights and place a high value on having them.

Having an official voice in the workplace has a real effect on whether the rights that have been won by workers and codified in legislation are actually implemented.

For instance, occupational health and safety legislation mandates that workplaces over a certain size must establish joint health and safety committees made up of worker and management representatives. Together, these joint committees are responsible for ensuring that workplaces conform to occupational health and safety laws; having processes in place for informing workers about hazards; providing training on how to work safely; ensuring workers have the materials they need; and inspecting workplaces to identify violations. However, many studies have shown that the legislation is no guarantee that such committees function effectively. What is needed is significant worker empowerment to ensure that joint committees perform their roles—union presence is a key factor in ensuring that workers' legal rights to healthy and safe workplaces are actually realized (Yassi 2012). Without unions to organize workers' participation in joint health and safety committees and to ensure that no reprisals are taken against workers for raising health and safety concerns, there is no absolute guarantee that health and safety legislation is observed and implemented.

UNIONS PROVIDE SOCIAL BENEFITS FOR ALL

For union members, the outcomes of union activities in Canada have brought significant benefits. Union members enjoy a wage advantage over their non-unionized counterparts. They are protected by the rule of law in the workplace. Their collective agreements entrench their rights and entitlements, unlike the terms and conditions of employment of most non-unionized workers. These gains are undoubtedly one of the main reasons why unions have historically been opposed, and why they will continue to be opposed, by employers and governments.

QUESTIONS FOR DISCUSSION

1. What do you consider the union movement's most impressive achievement and why?
2. What is the union advantage, and in which ways does it benefit union members?
3. What are the broader economic and social benefits of a highly unionized workforce?

CHAPTER 9

WHO BELONGS TO UNIONS? WHO DOESN'T AND WHY?

The "union advantage" clearly provides unionized workers with better wages and greater benefit entitlements than their non-union counterparts. Furthermore, public opinion polls tell us that many workers, if given the choice, would opt to work in a unionized workplace. But if union membership is so desirable and the union advantage is so obvious, why are most workers not unionized and why don't more workers join unions?

FIGURE 9.1: UNION COVERAGE IN CANADA, PUBLIC VS. PRIVATE SECTOR, 2014

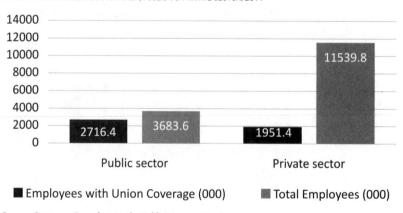

Source: Statistics Canada 2014b: Table 282–0078

In Canada, union density, or the percentage of workers that are unionized, has been hovering around 30 percent since the early 2000s, down from its high point in the mid-to-high 30s in the late 1980s (see Figure 9.1). However, that stable number masks significant differences in union membership across a number of important demographic factors. For example, workers in the public sector are far more likely to belong to unions than workers in the private sector. The public sector now accounts for 58.3 percent of union members but only 8.8 percent of non-unionized paid workers, while the private sector accounts for 41.7 percent of union members and 91.2 percent of non-unionized paid workers. In short, nine of every ten workers who are not unionized are in the private sector (Statistics Canada 2014b: Table 282–0078).

It is also undeniable that the labour movement is increasingly dominated by the public sector. Since the 1960s, the explosion of unionization in the public sector twinned with declines in traditional private sector union bastions—like manufacturing and resource extraction industries—has resulted in public sector workers making up the majority of union members. While this has been a long-term trend, it has only been since the mid 1990s that the public sector has eclipsed private sector unions.

Broken down by industry, there are wide variations in union coverage. While workers in education and public administration enjoy over 70 percent union coverage, those in agriculture, the insurance and real estate sectors, and accommodation and food services have levels of union coverage under 10 percent.

A key obstacle to unionization in many segments of the private sector is the relatively small size of the workplaces. Workplaces with under twenty employees have a union density rate of 14.4 percent, whereas those with over 500 employees have a rate of 55.2 percent. The problem for unions is that almost one third (33.1

FIGURE 9.2: SHARE OF UNION MEMBERSHIP, PUBLIC VS. PRIVATE SECTOR, 1997–2013

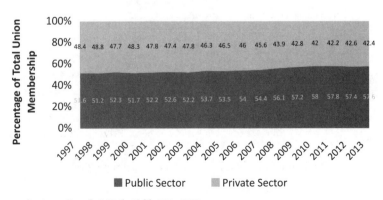

Source: Statistics Canada 2014b: Table 282–0078

percent) of paid employees are in workplaces with fewer than twenty employees, and close to one third (34.3 percent) are in workplaces with less than 100 employees. Moreover, 67.4 percent of all non-unionized workers are in workplaces with fewer than 100 employees (Statistics Canada 2014d: Table 282-0224). The costs to unions in terms of money and staff time involved in organizing small workplaces is much higher per potential member than in large workplaces. Small employers are also more likely to detect unionization drives in the early stages and to try to thwart them.

Within Canada, the level of union density also varies considerably from province to province. Alberta and Ontario, two of the most economically significant provinces in the country, have the lowest unionization rates. Even within provinces, there are important variations. For example, Hamilton is far more densely unionized than Toronto, while Edmonton is significantly more unionized than Calgary.

One major transformation in the make-up of the labour movement concerns the numbers and proportion of women in unions. In 2014, the labour force

FIGURE 9.3: UNION DENSITY BY INDUSTRY, 2014

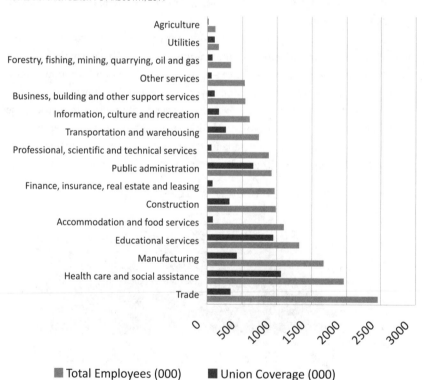

■ Total Employees (000)   ■ Union Coverage (000)

Source: Statistics Canada 2014c: Table 282-0077

participation rate of women—the proportion of women over age 15 in the labour force, either employed for wages or actively looking for waged work—was 61.6 percent. This is up from 22 percent in 1951; from just over 45.7 percent in 1976; from almost 59 percent in 1999; and from 61.7 percent in 2005 (Statistics Canada 2015b: Table 282-0002). While the rate of women's participation is still lower than that of men (70.6 percent of whom are in the labour force), women are slightly more likely than men to belong to unions, (32.8 percent and 30.3 percent respectively in 2012). As well, of the total number of union members in Canada, the proportion

FIGURE 9.4: UNION DENSITY BY PROVINCE, 2014

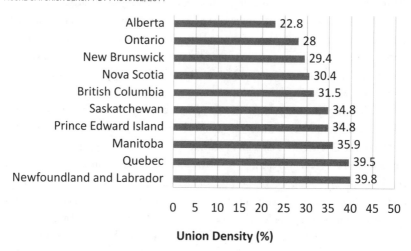

Source: *Statistics Canada 2014e: Table 282-0220*

FIGURE 9.5: UNION DENSITY IN SELECTED CANADIAN CITIES, 2014

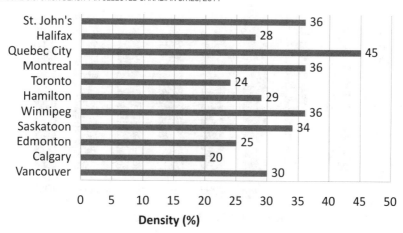

Source: *Canadian Labour Congress 2014*

of women has grown steadily over the past 40 years, from 16.6 percent in 1965 to 26.0 percent in 1975, to 36.2 percent in 1985, to 42.7 percent in 1995, to 49.2 percent in 2006, and to 51.7 in 2013 (Statistics Canada 2006a: 64–71; Statistics Canada 2014b: Table 282-0078).

How do we account for this dramatic change in the gender composition of union membership? The explosion of public sector union organizing in the 1960s and 1970s, combined with women's increased participation and the relatively stable levels of union density in that sector in the last few decades have really helped to boost union membership among women. Conversely, male-dominated sectors of the workforce, in particular manufacturing, have been very hard-hit, suffering massive job losses, thus applying downward pressure on union membership for men. The growth of public sector unionism and the growing proportion of women in the labour movement in Canada have turned the pop culture image of the white, male, hard-hatted industrial union member on its head. Today's typical union member is a woman who works in the public sector.

Gender is not the only source of demographic change in the union movement. A second challenge confronting organized labour is a demographic shift in the racial composition of the Canadian workforce—that is, the proportion of non-white workers is growing rapidly. This is the result of both a dramatic change in the composition of the immigrant population, and also of an increase in the proportion of Indigenous peoples moving to cities from reserves and rural communities.

Indigenous peoples made up 4.3 percent of the Canadian population in 2011, up from 2.9 percent in 1996, with the bulk of the growth in urban centres like Winnipeg, where the Indigenous population topped 10 percent of city dwellers

FIGURE 9.6: GENDER AND UNION MEMBERSHIP, 1978–2013

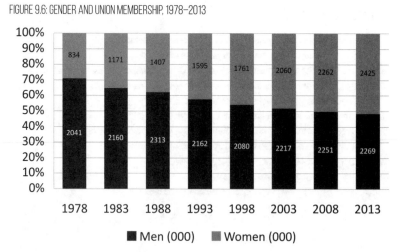

Sources: Statistics Canada 2006a: 64–71; Statistics Canada 2014b: Table 282-0080

in 2006 (Statistics Canada 1996: Table 109-0012; Statistics Canada 2011a). The proportion of racialized persons (non-white excluding Indigenous peoples) in Canada has grown from 4.7 percent in 1981 to 13.4 percent in 2001, and to 19.1 percent in 2011. Now and for the foreseeable future, immigrants will primarily feed growth in Canada's labour force, and the majority of these immigrants will be racialized (Jackson 2005: 101–22; Statistics Canada 2011b).

Along with immigrants who settle in the country as permanent residents and who in many cases eventually gain full citizenship rights, Canada also recruits migrant workers, normally from less developed countries, as part of a set of schemes that allow employers to bring them here to work for limited periods and without permanent status. These programs—the Seasonal Agricultural Workers Program, the Live-In Caregiver Program and the Temporary Foreign Worker Program—have grown tremendously in recent decades. For instance, the number of temporary foreign worker permits issued in Canada has risen from 13,999 in 1995 to 104,160 in 2013 (Citizenship and Immigration Canada 2014).

The federal government launched the Temporary Foreign Worker Program (TFWP) in 1973, in an effort to address very specific labour shortages, primarily in highly skilled occupations. The program was greatly expanded in 2006 when the newly elected federal Conservative government changed the system to make it easier for all kinds of employers to obtain temporary work permits, even in the absence of a demonstrable labour shortage. In 2013, the Royal Bank of Canada faced severe criticism when news broke that the bank's information technology workers were training temporary foreign workers to replace them. The public's heightened awareness of the TFWP shone a light on companies like Dairy Queen, A&W and Tim Horton's, all known to have used the program to hire migrant workers. In

FIGURE 9.7: TEMPORARY FOREIGN WORKER PERMITS IN CANADA, 1994–2013

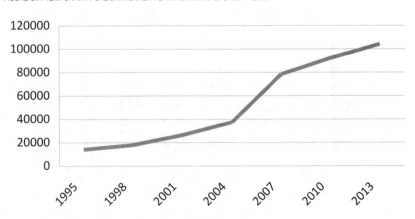

Source: Citizenship and Immigration Canada 2014

effect, according to the CLC (2013), the federal government "changed the purpose of the TFWP from helping employers fill specific labour shortages on a short-term basis to helping employers profit from a global supply of cheap, vulnerable and disposable labour for just about any job you can imagine."

The use of migrant labour is controversial, pitting groups against each other. Migrant workers themselves are provided with work opportunities in Canada that could help them lift their families out of poverty back home. These workers, however, are also placed in extremely precarious employment situations with fewer rights and protections than Canadian workers. Some Canadian workers complain that the use of temporary labour undermines their own ability to find paid employment. For their part, employers involved with the TFWP are provided with a relatively cheaper source of labour that is far more difficult to unionize and far less likely to press for increased workplace rights.

Unions are using several different strategies to fight the exploitation of temporary foreign workers in Canada. The need for unions to pursue solidarity initiatives in support of migrant workers is critical given the potential for governments and employers to use these programs to divide Canadian and non-Canadian workers, thus facilitating downward pressure on wages, working conditions and working-class power overall. First, some unions are advocating for a route to permanent citizenship for migrant workers based on the premise that if they are good enough to work in Canada, they are good enough to live here if they so choose. Second, unions are pushing the federal government to more strictly validate existing labour shortage claims with a view to scaling back the TFWP. Finally, some unions are fighting for increased federal investment in job training and apprenticeship opportunities to address any skills gaps among Canadian citizens that would contribute to the demand for skilled labour from abroad.

Despite Canada's growing economic dependence on immigrants and racialized and Indigenous peoples, workers in these groups are disadvantaged in the labour market relative to other workers. In brief, they are more likely to experience unemployment; be concentrated in jobs in service, clerical and unskilled or semi-skilled manual occupations; have lower annual earnings; and be poor (Galabuzi 2006).

While a number of factors contribute to these disparities, discrimination and racism play a critical role in determining the opportunities and rewards open to racialized and Indigenous workers. The challenge confronting the labour movement and its various components is to determine—and then follow through with— the action required to do away with the conditions in our society that nurture and sustain racism. Put another way, the challenge to unions is to obliterate the obstacles to racial equality, both in workplaces and within union themselves. The starting point for the labour movement must be to recognize that racism exists and is pervasive, and to resolve to work with the victims of racism to empower them and overcome the conditions that oppress them. "An anti-racist perspective begins by accepting that the perceptions of people of colour are real," and the struggle for racial equality must include "members of racial minorities as full and equal participants" (Henry et al. 2000: 379). The struggle to overcome racism must, as Galabuzi (2006: 235–36) suggests, be reflected in all union activities, including organizing, collective bargaining and the work of local labour councils to create communities that serve the collective interests of working people.

While the union movement in Canada has much work to do to ensure its leadership more accurately reflects the make-up of the membership, there are signs of positive change. In May 2014, Hassan Yussuff became the first racialized worker to be elected President of the CLC. In addition, more unions than ever have equity caucuses specifically promoting issues identified as important to racialized workers and fighting to make these issues a priority in bargaining and in the broader political sphere. For example, CUPE has a National Rainbow Committee that works to advance issues important to racialized workers and Unifor has a people of colour caucus that prioritizes and strategizes around issues of racial equality.

Union membership is affected by a number of other demographic factors. For example, workers with post-secondary credentials (certificates, diplomas or university degrees), full-time workers, workers with permanent jobs and workers with over five years tenure in a particular job are much more likely to be union members than are those with no post-secondary credentials, those with part-time or non-permanent jobs, and those with less than five years tenure in their jobs. Of these factors, the most critical seems to be the characteristics of the jobs held by workers, not of the workers themselves. One of the more pervasive labour market trends in recent decades has been the growing "casualization" of work, as reflected in increases in part-time and temporary jobs, both of which are concentrated among young people and women (Cranford and Vosko 2006; Silver 2014: 21–27). In 2014, 13.4 percent of paid workers were in temporary or non-permanent jobs, up from 11.3 percent in 1997 (Statistics Canada 2014: Table 282-0080). However, although the rate of insecure work is creeping up for workers of all ages, young workers aged 15–24 were the most likely to be in temporary employment. Fully 30.8 percent of younger workers were in temporary jobs in 2014, up from 25.1 percent in 1997 (Statistics Canada 2014: Table 282-0080). In 2011, unionization rates for part-time and temporary or non-permanent workers were 23.6 percent and 28 percent respectively, significantly lower than the average (Uppal 2011).

Young workers (aged 15–24) are very often employed in sectors of the economy and in the types of jobs where unions are least present. This means that, in 2015, the older one is, the more likely one is a member of a union. This is ironic given that young workers arguably have the most to gain from union membership. Moreover, surveys show that non-unionized young workers are more likely than their older non-union counterparts to want to unionize. While the contemporary disconnect between unions and young workers is significant, this was not always the case. In the 1960s, young workers fresh out of high school and university breathed new life into organized labour, bringing a renewed sense of radicalism and industrial militancy and leading wildcat strikes that altered the character of the union movement during this period (Palmer 2009: 216–19).

Changes to the political-economic order, however, have significantly altered union dynamics. The decline of the manufacturing sector has resulted in fewer jobs for young people in what was a relatively densely unionized part of the workforce. Higher unemployment in general and the shift to more precarious employment has resulted in a labour market that simply does not connect young people to unions as effectively as it once did. Where unionization has become more popular in professional occupations in the public sector, for example, very few younger workers are able to acquire the credentials for these jobs until their mid-to-late twenties. For their part, very few unions have made major investments in organizing new sectors of the economy dominated by young workers. All of these factors have contributed to low levels of youth engagement with unions in the current labour market.

UNION COVERAGE IN CANADA AND INTERNATIONALLY

Compared to other advanced capitalist countries, Canada ranks somewhere in the middle in terms of union density. The Scandinavian countries—where rates range from 53.5 percent in Norway to 82.6 percent in Iceland—all have higher rates than Canada does, while Australia, New Zealand, Germany, Japan and the U.S. have lower rates (OECD 2015). Overall, like Canada, most other countries have had stagnant or declining rates of union density, but the juxtaposition of unionization

FIGURE 9.8: AGE AND UNION DENSITY, 1998–2013

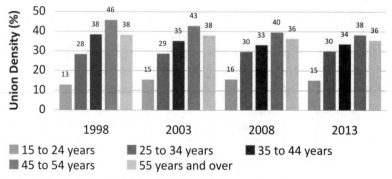

Source: Statistics Canada 2014e: Table 282-0220

rates in Canada and the U.S. is particularly interesting. In 1951, union density rates in the two countries were almost identical: 30.2 percent and 31.7 percent respectively (Murray 1995: 164). Since 1951, union density in the U.S. has declined continuously. In 2013, according to the OECD (2014), union density in Canada was more than twice that of the U.S.: 27.2 percent and 10.8 percent, respectively.

Given the similarities between labour relations regimes in Canada and the

FIGURE 9.9: UNION DENSITY IN CANADA, THE U.S. AND THE OECD (AVERAGE), 2013

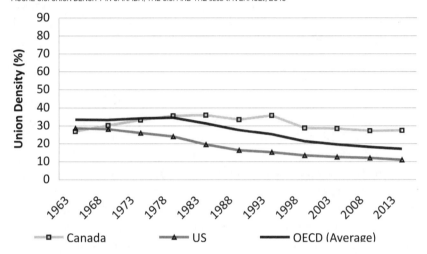

Source: OECD 2015

FIGURE 9.10: UNION DENSITY IN CANADA AND SELECTED EUROPEAN COUNTRIES, 2013

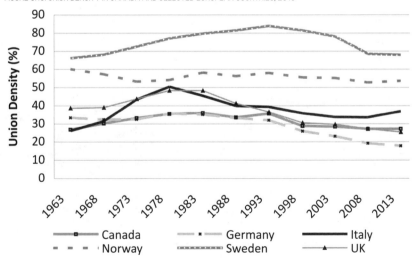

Source: OECD 2015

U.S., how do we explain the disparity in union density between the two countries? Researchers point to the existence of a social democratic party in Canada, which can account for differences in labour laws that promote unionization (in particular the use of card-based certification in some jurisdictions and the absence of right-to-work laws in Canada). Some researchers have argued that a more inclusive union movement in Canada and more effective unionization strategies by Canadian unions help account for the divergence, while others still point to the larger public sector in Canada, and a stronger anti-union bias by employers in the U.S., to explain the differences (see Murray 1995: 164-65; Goldfield 1987; Kumar 1993; Riddell 1993; Robinson 1993).

WORKERS' ATTITUDES TOWARDS UNIONIZATION

There is no consensus about which factors are most likely to sway employee support for unionization, but there does exist a range of hypotheses, from deeply personal to more general societal explanations (McQuarrie 2011: 165–73). Some workers develop specific attitudes towards unions based on their family background or self-perception as workers. For example, people whose parents have been active in their own unions are themselves more likely to hold pro-union attitudes (Hester and Fuller 2001). In some cases, workers' socioeconomic status, sex and race can positively predispose them towards unionization. Larger economic factors like the rates of unemployment and inflation can also influence whether a worker is more or less likely to join a union. So too can the absence or existence of a legal framework

FIGURE 9.11: UNION DENSITY, CANADA AND SELECTED ASIAN AND OCEANIC COUNTRIES, 2013

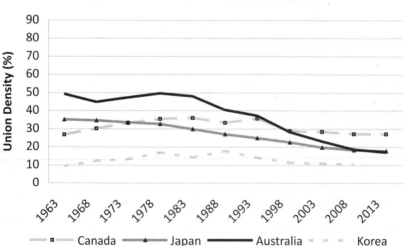

Source: OECD 2015

that encourages union membership or management's resistance (McQuarrie 2011: 166). To be sure, dissatisfaction with the terms and conditions of work may spur employees to demand a union. Overall, however, workers must buy into the union's instrumentality—the idea that unionization offers a vehicle to achieve certain ends that could not be achieved otherwise—to transform pro-union beliefs into concrete workplace action.

Surveys of workers' feelings about unions consistently generate two primary results: the majority of workers already in unions are relatively content with their status and prefer to remain union members; and a significant minority of non-members are favourably disposed to joining unions (Murray 1995: 169; Riddell 1993: 118–22). The results of a 2003 CLC survey confirmed this tendency: "Two-thirds of current union members are satisfied with their own national union and three-quarters [are] satisfied with their local unions." The results of the survey showed that 43 percent of non-union workers "would be 'very or somewhat likely' to join a union if there were no grounds for fear of employer reprisal." This survey also revealed "underlying support for unions is even higher among young workers aged 18 to 29 (52 percent), visible minorities (54 percent), and women (50 percent vs. 37 percent for men)" (Jackson 2005: 182). The evidence certainly suggests that if workers are dissatisfied with their jobs, believe that unions can improve their situation, and have a positive view of unions, if given the opportunity they will join up (Murray 1995: 168–70). Canadians in general have more mixed views on unions. According to a 2013 Harris-Decima poll commissioned by the Canadian Association of University Teachers (CAUT), "most Canadians think unions play a positive role in society and are still needed today" but "are split on whether unions have too much power and whether public sector unions should be stripped of rights" (CAUT/Harris-Decima 2013). However, even if there is an individual propensity or desire to unionize, there are still significant structural barriers—legal, political, economic, social—that need to be overcome.

BARRIERS TO UNIONIZATION: LEGAL EXCLUSIONS AND THE LABOUR LAW REGIME

For some groups of workers, unionization is simply not an option. Senior managers, military personnel, independent contractors and the self-employed are all legally excluded from union representation in Canada. These categories of workers aside, for a growing proportion of the workforce, unionization is simply out of reach. Precarious workers, domestic workers, agricultural workers and migrant workers, although not technically excluded, find unionization very difficult due to the labour law regime in some jurisdictions.

Labour laws play a fundamental role in either facilitating or impeding union membership for certain groups of workers. For example, in Ontario, farm workers are permitted to form associations but not unions. The associations are entitled to make representations to employers, but other than to simply hear workers' views, there is no reciprocal requirement for employers to negotiate with the association, thus undermining one of the central purposes for forming a collective entity in the first place. Employers have become highly skilled at using the labour law regime to their advantage or pressuring governments into modifying labour laws in their favour. For example, in Ontario in 1998, Bill 31, dubbed the "Wal-Mart Bill" by its opponents, was passed by the anti-union Progressive Conservative government of Mike Harris to put an end to automatic union certifications, a remedy available to the Labour Board if it found an employer had engaged in unfair labour practices to derail a unionization drive. The legislative change was pushed by retail giant Wal-Mart, after one of its Windsor, Ontario, locations was unionized in this fashion (Schiller 1998). In December 2000, to further curtail union rights, the Harris government passed a law restricting unions to one certification drive a year in any given workplace, and what was previously an unfair labour practice—namely, employers' provision of information to employees on how to decertify their union—became required by law (Lancaster House 2000: 3–4). Interestingly, however, the law did not require employers in non-union workplaces to post information on how to unionize for their employees.

A similar example from Nova Scotia involves the infamous "Michelin Bill." Passed in 1979 at the behest of the Michelin tire company, the law retroactively rewrote the province's labour laws to force any union attempting to represent the company's workers to organize all three of the Michelin plants in Nova Scotia simultaneously, thus scuttling the union drive that was then underway at one of the plants and seriously undermining any union's ability to unionize Michelin workers in the future (Langille 1981). Nova Scotia was also the first province to do away with card-based union certification in 1984, replacing it with a system of mandatory votes, which further hobbled organizing efforts.

As discussed in Chapter 5, Canadian provinces use one of two systems for certifying unions: card-based certification or the mandatory vote system. Unions much prefer the card-based method of union certification because it gives employers fewer opportunities to interfere with the will of workers. Under the mandatory vote system, not only must workers twice demonstrate their desire to unionize but the additional time required for the Labour Board to organize a secret ballot also gives employers an important advantage. During the days between the date the union files the application for certification and the date of the board-supervised secret ballot certification election, workers are typically bombarded with anti-union literature and an assortment of management threats and promises designed to dissuade them from following through with unionization. For example, employers may circulate legalistic-sounding anti-union literature designed to confuse or inspire doubt in the minds of workers about the potential benefits of unionization. Employers may also use this time to offer incentives, like free food, staff parties or company swag to buy employees' loyalty. In effect, the secret ballot actually inhibits workplace democracy because it provides employers with both opportunity and incentive to influence the outcome of the vote—through intimidation, coercion, misinformation, empty promises or all of the above. Most provinces have now switched from a card-based to a mandatory vote system for union certification, thus stacking the deck in favour of employers who resist unionization efforts in the days leading up to mandatory certification votes.

On the other hand, ostensibly pro-labour provincial jurisdictions, like NDP governments in Ontario (1990–1995) and B.C. (1991–2001) or the first Parti Québécois government in Quebec (1976–1981), played an important role in promoting unionization through pro-union changes to the labour law regime, including mechanisms to facilitate certification and bans on the use of replacement workers during strikes, also called scab labour. However, even the most pro-union labour law reforms have not fundamentally challenged the power imbalance between employers and workers, especially in the growing retail and private service sectors (Coulter 2014). Indeed, in the past forty years, unions in Canada have experienced far more legislative losses than victories, thus further tilting the labour relations framework to the benefit of anti-union employers.

BARRIERS TO UNIONIZATION: UNION SUPPLY

Despite these legal barriers, many workers continue their efforts to unionize. Many others, however, simply cannot find a union willing to organize them. This is known as a problem of union supply.

Charlotte Yates (2006) argues that there is a mismatch between workers who want unions and the groups of workers that unions seek to organize. Some groups are viewed as too small, too difficult or too expensive to organize, which can result in bargaining units with very little bargaining power or insufficient dues money to cover their basic costs. As Craig Heron (1989: 144) observes, part of the problem is that:

> The modern labour movement has inherited a model of organizing based on the large mass-production factory with a fairly stable, semi-skilled, male workforce ... This model is not helpful for signing up the thousands of highly transient, part-time workers in the booming service industries, where most of the new jobs are now being created.

This problem is related to broader questions about how unions decide which groups of workers are worthy of support to organize and how various groups of workers view the unions seeking to organize them. Yates (2004: 173–74) argues that unions could do a much better job at ensuring their organizers more closely resemble the workers targeted for organizing. Her research shows that "87 percent of campaigns studied in Ontario and 79 percent of those in B.C. were headed by white organizers (women or men). B.C. has a noticeably higher number of women heading up organizing drives than does Ontario: 41 percent in B.C. versus only 22 percent in Ontario" (Yates 2006: 108). This is a problem, according to Yates, because if union staff does not resemble the target membership, some workers will question whether the union can ably represent their interests. For example, are male organizers best suited to pitch unionization to a predominantly female group of child care workers? Or can white organizers effectively unionize migrant agricultural workers from Jamaica and Mexico?

BARRIERS TO UNIONIZATION: SOCIO-CULTURAL DYNAMICS

Workers seeking to unionize also face a hostile social and cultural climate that is increasingly anti-union and primarily driven by the corporate mainstream media. The news media constantly bombard the public with anti-union views that undermine support for organized labour by portraying unions as organizations of privilege and excess, and in the case of the public sector, seeking to bleed taxpayers dry. They are portrayed as outdated, out of touch and resistant to technological change at work for the sake of preserving jobs. Organized labour is sometimes depicted as a harmful or corrupt force in society, a direct nod to historical connections between unions and organized crime in the U.S. Unions are also painted as radical, trouble-making organizations, intent on strike action no matter the consequences for the public. Finally, unions are sometimes depicted as irrelevant and powerless, unable to improve the lives of workers in the face of globalization.

In some ways, this anti-union bias should come as no surprise. Journalist Linda McQuaig (1995: 12) reminds us, "all media outlets are owned by rich, powerful members of the elite. To assume that this fact has no interference on the ideas they present would be equivalent to assuming that, should the entire media be owned by, say, labour unions, women's groups or social workers, this would have no impact on the editorial content." On a more abstract level, Italian political theorist Antonio Gramsci (1971) used the concept of cultural hegemony—the state's use of cultural institutions to gain and maintain widespread influence over the public through the production of "common sense"—to explain why working classes are not physically coerced by wealthy elites into their own domination but rather consent to a subordinate position in society.

Inspired by Gramsci's work, contemporary labour studies research has explored the media's influence over society's attitudes and opinions about unions. Political scientist Michael Parenti (1986) developed seven generalizations about media coverage of labour disputes through an analysis of newspaper coverage of a Philadelphia transit worker strike. Parenti argued that media (1) portray labour struggles as senseless, avoidable contests brought on by unions' unwillingness to negotiate in good faith; (2) focus on company wage "offers," omitting or underplaying references to take-backs and employee grievances, thus making the workers appear irrational, greedy and self-destructive; (3) provide little to no coverage of management salaries, bonuses or compensation nor how they are inconsistent with concessions demanded of workers; (4) emphasize the impact rather than the causes of strikes, blaming the union for inconveniencing the public; (5) fail to consider the harm to workers if they were to give up their strike; (6) demonstrate an unwillingness to cover stories of union solidarity and mutual support; and (7) portray government as a neutral umpire, upholding the public interest, when in fact governments tend to protect corporate interests.

Along similar lines, Christopher Martin (2004) has identified five frames used by the media to dictate how they report on labour disputes. First, media always treat the consumer as "king," focusing their reporting on how the dispute impacts consumers and the broader public. For example, media reporting about teachers' strikes tend to revolve around how the dispute inconveniences students and their parents. Second, the focus on the consumer ignores the actual process of production involving workers and their work. Third, media also provide an overarching narrative that presents business leaders and entrepreneurs, not workers, as the true drivers of the economy and thus as the "good guys" in disputes with workers. Fourth, the media promote the idea that the workplace is a meritocracy to undermine the collective demands of unions, even though many people are hired because of who, rather than what, they know. Finally, media reports tend to portray any type of collective economic action, like strikes, in negative terms, favouring instead individual heroic acts that do not to fit in with union discourses.

The work of Martin, Parenti and others demonstrates how the media routinely uses unions and their members as scapegoats for many of society's ills, from unemployment to inflation and public debt. Media coverage of union activities tends to focus almost exclusively on strikes, picket-line battles, confrontations with governments, attacks on unions by politicians and conflicts within and between unions. More often than not, media reports of such incidents obscure both the issues involved and their significance while conveying the message that unions and their members do nothing but strike, demonstrate, and fight amongst themselves. Reports also often misrepresent the position and objectives of unions and create an impression that their activities and actions are invariably contrary to the "public interest." Working-class people themselves are often portrayed in films and on television as clownish, greedy, stupid and racist, and their unions are often portrayed as corrupt and self-serving.

Working-class people and their organizations are forced to confront these issues in a hostile political and ideological climate in which, rightly or wrongly, unions are seen as defenders of sectional rather than of general interest. The negative effects of the Great Recession of the late 2000s and the longer-term decline in working-class wages and living standards have made it much more difficult for unionized workers in general, and public sector workers in particular, to defend their collective agreements and their rights to dignified and secure work. As Tom Walkom (2010) has argued, the political right has mastered the art of mobilizing "reverse class resentment" based on the real feelings and experiences of insecurity of many working-class people:

> Today, class resentments have been turned on their head. The focus of anger is not the silk-hatted capitalist but his unionized workers, with their job protection guarantees, their pension plans and their good wages … Increasingly, in the world of media and popular culture, it is not the rich who are blamed for their excesses but the poor – the undeserving welfare recipient, the shiftless single mother, the employment insurance cheat. Resentment has become a potent tool of the right … The left's resentments were predicated on the notion that if some are privileged, all should be. For all of its problems (and resentment is a difficult force to control), it was at least optimistic. At its best, it encouraged people, through their governments, to improve the lot of those who were hurting. The new resentment is based on the presumption that if I don't have something, neither should you. Its aim is not to improve anyone's lot but to cut down to a common level of misery those uppity enough to think they deserve better.

BARRIERS TO UNIONIZATION: EMPLOYER UNION AVOIDANCE STRATEGIES

Employers intent on resisting unionization frequently exploit social-cultural biases, economic fears and weaknesses in the law to build opposition to union certification within their own workforces. This is union-busting, an employer-based line of attack used to prevent workers from organizing a union or to decertify an already existing union. While many forms of union-busting are illegal, employers are often less fearful of the penalties they may face for engaging in union-busting activities than of the consequences of unionization. Union-busting is a multi-million dollar business, involving lawyers and consultants responsible for devising strategies and tactics for employers, managers and supervisors to maintain union-free workplaces.

Union-busting can take various forms, including active intimidation of union supporters, captive audience meetings, sowing dissension in the workplace, exploiting divisions between workers, spreading misinformation about unions or smearing union supporters. Orchestrating an effective anti-union campaign often relies on a combination of union substitution (carrots) and union suppression (sticks).

Union substitution techniques are designed to increase worker loyalty to the employer, making employees less likely to identify with the union and less able to see their interests as distinct from the employers'. Union substitution techniques include voluntary provision of extras like signing bonuses, free dry-cleaning services, educational reimbursements, employer-sponsored sports leagues, holiday parties and family picnics. Employers' use of social activities has a long history, designed to foster workers' feelings of belonging to a workplace "family" and gratitude to a generous employer. Some non-union companies, operating in sectors with higher union density, try to keep wages and working conditions in line with those of unionized workers in the same sector. Historically, this was the case with steel companies Dofasco (non-union) and Stelco (unionized) in Hamilton, Ontario (Storey 1983), and it is happening now with casinos in Niagara Falls (non-union) and Windsor (unionized). The desire to remain union-free has created a situation wherein casino workers in Niagara receive wages and vacation time provisions comparable to those of workers in Windsor without having to pay union dues, thus creating a disincentive to unionize (Patrias and Savage 2012: 152).

Some employers also use mechanisms for employees to air their grievances and resolve disputes without having to formalize them in a legally binding collective agreement. These include open-door policies and formalized complaint procedures, which, while not legally enforceable as a union-negotiated grievance procedure would be, give the impression that employee complaints are dealt with fairly and consistently and that employee input is valued.

If union substitution represents the carrot, union suppression techniques represent the stick. Union suppression is designed to plant anti-union seeds of doubt in workers' minds and to play on their fears concerning the impact of unionization on job security. The strategy typically casts the union as a self-interested and disruptive third party whose involvement in the workplace will interfere with the existing workplace dynamic. Suppression techniques can include the targeting of pro-union employees for discipline and dismissal, captive audience meetings, which workers are required to attend and where they are subjected to the employer's anti-union perspectives, or the screening of anti-union videos designed to fill workers' heads with anti-union talking points and ways of thinking. In recent years, retail giants Target and Home Depot had their slick anti-union videos leaked on social media, providing insight into how much money and effort employers are willing to pour into anti-union initiatives.

Unsurprisingly, the threat of job loss is the most effective union suppression tactic. A 1997 study done for the labour ministries of Canada, the U.S. and Mexico found that between 1992 and 1995,

> more than one-third of US employers faced with NLRB [National Labor Relations Board] representation elections discharged workers for union activity, more than half threatened a full or partial shutdown of the company if the union succeeded in organizing the facility, and between 15 and 40 percent made illegal changes in wages, benefits, and working conditions, gave bribes or special favors to those who opposed the union, or used electronic surveillance of union activists during organizing campaigns. (Bronfenbrenner and Juravich 1998: 5)

In the 1980s and 1990s, attempts to unionize companies such as McDonald's and Wal-Mart were met with fierce union suppression campaigns. In the case of McDonald's, repeated attempts to unionize the restaurants have floundered. Following four earlier failed attempts to unionize outlets in Quebec and a similar failed attempt in Orangeville, Ontario, in the early 1990s, in 1997 the Teamsters signed up 82 percent of the sixty-two employees at a McDonald's in Saint-Hubert, a suburb of Montreal. Success seemed imminent. Then management pulled out its well-worn bag of anti-union tricks. According to writer Christian Huot (1998: 25),

> First, they tried the classic methods of harassment and reduction of working hours of union sympathisers. They also started giving special gifts and privileges to the 'soft' elements of the staff to try to rally their support ... The owners of the franchise also tried to argue that the union had to recruit a majority in the four other restaurants they owned, since all of these restaurants had to be considered together as one business.

After a year-long fight, the workers did win certification "and became the only McDonald's employees in either Canada or the US to be unionised workers" (Huot 1998: 25). But two weeks before, knowing what was coming, the owners had shut the restaurant down—permanently. Better, McDonald's believes, to sacrifice one restaurant than to let unionization get a foot in the door.

Workers who want to be in unions face several serious obstacles. Their gaining union membership has been blocked by legislation, or has been made difficult through problems like the labour relations framework, union supply, employer-based union avoidance strategies or broader socio-cultural anti-union biases. These factors are not mutually exclusive but rather mutually reinforcing, thereby lowering workers' expectations about the possibility of achieving secure and dignified work in a unionized environment.

QUESTIONS FOR DISCUSSION

1. How is the composition of today's labour movement different from that of the late 1800s and the mid 1950s respectively?
2. Do the media have an anti-union bias?
3. Have today's unions overcome their history of excluding certain kinds of workers?
4. Why do so many employers fight to remain "union-free"?
5. What is the difference between union substitution and union suppression?

CHAPTER 10

THE FUTURE OF UNIONS: DECLINE OR RENEWAL?

C apitalism generates change—the constant, never-ending "creative destruction" that is the inevitable consequence of its competitive search for profit, which, in turn, influences the making and unmaking of working-class solidarity. In recent decades, change has become so rapid and so dramatic that it would be foolhardy to try to predict the challenges that unions might be facing by the middle of the twenty-first century.

Some of the challenges that unions will have to grapple with in the immediate future are clear enough, however. These include: reviving labour's bargaining power in both the private and public sectors; organizing the new kinds of jobs and workplaces created by the continuous restructuring of capitalism; meeting the needs of an increasingly diverse working class, both in the labour force and in unions; educating and mobilizing members and democratizing unions to create a stronger and more effective labour movement; building alliances with social justice activists in response to challenges such as persistent poverty and income inequality, racial and gender discrimination, and environmental destruction; working internationally, not just domestically, to counter the global reach of transnational corporations (TNCs); and determining how best to promote workers' political interests.

This is a formidable set of challenges—but the labour movement has always had to overcome formidable challenges. At the beginning of the twentieth century, when monopoly capitalism was dramatically changing the structure of industry and the labour force, the movement took up new forms of organization. Efforts to build industrial unionism were met with unrelenting opposition. Early attempts failed.

Workers experimented with different organizational forms. The struggle was bitter and long-lasting. But in the end, the desire of working people to come together to protect and advance their common interests in the face of the unrelenting demands of competitive capitalism prevailed, and new kinds of unions were created that gained them significantly more respect and stability at work. Today we see similar patterns: formidable challenges posed by neoliberal globalization; determined and creative organizing by labour, with success coming only after experimentation with different and innovative approaches to organizing; and similar experimentation with forms of political representation.

These determined efforts by workers continue to occur despite the predictable and continuing claims that unions are the product of earlier times and circumstances, and have now "outlived their usefulness." Employers and those who represent their interests, however, always make such claims. After all, *The Globe and Mail*, for example, was editorializing about unions' obsolescence as far back as 1886. Anti-union ideology will remain a constant and inevitable feature of capitalism because the interests of those with economic and political power are threatened by the counter-power that unions provide to working people. Far from outliving their usefulness, unions are more needed than ever, both by workers and by society at large. The question is: how will unions respond to the challenges of twenty-first century capitalism?

UNIONS IN DECLINE, UNIONS IN RENEWAL

The debate about how unions should respond to challenges presented by twenty-first century employers and governments is generally framed as a crisis of unions. Many important indicators show that unions' effectiveness in the workplace and the political sphere has declined in recent years. Although there is still a significant union advantage in wages and benefits compared to non-unionized work (as discussed in Chapter 8), negotiated increases in base wage rates of large bargaining units (500 or more employees) have struggled to keep pace with inflation, particularly between 1979 and 1999. The situation has improved marginally since 1999. Overall, however, unions have experienced declining bargaining power relative to employers. This refers to the extent to which withdrawal from the labour–management relationship by one party entails costs for the other. In recent times, unions are finding postwar strategies increasingly irrelevant in their efforts to impose on their employers sufficiently high costs either to defend past gains or to make improvements for their members. This is due to greater employer mobility and governments' increasing willingness to use legislative means to end labour disputes.

This situation is linked to a gradual decrease in time lost due to strikes. The causes of this phenomenon are different for various sectors of the economy. In the public sector, where workers have become increasingly militant since the 1970s, governments have suspended bargaining rights and in practice curtailed the right to strike for many workers (Panitch and Swartz 2003; Briskin 2007). In the private sector, higher rates of unemployment, a dramatic reduction in access to Employment Insurance benefits since 1996, and threats of corporate mobility have effectively regulated private sector workers' organizing attempts, bargaining demands and propensity to strike. As free trade has made it possible to reorganize production chains at a global level, TNCs now have access to a highly unequal global labour market and can effectively use the threat of plant closures and job flight to lower-wage jurisdictions as a lever against all union efforts. For example, one U.S. study found that between 1993 and 1995, "employers threatened to close the plant in 50 percent of all union certification elections" and carried out the threat in 15 percent of cases—three times the pre-NAFTA level (Bronfenbrenner 1997: 8).

As discussed in Chapter 4, since the late 1970s, union acquiescence to management prerogatives has often taken the form of concession bargaining, where employers demand various givebacks from workers. Concessions take various forms: wage and benefit cuts; changes to work rules that increase the intensity of work and reduce employment; two-tier contracts that provide lower rates of pay and benefits to new hires; and the end of pattern bargaining and master agreements that create equal working conditions across firms in the same sector. Concession bargaining reverses the tenets of postwar labour relations, that workers could expect to share in economic growth and that past gains would become a permanent base upon which to make future improvements.

All of the above not only contribute to the decline of existing unions but also stunt the growth of new unions because prospective members may not see the benefit of joining a union. As the working population grows in non-unionized sectors of the economy, the union density rate declines, reducing unions' economic and political weight. Union responses to the decline of union density and union power have taken several forms.

MERGERS, SPLITS AND UNION REORGANIZATION

One response to union decline, and particularly to membership losses, has been existing unions combining into new organizations with larger memberships and more resources. This can take the form of a merger of unions to create a whole new organization, or absorption of smaller unions into a larger one that keeps its name, structure and identity. These moves are meant not only to overcome the financial losses that come with a declining membership and dues base, especially in the case of smaller unions, but also to combat the longstanding problem of an organizationally fragmented labour movement. It is argued that mergers remove unnecessary union competition and duplication of efforts, potentially create increased bargaining power along sectoral lines, and provide more political clout in electoral politics and coalition work (Chaison 1996). Often, mergers beget absorptions, as other smaller unions seek to join what is perceived as a revitalized union on the upswing.

Since the 1990s there have been several important mergers in North America that have reduced the overall number of unions. The number of union mergers in Canada has increased consistently since the 1960s: fifteen in the 1960s; twenty-six in the 1970s; twenty-nine in the 1980s; and nineteen between 1990–1993 (Chaison 1996). An increasing proportion of mergers over this period consisted of outright absorption as opposed to amalgamations. The proportions of total mergers taking the form of outright absorptions were 53 percent in the 1960s; 81 percent in the 1970s; 79 percent in the 1980s; and 95 percent between 1990–1993 (Chaison 1996: 58). There are many examples of union mergers and amalgamations in Canada. Perhaps the most interesting recent example, however, began as a split. A wave of amalgamations followed the withdrawal of the Canadian region from the UAW in 1985 and the subsequent creation of the CAW. Over twenty-three unions representing 100,000 workers—including the Fish, Food and Allied Workers and the Sudbury local of the Mine, Mill and Smelter Workers—joined the CAW in its first ten years (C. Yates 1998: 94). In 2013, the CAW and the Communications, Energy and Paperworkers Union merged to create Unifor, the largest private sector union in Canada.

Mergers have several positive implications for unions. They are a relatively quick and much easier way to make a major expansion in membership. Mergers consolidate resources and get rid of smaller, less effective unions whose bargaining power may be declining. Today's mergers also call to mind the argument made by radical unionists in support of industrial unionism in the early twentieth century: unity is power. Mergers create mini-versions of the one big union, representing large numbers of workers in multiple industries. The power of these merged unions is considerable because they have the potential to shut down important sectors of the economy. These mergers also go one step beyond industrial unionism and represent a movement towards general unionism, in which industrial or craft jurisdictions no longer define the boundaries of union membership. This can reduce sectionalism and build broader forms of solidarity, collective identity and (potentially) class consciousness, since union members are exposed to workers in very different occupations and have the opportunity to discover shared common interests that go beyond their own jobs, workplaces, or sectors.

However, mergers also create new challenges and do not necessarily resolve the underlying sources of union decline. First, they don't increase union density but rather reallocate existing union membership amongst fewer organizations. While this may be good for a particular union's organizational stability, its positive effect may be short-lived if it is not accompanied by serious efforts to organize new union members. There is no consensus on whether larger, better-resourced unions actually use their capacities for new organizing. Second, the loss of clear jurisdictions can intensify rather than reduce competition, since all unions are increasingly competing to organize all workers with less regard for sector. Third, mergers and the negotiations that produce them are often leadership-driven. While the union's members must vote to approve mergers, deals are often made at the top to facilitate mergers that aren't always in the best interests of the membership. Furthermore, size and greater diversity increase the challenge of ensuring membership participation and leadership accountability, the effective representation of various sectors, and the creation of a new collective identity to which all members can relate. Finally, mergers often don't take into account problems with the way unions carry out their key work of organizing, bargaining and engaging in political action, and so their contribution to union renewal is at best mixed.

NEW APPROACHES TO ORGANIZING

Some unions have placed a renewed emphasis on organizing new members into their fold, both to compensate for the loss of members in traditionally unionized sectors (like resource extraction and manufacturing) and to make inroads into those growing sectors of the economy that remain largely unorganized. There is increasing recognition that unions are in decline partly because they represent only a minority of the working population, which gives the non-union sector a competitive advantage and a capacity to place downward pressure on wages and conditions in unionized workplaces. It is clear that the majority of non-unionized workers are more poorly paid, have fewer benefits, and are given little effective control over their work lives. Unions are thus focusing on organizing the unorganized for both pragmatic and moral reasons.

Organizing in traditionally non-union sectors presents a particular challenge for unions. Employers in general have moved to a more "flexible" labour force through the creation of part-time, non-permanent and/or lower-waged jobs. Most new jobs are non-union, in relatively small units in the private service sector, and are more often staffed by women and/or workers of colour. These jobs, workers and sectors of the economy have not traditionally been the labour movement's main targets, and the established models of organizing don't easily apply. These sectors are also populated by exceptionally aggressive, anti-union employers whose business model depends on remaining both low-wage and "union free," and who have been willing to spend significant resources to block unionization efforts (see Chapter 9 for a discussion of union avoidance and union busting). In other words, a high proportion of new jobs are in areas that unions have traditionally faced the greatest difficulties in organizing.

However, service industries also present real opportunities for the labour movement in a globalizing economy because they simply aren't as mobile as manufacturing. Whereas manufacturing facilities can move offshore or relocate, restaurants, hotels and other personal services need to be located where the consumers are. If organized, the potential for bargaining power for these workers is significant.

Some argue that unions need to put more effort into organizing, including developing resources and training for both union and community-based organizers, and coordinating organizing campaigns and pooling resources across unions. In 2005, frustration with the gap between organizing efforts and results led to a major internal conflict in the U.S. labour movement. Alleging that the AFL–CIO overemphasized lobbying and political action at the expense of new organizing, seven unions—including the SEIU, Teamsters and UNITE HERE, representing more than 40 percent of AFL–CIO membership—broke away and formed the Change to Win Federation (CTW) in September 2005. CTW promised a greater commitment to organizing, especially in the growing service sector, experimentation with different organizing and union models, structural changes like mergers to create stronger unions and more centralized decision-making, and coordination of sectoral organizing activities. Critics of CTW argued it would actually undermine union solidarity, introduce competition between the federations, and promote more of the "same old" business unionism (Estreicher 2006; Greer 2006). In 2014, however, only three unions were still affiliated with CTW—the others had returned to the AFL–CIO. Neither Change to Win nor the AFL–CIO have yet found the key to unleashing a successful mass upsurge in unionization, both in general and in the precarious and increasingly racialized sectors of the labour market that are growing most rapidly. Canadian unions have been slower to allocate more resources to organizing, largely due to the relatively stable levels of union density overall, especially in the public sector. However, at its founding convention, Unifor committed $50 million in its first five years to organizing new members, recognizing that something had to be done about plummeting private sector unionization in Canada (Unifor 2013: 7–8).

At the same time, unions have to confront their long-term lack of attention to organizing and their approach to organizing, which clearly doesn't produce the kinds of dynamics needed to withstand employers' anti-union strategies. As discussed in Chapter 5, the "traditional" model of organizing is sometimes reactive, responding to a call from a "hot shop" where workers are very upset and conditions are very bad. This typically means the union is dealing with a hostile and volatile organizing environment. The organizing drive is therefore likely to take place under a veil of secrecy (to protect workers from reprisals) and to focus on the individual signing of cards. Campaign material is general in its purpose and distributed en masse, often at the "plant" gate or through mass meetings, and the appeal is based on union services and improvements. Union staff also plays a large role in traditional organizing strategies (Bronfenbrenner and Juravich 1998: 24). Simply investing in more organizing doesn't guarantee that organizing tactics or strategies have been rethought, or that enough has been done to help workers stay organized and actually negotiate successfully.

Since the late 1980s, the U.S. labour movement has sought to reverse its legacy of failure to organize new members through a great deal of debate and experimentation. Several important new approaches to organizing have emerged from these debates. The organizing model of unionism, which emphasizes the need to include union members in organizing, is premised on the idea that union power is enhanced by active membership participation, which must begin in the process of creating the union. Because employers are willing to invest so much money into anti-union campaigns, workers' connection and commitment to the union needs to be deeper to withstand these tactics. Bronfenbrenner and Juravich (1998) and Charlotte Yates (2000) show that heavy membership participation—with member-organizers drawn from existing bargaining units, for example, and with extensive personal contact between union organizers and prospective members—produces a higher percentage of certification wins.

The organizing model also focuses on the creation of an "organizing culture" that extends past the unionization drive, emphasizing the ongoing involvement of members in solving their own problems. UNITE HERE, which represents many hotel workers across Canada, takes an organizing approach to grievance handling, viewing some workplace problems as opportunities to organize, mobilize and politicize members through direct workplace actions rather than long, drawn-out dispute resolution mechanisms. For example, workers may sign a petition or march en masse to confront a manager over an unfair decision. Such continued activism is crucial to negotiating a first collective agreement, which can be very tough in the U.S. where there is no provision for first contract arbitration. Much new organizing fails, not because the union doesn't win the vote but because it is unable to get a contract. In short, experimentation with new organizing techniques for the new labour force can yield positive results.

Organizing success also often depends upon tapping into broad notions of workplace justice. According to Bronfenbrenner and Juravich (1998: 24), "Unions that focused on issues such as dignity, justice, discrimination, fairness, or service quality were associated with win rates that were nearly 20 percentage points higher than those that focused on more traditional bread-and-butter issues, such as wages, benefits and job security." In other words, workers see unions as vehicles for achieving improvements in their lives that cannot be measured in dollars and cents, and unions that tap into this perception can be more successful.

The corporate campaign strategy, which also supports bargaining, focuses on unions analyzing the structure of the corporation to better understand where the sources of power, weakness and leverage might be. Unions use this knowledge to pressure key individual or institutional investors or shareholders, lenders, suppliers, distributors, clients and governments to influence the target company not to resist unionization. Sometimes unions also use public campaigning techniques to expose corporate wrongdoing and attack their brands to pressure them into neutrality agreements. This approach is far more pervasive in the U.S., where unions like SEIU and UNITE HERE routinely launch corporate campaigns to blame and shame employers in an effort to obtain leverage in bargaining or extract a commitment from employers to remain neutral in the event of a union organizing drive. In 2012, UNITE HERE organized a global boycott of the Hyatt hotel chain in response to the latter's prominent opposition to a California bill that would have improved health and safety standards for hotel workers. The "Hyatt Hurts" campaign spread to cities across the U.S., India, the U.K., Israel and the Philippines (Wolf 2012). Pressure from this campaign led directly to the signing of a national labour "peace agreement" between the union and the hotel chain in 2013. The employer agreed not to actively campaign against new unionization efforts in exchange for the union lifting the boycott (Vail 2013).

Neutrality agreements, sometimes referred to as "bargaining to organize," use an existing collective bargaining relationship in one location to get the employer to agree not to oppose an organizing drive at one of their non-union workplaces or new outlets. Such agreements can also commit an employer to using its influence with a subsidiary or supplier to discourage them from conducting an anti-union campaign. Sometimes, in the U.S., these agreements also secure an election procedures agreement, whereby the company voluntarily accepts the card check method of determining majority support for the union (rather than the second step, voting, which is required by law in the U.S. and most of Canada). Unions also bargain for access to employee lists (which employers prefer to keep secret) and worksites (which are usually no-go zones for union organizers). In the U.S., union support for neutrality agreements has grown steadily in response to the failure of the country's labour laws to adequately protect the rights of workers to unionize. Neutrality agreements, with a card-check recognition procedure, result in union organizing success rates of 78 percent, compared with success rates of between 45 percent and 55 percent in typical NLRB recognition applications (Eaton and Kriesky 2001: 53). This is a promising result, but it also shows how unfavourable the legal certification process is for U.S. workers and unions today. As a result, UNITE HERE, the UAW, Steelworkers, the Communications Workers of America and SEIU have used neutrality agreements widely in their new organizing efforts.

The most successful example of bargaining to organize in Canada was the Canadian Union of Postal Workers' (CUPW's) negotiation in 2003 for recognition of rural route postal carriers, who Canada Post had misclassified as independent contractors and thus rendered ineligible to unionize under the *Canada Labour Code* (Clark and Warskett 2010: 247–48).

The use of neutrality agreements has also been quite controversial. While such agreements can be an important tool for neutralizing the company's anti-unionism and drawing on the bargaining power of some workers to support others, these deals can come at a price. Unions can agree to poorer collective agreement standards, or not to strike or be militant in exchange for neutrality, arrangements that call into question the kind of union workers will be getting. The SEIU's approach to neutrality agreements in California has also included acceptance of a template contract without involving workers. However, the most potent Canadian example was the CAW's 2007 negotiation with Magna Manufacturing of the "Framework of Fairness" (previously discussed in Chapter 4), which generated significant external criticism and internal discontent but in the end failed to produce any additional organized plants at Magna.

Some unions have sought community support to strengthen organizing efforts. Such efforts involve using the various webs of relationships that prospective union members bring with them to provide moral and practical support and to mobilize political pressure against anti-union employer efforts. These relationships can be with churches and faith-based organizations, and a range of social, cultural, ethnic or immigrant organizations. Jane McAlevey (2012) calls this "whole worker organizing," whereby all of a worker's priorities and social ties are mobilized to create strong organizations that fight on all the issues that matter to them. Unions that mobilize these social ties can also gain strength in workplace organizing campaigns as workers tend to be supported by their wider community in confrontations with employers. Community-based organizing efforts also tend to use a "social movement repertoire" of tactics such as public demonstrations, rallies, picketing (to put public pressure on employers who resist union drives), job actions and media engagement. A prominent example of this approach was the Stamford Organizing Project in the late 1990s, which brought together four unions in Connecticut to collaborate on organizing low-wage service sector workers. What made this project different—and therefore historically important—was that it began by organizing workers on issues they confronted *outside* their workplaces, namely the high cost of housing. Workers' successful efforts to secure the building of affordable housing, especially with the support of their church communities, later provided the basis for unionization drives in several low-wage workplaces (Clawson 2003: 110–24).

The AFL–CIO and many of its affiliates have also turned to industry or "sectoral organizing," which attempts to reach all the workplaces in a particular industry as opposed to organizing on a shop-by-shop basis. Sectoral organizing can also be geographical—a union may decide to focus on "wall-to-wall" organizing, aiming to completely unionize a company or sector in a particular regional market. Sectoral organizing can help to reestablish pattern or master bargaining by lining up common expiration dates in collective agreements, and also by making possible city-wide bargaining rounds and strikes with significant leverage because they eliminate competition from non-unionized facilities. When it works, sectoral organizing can set wages and conditions across the industry so that companies are no longer competing on that basis (Lerner 2003). This strategy is especially suited to those sectors that are less mobile, such as the hotel and cleaning services industry.

Some argue that the most successful organizing uses comprehensive campaigns, which combine many of the strategies discussed above. Comprehensive campaigns involve multiple strategies to strengthen workers' resolve to resist employers' anti-union actions, place political and economic pressure on employers from different directions, and leverage the power of community allies in supporting unionization efforts (Bronfenbrenner and Hickey 2004).

Perhaps the best-known example of a successful comprehensive campaign is the SEIU's Justice for Janitors (J4J) campaign, which began in Los Angeles in 1985. J4J targeted all non-union building owners and cleaning contractors in a given city, involving them in mass direct action tactics, like daytime sit-ins designed to disrupt business as usual and make normally invisible night workers visible to the public. In particular, the tactic was designed to convince the building's tenants to pressure the landlord into dealing only with unionized cleaning contractors. J4J's campaign for union recognition has also involved significant struggle. On June 15, 1990, Los Angeles janitors were beaten by police during a peaceful demonstration against the cleaning contractor ISS. Public outrage over this incident resulted in ISS recognizing the union. SEIU janitors and supporters now take action every June 15, Justice for Janitors Day, in cities nationwide and in countries around the world.

Despite important inroads in some sectors, these organizing efforts have not produced much change in the overall level of unionization. Part of the challenge is that new organizing, whether using traditional or new models, is both expensive and labour-intensive, and the scale of what is needed to keep union density stable (let alone growing) is daunting. By some estimates, each worker organized costs $1000. To raise union density by one percentage point in the U.S. would require organizing an additional 1.3 million workers at a cost of $1.3 billion—a daunting investment. The expense is partly because even innovative organizing still involves heavy reliance on paid union staff; while their duties may change, the organizing model requires a lot of work to mobilize and coordinate member-organizers' activities (Fletcher and Hurd 1998). Some are not sure that the comprehensive campaign model of organizing is yielding the kind of results that warrant such investment (Yeselson 2013).

As with mergers, simply adding more union members does not automatically translate into more union power. An expanding union must rethink and renegotiate the basis of its core values, goals and interests, symbols and heroic actions—in other words, its collective identity (C. Yates 1998)—a process that can involve significant internal conflict. On the one hand, more diversity can undermine previously created and powerful solidarities based on a homogenous membership or common experience of struggle. On the other, insisting that new members assimilate into an older union culture can be a real barrier to expansion.

NEW APPROACHES TO REPRESENTATION AND INCLUSION

The exclusion or marginalization of certain types of workers has always weakened the labour movement. Craft unions excluded industrial workers and, at some point in their history, most unions have excluded or marginalized women, newly arrived immigrants, workers of colour, Indigenous workers, people with disabilities and members of the queer community. As the workforce becomes increasingly diverse, a central challenge for unions is to create a labour movement that is inclusive, representative and responsive to the needs of all members and all workers. This is not only a question of which sectors of the economy unions prioritize for new organizing (as discussed above), but also of the role, voice and decision-making power those new union members will have within their organizations. Renewing unions is therefore also about creating and supporting union activists who are prepared and able to play leadership roles around issues of inequality, exclusion and marginalization at work, in the economy and wider society, and in the labour movement itself. In Canada, the struggle to foster greater inclusion in the labour movement is generally called equity politics.

Beyond the labour movement's moral commitment to equality (even if it has been unevenly applied in practice), there are two strategic reasons why greater inclusion matters to unions and to their renewal. First, an important part of the capitalist dynamic is to seize upon social differences between groups of workers and use them to pit those workers against each other. Employers have often self-consciously organized work in such a way as to create hierarchies amongst workers, with some accessing better jobs and wages while others are relegated to the worst jobs. As we saw in Chapters 3 and 4, employers often use these inequalities to play different groups against each other and undermine their potential for solidarity. Sexist, racist, homophobic and ableist (favouring the able-bodied) ideologies are used to justify which workers are "valuable" and which offer "rightfully" cheap labour. When unions accept rather than challenge those inequalities, they allow employers to weaken working-class community, solidarity and power. It is therefore in organized labour's interests to improve the wages and working conditions of *all* workers, so that one group cannot be used against another.

Second, these divisions are not random: they are gendered, racialized and pervaded with other inequalities. Thus there are patterns to the opportunities and limits experienced by different workers in the labour market and the workplace. Even though all workers experience class inequality because of their need to work for wages, they experience that inequality in different ways. The workplace issues and priorities for women, Indigenous and queer workers are not the same as those for workers in relatively more privileged positions in the division of labour. Women, for example, are more likely than men to prioritize gender pay equity. Indigenous or queer workers are more likely than their white or straight counterparts to be concerned with policies that ensure a workplace is free of harassment. Thus, if unions want to appeal to the full range of workers, whether in traditional or new industries, they must have an agenda that takes equity issues seriously and seeks to combat the systems of oppression, like racism, sexism and homophobia, that reproduce these inequalities.

As workers from equity-seeking groups have long understood, unions are key institutions in the fight for social equity. As Grace-Edward Galabuzi (2006: 235) puts it, "perhaps no institution represents as much promise in empowering racialized workers to overcome their oppression in the labour market as does organized labour ... For Canada's racialized group members to make significant progress in the labour market, they need the union advantage—the power of collective bargaining." Despite much frustration and internal resistance, unions in Canada, as previously discussed in Chapter 8, have made considerable gains in internal equity and inclusion in recent decades. These gains have taken the form of union education programs; shifts in union policies and collective bargaining priorities; and changes in internal union structures, including constitutional requirements for the representation of equity-seeking groups in executive positions. This has largely been due to the hard work of dedicated union activists using strategies of both separate organizing and alliance building.

According to Linda Briskin (1993), separate organizing is a strategic response to differences in power within an organization that make it difficult for historically marginalized groups to influence those who have power in that organization. Separate organizing—the creation of separate structures or spaces that allow equity-seeking groups to explore and define their own issues and priorities, develop strategies and tactics for working on them, and strengthen their own leadership capacities—has been used to challenge these power differentials. As such, separate organizing, usually in the form of separate equity caucuses, committees and conferences, is a strategy of empowerment that is used to make unions more inclusive.

Examples of separate organizing are now pervasive in Canadian unions and include women's committees, racialized worker caucuses, youth committees and queer worker groups. Separate spaces have also been created to link equity activists across unions. For instance, Ontario-based feminists created Organized Working Women, which between 1976 and 1990, brought women unionists together to strategize interventions in their own unions, the provincial labour federation and in government policy-making. The Ontario Coalition of Black Trade Unionists, established in 1986 and still active in 2015, is also autonomous from unions but has played a central role in struggles for anti-racist policies and equity representation in both the provincial and national labour federations. Similarly, activists founded the Asian Canadian Labour Alliance in 2000 and the Latin American Trade Unionists Coalition in 2009, both to create similar cross-union communities.

A second major set of initiatives put forward by equity-seeking activists was internal union education, of which there have been two major types. First, activists have pressured unions to deliver courses that raise awareness and develop an analysis of patterns of inequality amongst the general union leadership and membership. Second, equity activists have sought education that builds their own leadership skills, knowledge and confidence, so as to be more effective advocates and to be considered capable of holding elected office within the union.

A third set of equity strategies has more directly challenged union power structures and decision-making practices. These have come in the form of union convention resolutions and policy statements calling for anti-harassment training and codes of conduct within unions, prioritization of equity issues in collective bargaining, establishment of equity departments and staff roles, designated equity positions on executive boards and employment equity hiring policies for union staff. All of these initiatives are aimed at renewing unions' relevance to social equity struggles, anti-racism, pay and employment equity, human rights legislation and same-sex and trans-gender rights.

Equity organizing also entails some important tensions and contradictions, including backlash from some segments of the union that do not support equity issues, on one hand, and accusations of tokenism from segments of the union who feel the equity agenda is not taken seriously enough, on the other. Conflict can also arise between different notions of union democracy, raising the question about whether unions should operate under the principle of representativeness or majority rule. In the former case, the union might reserve elected positions on its executive board for members of equity-seeking groups; while this means not every position is open to every member, it would ensure the leadership reflects its membership with relative accuracy. In the latter case, the union might simply allow the will of the majority to rule on all positions, without any consideration for the inequities or exclusions that might produce. For example, members may elect an all-white or all-male executive board despite a significant minority of its members being women or racialized persons, because those members cannot muster an electoral majority to get their non-white or non-male candidate elected. The question of how to unite across difference can be difficult, particularly because experiences within marginalized groups are also diverse and unequal, thus potentially reinforcing divisions based on identity in the absence of conscious cross-constituency organizing (Briskin 2006: 106). For instance, "women's" organizing has not always reflected diversity and inequalities based on race, sexual orientation and ability between women, instead privileging what many would consider a white middle-class feminist perspective.

RENEWING SOCIAL UNIONISM AND COMMUNITY ENGAGEMENT

One important lesson from neoliberalism and its reversal of the postwar framework for industrial relations and social welfare has been that unions cannot confine themselves to the economic realm. Although "pure and simple" unionism did deliver the goods for some workers and for a given period (as previously discussed in Chapter 4), the conditions that made such advances possible—namely rapid economic growth and the postwar consensus that labour should share in that growth—no longer exist. That is why, more than ever, unions must mobilize their members as part of a broader movement for social change.

Much union activity is already concerned with broader social change. As we saw in Chapters 6 and 8, the labour movement in Canada has long engaged in social unionism, the pursuit of broader social and political reforms that will serve the interests of all working people, and not just union members. It has also been very successful at winning transformative policies like occupational health and safety laws, unemployment insurance, public health care, pay and employment equity legislation, and same-sex rights to name but a few. However, the rise of neoliberal policy has further promoted the adoption of social unionism as a union orientation and strategy, as it has become clear that workers' problems are caused by processes outside the workplace and can only be solved by dealing with those processes directly. Thus, the renewal of the labour movement is closely linked to the development of effective social unionist strategies both to contest policies that harm working-class people and to bring into existence the political economic arrangements that will sustain a socially just and equitable society.

Here we focus on a key social unionist strategy that is strongly linked to labour movement renewal, namely building alliances with other progressive social movements. Such alliances combine different forms of power to amplify the effect of coalitions. As membership-based bodies with regular dues and staff, unions are organizationally the strongest of social justice groups and bring important capacities to coalitions. While other organizations may have less money or less organizational stability, they often have stronger social relationships than unions and can mobilize larger numbers of people. Usually organized to tackle particular issues, these alliances are often called union–community coalitions. However, as Jane McAlevey (2012) has argued, this is a problematic formulation since union members are both in the workplace and in the community, and their interests overlap both spaces. Dividing "union" and "community" produces a false separation between organizations that in fact represent different aspects of workers' own interests. Nonetheless, efforts to expand the numbers of people and groups working together on common issues have become an important union renewal strategy.

The Canadian labour movement has a history of coalition work, going back at least to the free trade fights of the late 1980s (Bleyer 1997). Since then, coalition work has become a key part of the movement's repertoire. Coalitions have emerged on the myriad of issues in which union members' interests overlap with those of community members, such as in fights against plant closures or sweatshops, anti-privatization struggles and the need for higher wages, better services or environmental protection in the community.

Some coalitions are temporary, created to conduct a specific campaign over a particular issue. For instance, cupw's 1987–1988 campaign to keep rural post offices open was propelled by an alliance between cupw workers who would lose their jobs to contracting out and rural residents who would lose services (Tufts 1998: 235). The union's 2014–2015 Save Canada Post campaign similarly mobilized residents and municipalities in a coalition to save door-to-door urban delivery and prevent privatization of the mail service. The caw's Manufacturing Matters campaign, which highlighted the importance of the manufacturing sector to the overall health of the economy, similarly generated a community coalition to fight plant closures in Windsor, Ontario, in 2007 (Ross 2011). All are examples of unions using a social unionist repertoire to mobilize union and community members politically to save jobs and stave off union decline.

Unions also participate in coalitions whose aims more directly benefit non-union workers, rather than their own members, in the community. "Living wage" campaigns are a powerful example of this kind of social unionism. Such coalitions attempt to get local governments to pass municipal bylaws or living wage ordinances that require any private business benefitting from public money to pay their employees a living wage as a condition of winning a contract. A living wage is usually defined as an hourly rate that will permit workers (and their families) to meet their basic needs and live in dignity within that community. The living wage is thus different from the legal minimum wage, because it varies depending upon the cost of living where someone lives. Living wage campaigns have become pervasive in the U.S., bringing together coalitions of anti-poverty organizations, youth advocacy groups and unions in an effort to convince municipalities to adopt living wage ordinances. In Canada, the most prominent living wage campaigns have taken place in Toronto, through the Toronto and York Region District Labour Council's Good Jobs for All Coalition, and in New Westminster, B.C., led by the Association of Community Organizations for Reform Now (ACORN). In 2009, New Westminster became the first living wage municipality in Canada, requiring the city to pay both city and contract employees an hourly family living wage (Coulter 2012).

Other coalitions develop permanent structures for organizing ongoing advocacy on a particular issue or series of related issues, such as the Equal Pay Coalition (focused on gender pay equity) or the Ontario Health Coalition. The Ontario Health Coalition is an alliance between public and private sector unions, including CUPE, Unifor and OPSEU, and an assortment of community groups, all opposing the privatization of health care in Ontario. The Ontario Health Coalition has played a central role in exposing long-term consequences of public–private partnerships in Ontario. It has also engaged in a massive community outreach campaign to mobilize the public to defend medicare, through door-to-door canvassing, town hall meetings and public forums, and campaigns to get municipalities to pass resolutions of support for preserving public health care (Mehra 2006).

NEW WORKER ORGANIZATIONS

Labour movement renewal has also taken the form of non-union worker organizations, variously referred to as community unions or, more recently, "alt-labour." As Simon Black (2012) explains, community unionism is based on the practice of community organizing, in which people living in proximity come together to advocate over shared problems and interests. Labour organizing has moved outside the workplace to include the community because of the transformations to employment relationships that have characterized the neoliberal era. As workers face more unemployment, underemployment and precarious work arrangements, they are less likely to be attached to particular workplaces long enough to be able to organize. Workers therefore need to find other sites to organize themselves. The "community" is one such site, which can mean organizing workers around a shared geographic location or identity (like ethnicity or language). Often these two overlap, given the patterns of segregated living that concentrate low-income, ethnic communities in particular places; while community members may not share a workplace, they do share common economic problems that can be addressed through community action, such as challenging the high cost of housing (Clawson 2003: 112). Some forms of community unionism therefore focus on building power amongst working people in the community, not necessarily in the workplace as such.

Other community unions specifically aim to represent workers in the workplace but do so through organizations that exist outside the legal framework that certifies unions. In some cases, these are pre-union workers' organizations that may one day want to certify as a union but who at present don't have sufficient support in a given workplace to meet the legal hurdle of 50 percent plus one. In the meantime, such organizations advocate for improvements to workers' conditions, provide various supports and services and foster social connections between members.

Some of these pre-union organizations involve associate membership in existing unions—individual workers can join the union and receive services and support even though they haven't created a collective bargaining relationship with an employer (Fiorito and Jarley 1992).

Other community unions have no intention of ever becoming legally certified, not because they don't want to, but because they represent workers who are unlikely to be able to establish a collective bargaining relationship with an employer. Such workers are most likely to suffer from violations of basic employment standards, and therefore need support to enforce the law when governments won't. The most common form of community union is the worker centre.

Worker centres engage in economic and political advocacy without being formally certified by the labour relations system. They usually combine service provision; legal support and representation around workplace rights; education and research on industry conditions; advocacy, political action and lobbying for labour standards improvements or enforcement; and direct action organizing. According to Janice Fine (2005), workers' centres have emerged because workers' economic power had become so weak in some sectors they could no longer effectively use strikes to change employers' behaviour. Workers' centres tend to mobilize political forms of power instead. The worker centre model is highly developed in the U.S., perhaps because their certification system has been so much more hostile to unionization efforts. By necessity, workers have had to seek other forms of organization to advocate for their collective interests, leading some to dub them "alt-labor" (Eidelson 2013). Fine has documented the existence of over 200 such organizations in the U.S., including the Carwash Workers Organizing Committee, the Restaurant Opportunities Center, the National Day Laborer Organizing Network, OUR Walmart and Fast Food Forward.

Worker centres have now opened in several Canadian cities, including Toronto, Montreal, Winnipeg, Calgary and Windsor, Ontario. Winnipeg's Workers' Organizing and Resource Centre, funded largely by CUPW, provides space for community organizations to meet, organize and form coalitions. Their mandate includes advocacy for unorganized workers and a commitment to organize the unorganized (Bickerton and Stearns 2002). The Windsor Workers' Education Centre has a similar mandate. Perhaps the most successful to date has been the Workers' Action Centre (WAC) in Toronto, which organizes low-wage, precarious and temporary workers whose employers do not comply with employment standards. Established in 2005 through a merger between Toronto Organizing for Fair Employment and the Worker's Information Centre, WAC provides individual workers with advice and support in dealing with employers that violate employment standards, but it also encourages workers' involvement and activism in campaigns to build their leadership and organizing skills (Cranford et al. 2006: 408). In WAC's early days, it emphasized direct action methods to target employers engaging in violations and wage theft, pressuring them through pickets and boycotts to comply with the law. More recently, WAC has focused its campaigning on new legislation and better enforcement, successfully pressuring the Ontario government to pass laws regulating temporary employment agencies, raising the minimum wage, improving workers' ability to claim wages lost to wage theft, and increasing the number of employment standards enforcement officers and using proactive (rather than complaints-driven) enforcement.

Some worker centres focus specifically on immigrant and migrant workers, some of whom do not have legal status in Canada or are working in Canada under restrictive conditions, as with the Temporary Foreign Worker Program, Seasonal Agricultural Worker Program or the Live-In Caregiver Program. The Montreal Immigrant Workers' Centre is the leading example here, providing support and information about workplace rights, developing campaigns for individual and collective demands and most importantly, creating a safe and democratic space for immigrant workers to self-organize (Choudry and Thomas 2012). The UFCW has also established Migrant Agricultural Workers' Support Centres in agricultural communities across Canada to provide support for primarily Mexican and Jamaican migrant workers in greenhouses and vineyards. The centres document harsh working conditions, provide information on health and safety, and engage in various forms of outreach and advocacy (Cranford and Ladd 2003; Patrias and Savage 2012: 169).

While alt-labour organizations have clearly grown in size and significance over the last few decades, their relative influence and long-term sustainability are very much case-specific. Those operating without the same dues-paying base that traditional unions enjoy, or without significant financial backing from organized labour, arguably lack the organizational capacity to effect significant change over the long term. On the other hand, those alt-labour organizations that do enjoy strong union backing are likely to feel beholden to the unions footing the bill, thus undermining their own independence and possibly effectiveness, especially in cases where their priorities do not align with those of their union sponsors. While these dynamics play out in different ways depending on the organization, it is unlikely that alt-labour organizations will supplant unions as the main voice for workers in the near future, largely because the availability of a consistent and predictable level of revenue is critical to funding the political activities and organizing efforts required to make social change.

INTERNATIONAL SOLIDARITY

Since the 1800s, the labour movement has recognized that capitalism is a global system, always seeking new markets and new pools of labour, and that workers must overcome their divisions and unite across international borders to defend their common interests. Since 1889, workers around the world have celebrated May 1 as International Workers' Day in commemoration of the 1886 deaths at the hands of Chicago police of an unspecified number of workers struggling for the eight-hour workday (Panitch 2009). Moreover, given how integrated our economy has been with that of the U.S. and given the longstanding presence in Canada of U.S.-based "international" unions, Canada's labour movement has also always had an international character. However, the capacity for capital to act on a global scale has never been greater and presents real challenges for workers and unions, who are much more rooted in local and national locales. Other union renewal strategies, even when successful, don't address the real problem of capital mobility in significant areas of the economy, such as the manufacturing, technology and communication sectors. Creating the capacity for effective international solidarity amongst workers and strategies that regulate the actions of global employers is therefore a pressing issue.

In addition to the International Trade Union Confederation (ITUC), which provides a global forum for national labour movements to advocate internationally for workers' rights and economic justice, there are the Global Union Federations (GUF). These international sectoral organizations link workers from different countries who work in the same global firms or production chains. In 2014, there were nine GUFs representing workers in manufacturing, public services, education, journalism, arts and entertainment, transportation, food, building and private services (Global Unions n.d.). Like the ITUC, GUFs share information and advocate for their members in global institutions. They also help coordinate the activities of national unions dealing with international industries or multinational companies. This is done through global industry councils for unions in the same industry, and world company councils that bring together unions representing workers at the same global firm.

The GUFs' world company councils have attempted to bring collective bargaining to the global level through international framework agreements (IFA) with transnational corporations. IFAs between global unions and transnational corporations generally include the company's commitment to uphold the International Labour Organization's core labour standards on union rights and collective bargaining, bans on child labour, forced labour and forms of discrimination, and conventions on working time and health and safety, no matter where they are operating. They also can include commitments on the part of the company to ensure their suppliers and sub-contactors also abide by core labour standards, as well as mechanisms for conflict resolution. While not a legally binding collective agreement or a substitute for national legislation, IFAs can supplement these documents, working as moral documents that participating unions can use to mobilize support and place pressure on a given company to improve conditions or to recognize and bargain with a local union.

There is some evidence that IFAs can indeed be useful to unionists at local, national and international levels when used strategically. One powerful case is that of workers at Ditas, an auto parts manufacturer in Turkey and a supplier to DaimlerChrysler in Germany. In December 2000, the entire Ditas workforce was fired after successfully organizing a union. Workers engaged in repeated efforts to secure recognition from the employer, including an eight-month recognition strike in 2002. In the middle of that strike, Turkish workers discovered Ditas' connection with DaimlerChrysler. They appealed to the International Metalworkers Federation affiliates, who had signed an IFA with DaimlerChrysler in 2002. The IFA stated that its suppliers were expected to respect workers' rights to unionize. The Metalworkers pressured DaimlerChrysler to intervene with their supplier, which they eventually did, resulting in recognition and a new collective agreement for Ditas workers in March 2003 (Gibb 2005: 45–49). While Ditas workers still face a hostile employer, their achievement of a collective agreement was significantly aided by the existence of an IFA and the willingness of unions in other countries to place pressure on their employer to enforce that agreement.

Unions, whether through their national or international labour federations, have also sought the inclusion of social clauses in free trade agreements as an attempt to mitigate the negative effects that free trade has on workers. Such clauses define workers' minimum rights in the free trade zone and set up complaints processes that allow either unions to contest violations or importing countries to take trade measures against exporting countries that fail to observe a set of internationally agreed minimum labour standards. For instance, the North American Agreement on Labor Cooperation, the labour side agreement that accompanied NAFTA, commits Canada, the U.S. and Mexico to promote eleven "Labor Principles," including freedom of association and the right to organize, collectively bargain and strike; the abolition of forced and child labour; nondiscrimination and equal pay for equal work; occupational health and safety and workers' compensation; and migrant worker protection (Compa 2001: 453). The idea is to use the international enforcement processes in free trade agreements, which typically protect the ability of transnational corporations to move investments and production freely across borders, to also protect workers' rights internationally. However, left-wing critics of such social clauses argue that in promoting them, unions risk accepting the overall logic of free trade by viewing workers' rights as an "add-on" rather than challenging the basic political and economic assumptions behind free trade. Moreover, few of these side clauses have any significant enforcement mechanisms.

Beyond the level of international trade deals, unions have also developed more direct forms of solidarity with workers in the Global South, particularly to foster conditions there that will support worker organizing. As we have seen, the combination of very low wages, high levels of poverty and unemployment and hence large reserves of cheap and desperate workers make countries of the Global South very attractive to TNCs, who have enormous bargaining power to extract extremely favourable conditions from host governments. In practical terms, this means both very harsh working conditions and extremely coercive measures by both TNCs and repressive governments to prevent unionization. Such conditions hurt workers in both the Global South and the Global North. One important response is to promote union organizing in the low-wage jurisdictions to which corporations are moving. The establishment of effective unions benefits workers in the Global South by improving their wages and working conditions. But it will also benefit workers in Canada and other higher-wage jurisdictions by reducing the incentive for TNCs to relocate in pursuit of low-cost labour and stopping the erosion of unions' bargaining power.

One means to support worker organizing abroad is through union international solidarity funds. In some cases, each member of the union contributes one cent per hour from their wages to the fund via payroll deduction, in others the employer makes the contribution. These funds are used to support development projects that reduce poverty, worker-to-worker exchanges to raise mutual awareness, and union organizing and workers' rights campaigns in other countries. As of 2015, the Canadian unions that have established international solidarity funds include CUPE, CUPW, National Union of Public and General Employees (NUPGE) and many of its provincial components, PSAC, Unifor, USW and the Canadian Federation of Nurses' Unions.

In the private sector, both the former CAW and the Steelworkers have made notable efforts at building international networks with their solidarity funds. The CAW was a member of the North American Ford Workers' Solidarity Network, which "supported Ford workers in Cuautitlán, Mexico, where thugs from the state-dominated labour federation killed a union activist" (Wells 1998: 34). The Steelworkers' Humanity Fund, funded by 600 bargaining units across Canada, has supported exchanges with miners' unions in Chile (Marshall and Garcia-Orgales 2006).

In the public sector, unions have built solidarity relationships with other unions around the common threat of privatization and restructuring of public services. Teachers' unions in Quebec, English-speaking Canada, the U.S. and Mexico established the Tri-National Coalition in Defense of Public Education in 1994 to monitor the impact of the NAFTA on public education and to develop common strategies.

These efforts more closely resemble what Kim Moody (1997) terms "rank-and-file internationalism," the organization of ongoing contact, exchange and joint action among groups of rank-and-file workers in different countries. Sometimes referred to as "transnational workers' networks," these represent attempts to foster common understanding and consciousness, overcome the often protectionist response of northern workers, and connect workers in regions of the global economy in ways that are direct (rather than mediated through unions leaders or official global union organizations). Transnational networks have developed between workers in different parts of a common production chain. A key example is the Transnational Information Exchange, which carries out grassroots research on multinational production chains, whether in auto, cocoa-chocolate or textiles, and creates regional linkages between workers in various parts of these chains (Moody 1997: 255–64). Such efforts are based on the conviction that international solidarity work can't be done by union leaders alone; instead, workers themselves need to be committed to common interests and strategies, actively engaged in meeting others, learning about conditions elsewhere, and taking concrete actions.

Sympathy strikes, especially by workers in the same production chain or global company, are perhaps the most potent form of rank-and-file internationalism. Such strikes, in support of a particular group of workers in another country, can intensify pressure on a corporation by targeting multiple weak spots or important profit centres in their global production chain. Perhaps the most famous example of this kind of international solidarity is the series of actions that occurred in support of Liverpool dockworkers between 1995 and 1998. These workers were locked out and replaced by scabs after refusing their employer's demand to implement lean production. In 1996, the dockworkers called a conference of rank-and-file dockers from twelve unions and eight different countries; all put pressure on their own unions to refuse to handle "hot cargo" from Liverpool and to engage in coordinated work stoppages on international "days of action" (Moody 1997: 249–50). However, the use of coordinated strike action across borders is rare. This is partly because it is risky: Canadian labour law explicitly restricts sympathy strikes, so workers would have to defy the law to engage in such actions on behalf of other workers.

Beyond the level of the workplace, labour internationalism can and does take on broader, human rights-based dimensions. In the mid to late 1980s, for example, the CLC played a key role in pressuring the Canadian government to push South Africa to end apartheid and release human rights activist Nelson Mandela from prison (Pratt 1997). In 2006, CUPE Ontario's convention adopted a resolution supporting an international campaign of boycott, divestment and sanctions against the state of Israel in an effort to pressure Israeli officials to end the occupation of the Palestinian territories (Leong 2009).

All of these embryonic attempts at global labour solidarity, and more, will have to be nourished if Canadian unions are to successfully meet the challenge of globalization. Rank-and-file union members, not just union leaders and staff, will need to become directly involved; if they don't, the result will be not only resentment of leaders' international travels but also fears about the neglect of local concerns. It is essential that union members see that global concerns *are* local concerns, and vice versa.

EDUCATION, MOBILIZATION AND DEMOCRATIZATION

Whether unions grow through mergers, new organizing or attention to inclusivity, broaden their agenda to include social justice or international solidarity, or experiment with new kinds of worker organizations, what matters in all cases is what happens once workers are part of the union. As Bill Murnighan (2003) points out, "simply having more members is not enough to build and maintain a strong, democratic, vibrant labour movement." This poses yet another challenge for the union movement: the need to actively involve the membership in the many aspects of their unions' work.

Even though they offer more opportunities for people to be directly involved in democratic decision-making processes than in any other institution, unions still face important challenges when ensuring active membership involvement and control. Apart from anti-union ideas that spread the false notion of the "union boss," there are real concerns that unions could be more participatory and democratic. With few exceptions, the more bureaucratic form that unions took on in the postwar period meant that the negotiation and servicing of collective agreements by expert leaders and staff took priority over members' education, mobilization and involvement.

The perception that unions are not democratic enough is a barrier to new organizing. In a 2003 poll conducted by the CLC and Vector Research, 43 percent of those unorganized workers who said they were "unlikely" to vote for a union gave the "lack of internal democracy" as a reason for their reluctance. Furthermore, a significant number of existing union members—45 percent—reported that they felt they had "no say in how their union operates" (CLC/Vector 2003: 41). Union leaders and activists often have a defensive reaction to such statements, not least because many of them have put their hearts and souls into building the movement. A common response is to argue that these are misperceptions, either due to lack of knowledge or a negative media portrayal of unions, and what is needed is "education" showing how democratic unions really are. This may be true, but it is also crucial that unions take stock of where they fall short democratically and take real steps to change practices that disempower members.

If unions are to be a powerful force for advancing the interests of workers, they must be open and democratic institutions in which members feel genuinely involved. They must be committed to educating and mobilizing members to create an alternative culture to the one established by the wealthy and powerful few who control our society's sources of information and entertainment. The case for prioritizing deep union democracy in the form of membership participation and empowerment is very strong, particularly if we are concerned with renewing the labour movement's energy and power. Contemporary social movement research has shown that members who feel they have real control over their organizations participate more and open the organization up to more and potentially innovative solutions to unforeseen problems. Greater involvement also means creating stronger bonds of solidarity and mutual commitment that come from ownership of decisions and the experience of working together. Such involvement enhances the legitimacy of unions' actions in the eyes of both members and outsiders (Polletta 2004; Parker and Gruelle 1993).

Union members themselves are also transformed through the experiences of participatory democracy. By participating in debate and decision-making, workers develop the organizational and critical capacities, the forms of collective consciousness and the individual attitudes needed for full and equal participation in a self-governing society. Unions can develop the capacities of individual workers by consciously setting about to increase the number of activists within the union—and especially the number of those actively involved in the running of the union. As Gindin (1995: 275) argues: "building that cadre of activists and activists-to-be is achieved by expanding educational opportunities, by establishing the widest range of forums and conferences, and, above all, by maintaining the union's constant involvement in campaigns and struggles. Activism creates activists."

Deepening union democracy also begins to construct the very democratic institutions many would like to see in the rest of society, and in that sense starts to build the future in the present. More democratic unions could easily raise peoples' expectations of other institutions, providing models for how we might deepen our society's democracy. Panitch and Swartz (2003: 237) call on unions to become "centres of working class life and culture," not only to sustain oppositional cultures that make resistance possible but also to model how our communities could be.

Several unions have adopted conscious programs of membership engagement, in which they apply the organizing model in the internal life of the union. Such efforts generally include involving membership in activities traditionally carried out by staff, and training member-organizers (discussed above) and member-educators or instructors. Instead of staff developing and delivering the union's educational program, union activists participate in the design of the programs and are then trained to deliver the courses in their own locals/regions. Leadership and activist training is potentially democratizing because it prepares the next generation of leaders and, if made widely accessible, interrupts the way that "expertise" is reproduced amongst a small number of people who remain entrenched in outmoded leadership roles.

In some unions, members have had to organize rank-and-file reform movements to make union structures and practices more democratic. Such movements, whether informal caucuses or formal organizations like Teamsters for a Democratic Union, organize collectively to make leadership more accountable, to democratize union constitutions or bylaws, or to challenge incumbent leaders by running opposition candidates. Such organizations are more common in the U.S., perhaps because the business union model is more deeply entrenched there, but there have been similar, if more ephemeral, efforts in Canadian unions.

Although it is widely understood that greater membership involvement is needed to revive union power, there are deep attachments to the postwar model of unionism, by leaders, staff and members alike. The passivity of the service model of unionism was also easy and many are accustomed to its routines. Workers' training and skills are designed to support this model, and membership engagement can require moving outside of one's comfort zone. In some unions, overt opposition to democratization initiatives isn't needed—leaders and staff simply fail to follow through on commitments to greater activism and new policies gather dust as the day-to-day pressures of servicing and collective bargaining take precedence.

Ultimately, however, labour movement renewal strategies must take seriously the need to democratize union structures, and membership mobilization and participation must be accompanied by membership control and ownership. Otherwise, members won't remain committed to their unions if they aren't included in meaningful ways. Moreover, if the labour movement's goal is to help working people build the capacities and self-confidence to become strong agents for social change, it follows that this process must be inclusive and participatory. That commitment, amongst large numbers of workers, is essential to any renewal of workers' collective power.

UNIONS ARE THE KEY TO BUILDING A BETTER WORLD

Which path to renewal holds the most promise? The answer to that question depends on the kinds of unions workers want and need. By the early part of the twenty-first century, following thirty years of unrelenting attacks by capital and the state, the Canadian labour movement was holding its own, having suffered much less than its U.S. counterpart. Still, many formidable challenges confront the Canadian labour movement today as dynamic changes at the heart of capitalism continue to alter the economic world in which unions operate.

It is important for all of us that unions succeed in meeting these challenges. Building a better world depends on a healthy and vibrant labour movement.

Unions increase wages, improve benefits and working conditions, promote social and economic equality, reduce the arbitrary power of owners and managers by bringing the rule of law to the workplace, and increase working people's sense of dignity and self-respect. In these ways unions are a force for democracy, which, again, is not merely a matter of casting ballots in general elections from time to time, important though that is. In Canada, democracy is advanced by a host of institutional arrangements and practices that protect and extend our rights and freedoms. Labour unions are one of those institutions. They protect and extend the rights of working people. They are an *essential* element of democracy. This is especially so now, early in the twenty-first century, in a period of unparalleled corporate power that threatens workers' rights and democracy everywhere on the globe.

Despite or perhaps because of their essential role in democracy's well-being, labour unions have always been opposed by those with power. It is no coincidence that one of the first priorities of all extreme right-wing governments is to crush or severely undercut union power. Even more moderate governments are forced to contend with powerful corporate interests that exert enormous pressure to erode union rights and weaken labour laws, using the threat of capital flight and associated job losses to their advantage. These corporate interests have enormous advantages in the conflict between classes because they own the means of production as well as most of the media. The result, not at all surprisingly, is that unions are consistently portrayed in a negative light despite the critical humanitarian role they play in curbing unbridled corporate power.

Reversing the anti-union tide will not be easy. Indeed, building union power has *never* come easily. Union gains are always the result of the hard work, militancy and creativity of workers, and especially of skilled and dedicated labour movement activists. Not all unions have the same priorities or modes of organization. But the *idea* of a union—that the people who do the work should have a voice in how the work is to be done and what they are to be paid for that work—is an intrinsically democratic idea. Those struggling to build strong and effective unions in the twenty-first century are working not only to advance social and economic justice but also to build democracy. They are working together to build a better world.

QUESTIONS FOR DISCUSSION

1. What are the key factors that explain the decline of union power and effectiveness?
2. What forms of union renewal are being adopted today? What are the strengths and weaknesses of different union renewal strategies?
3. Which renewal strategy should be the highest priority for the labour movement and why?

REFERENCES

Abella, Irving. 1973. *Nationalism, Communism and Canadian Labour: The CIO, the Communist Party, and the Canadian Congress of Labour, 1935–1956*. Toronto: University of Toronto Press.

Adams, Roy J. 2003. "Voice for All: Why the Right to Refrain from Collective Bargaining Is No Right at All." In James A. Gross (ed.), *Workers' Rights as Human Rights*. Ithaca: Cornell University Press.

Akyeampong, Ernest B. 1998. "Unionization — An Update." *Perspectives on Labour and Income*. Ottawa: Statistics Canada, Catalogue No. 75-001-XPE, Winter.

____. 2002. "Unionization and Fringe Benefits." *Perspectives on Labour and Income* 3, 8.

Albo, Greg, Sam Gindin and Leo Panitch. 2010. *In and Out of Crisis: The Global Financial Meltdown and Left Alternatives*. Oakland, CA: PM Press.

Allen, Richard. 1971. *The Social Passion*. Toronto: University of Toronto Press.

Alvaredo, Facundo, Tony Atkinson, Thomas Piketty and Emmanuel Saez. 2014. *The World Top Incomes Database*. <topincomes.parisschoolofeconomics.eu/#Database:>.

Archer, Keith. 1985. "The Failure of the New Democratic Party: Unions, Unionists and Politics in Canada." *Canadian Journal of Political Science* 18, 2.

Archer, Keith, and Alan Whitehorn. 1997. *Political Activists: The NDP in Convention*. Toronto: Oxford University Press.

____. 1993. *Canadian Trade Unions And The New Democratic Party*. Kingston: Queen's Industrial Relations Centre.

Avakumovic, I. 1978. *Socialism in Canada: A Study of the CCF–NDP in Federal and Provincial Politics*. Toronto: McClelland and Stewart.

Bakan, Abigail, and Audrey Kobayashi. 2007. "'The Sky Didn't Fall': Organizing to Combat Racism in the Workplace—The Case of the Alliance for Employment Equity." In Genevieve Fuji Johnson and Randy Enomoto (eds.), *Race, Racialization and Antiracism in Canada and Beyond*. Toronto: University of Toronto Press.

Baker, Patricia. 1993. "Reflections on Life Stories: Women's Bank Union Activism." In Linda Briskin and Patricia McDermott (eds.), *Women Challenging Unions*. Toronto: University of Toronto Press.

Barnetson, Bob. 2010. *The Political Economy of Workplace Injury in Canada*. Edmonton: Athabasca University Press.

Battye, John. 1979. "The Nine-Hour Pioneers: The Genesis of the Canadian Labour Movement." *Labour/Le Travail* 4: 25–56.

Bickerton, Geoff, and Catherine Stearns. 2002. "The Struggle Continues in Winnipeg: The Workers Organizing and Resource Centre." *Just Labour* 1: 50–57.

Black, Errol. 1984. "Canada's Economy, the Canadian Labour Movement, and the Catholic Bishops." mimeo.

____. 1982. "Just a Few More Notches." *Canadian Dimension* 16, 2.

Black, Errol, and Jim Silver (eds.). 1991. *Hard Bargains: The Manitoba Labour Movement Confronts the 1990s*. Winnipeg: Committee on Manitoba's Labour History.

Black, Simon. 2012. "Community Unionism and the Canadian Labour Movement." In Stephanie Ross and Larry Savage (eds.), *Rethinking the Politics of Labour in Canada*. Winnipeg: Fernwood Publishing.

Bleasdale, Ruth. 1981. ""Class Conflict on the Canals of Upper Canada in the 1840s." *Labour/Le Travail* 7.

Bleyer, Peter. 1997. "Coalitions of Social Movements as Agencies of Social Change: The Action Canada Network." In William Carroll (ed.), *Organizing Dissent: Contemporary Social Movements in Theory and Practice*. Toronto: Garamond.

Boehm, Marina. 1991. *Who Makes the Decisions? Women's Participation in Canadian Unions*. Kingston: Queen's University Industrial Relations Centre.

Boivin, Jean, and Ester Deom. 1995. "Labour–Management Relations in Quebec." In Morley Gunderson and Allen Ponak (eds.), *Union–Management Relations in Canada*, third edition. Toronto: Addison-Wesley.

Borins, Sandford. 1983. *The Language of the Skies: The Bilingual Air Traffic Control Conflict in Canada*. Montreal: McGill–Queen's University Press.

Bradford, Neil. 1989. "Ideas, Intellectuals and Social Democracy in Canada." In Alain Gagnon and Brian Tanguay (eds.), *Canadian Parties in Transition: Discourse, Organization, Representation*. Scarborough: Nelson.

Braverman, Harry. 1974. *Labour and Monopoly Capital: The Degradation of Work in the Twentieth Century*. New York: New York University Press.

Briskin, Linda. 2007. "Public Sector Militancy, Feminization, and Employer Aggression. Trends in Strike, Lockouts, and Wildcats in Canada from 1960 to 2004." In Sjaak van der Velden et al. (eds.), *Strikes Around the World, 1968–2005: Case Studies of 15 Countries*. Amsterdam: Aksant.

____. 1993. "Union Women and Separate Organizing." In Linda Briskin and Patricia McDermott (eds.), *Women Challenging Unions: Feminism, Democracy and Militancy*. Toronto: University of Toronto Press.

British Columbia (Public Service Employee Relations Commission) v. BCGSEU [1999] 3 S.C.R. 3.

Brodie, Janine, and Jane Jenson. 1988. *Crisis, Challenge and Change: Party and Class in Canada*. Ottawa: Carleton University Press.

Bronfenbrenner, Kate. 1997. "We'll close! Plant Closings, Plant-Closing Threats, Union Organizing and NAFTA." *Multinational Monitor* 18, 3: 8–14.

Bronfenbrenner, Kate, and Robert Hickey. 2004. "Changing to Organize: A National Assessment of Union Organizing Strategies." In Ruth Milkman and Kim Voss (eds.),

Rebuilding Labour: Organizing and Organizers in the New Union Movement. Ithaca, NY: Cornell University Press.

Bronfenbrenner, Kate, and Tom Juravich. 1998. "It Takes More than House Calls: Organizing to Win with a Comprehensive Union-Building Strategy." In Kate Bronfenbrenner et al. (eds.), *Organizing to Win: New Research on Union Strategies*. Ithaca, NY: Cornell University Press.

Brown, Larry. 2015. "Supreme Court Rulings on Labour Legislation: An Affirmation of Workers' Constitutional Rights." *Work Life: Labour Commentary & Analysis*, February 6. Winnipeg: CCPA Manitoba. <policyalternatives.ca/publications/commentary/work-life-supreme-court-rulings-labour-legislation>.

Byers, Barb. 2002. "Applying the Lessons to the Canadian Experience: Barb Byers, President, Saskatchewan Federation of Labour." In P. Leduc Browne (ed.), *Labour and Social Democracy: International Perspectives*. Ottawa: Canadian Centre for Policy Alternatives.

Camfield, David. 2007. "CUPE's Sympathy Strikes in British Columbia, October 2005: Raising the Bar for Solidarity." *Just Labour: A Canadian Journal of Work and Society* 11 (Autumn).

____. 2011. *Canadian Labour in Crisis: Reinventing the Workers' Movement*. Halifax: Fernwood Publishing.

Campaign to Raise the Minimum Wage. 2015. "About the Campaign." <raisetheminimumwage.ca/about-the-campaign/>.

Campbell, Peter. 1999. *Canadian Marxism and the Search for a Third Way*. Montreal and Kingston: McGill–Queen's University Press.

Canadian Labour Congress/Vector Research. 2003. "Canadians Talk About Unions." Ottawa: CLC/Vector Research.

CAUT (Canadian Association of University Teachers) and Harris-Decima. 2013. CAUT Harris-Decima Public Opinion Poll (November 29). <caut.ca/docs/default-source/better-funding/caut-harris-decima-public-opinion-poll-november-2013.pdf?sfvrsn=2>.

CBC News. 2014. "Essential Services Bill a Game Changer for Labour Relations." *CBC.ca*, April 4. <cbc.ca/news/canada/nova-scotia/essential-services-bill-a-game-changer-for-labour-relations-1.2597936>.

____. 2012. "Air Canada Wins in Contract Arbitration with Pilots." *CBC.ca*, July 30. <cbc.ca/news/business/air-canada-wins-in-contract-arbitration-with-pilots-1.1273060>.

CFLR (Canadian Foundation for Labour Rights). 2014. "Restrictive Labour Laws in Canada." <http://labourrights.ca/issues/restrictive-labour-laws-canada>.

Chaboyer, Jan, and Errol Black. 2006. "Conspiracy in Winnipeg: How the 1919 General Strike Leaders Were Railroaded into Prison and What We Must Now Do to Make Amends." *CCPA Review: Labour Notes*. Winnipeg: Canadian Centre for Policy Alternatives–Manitoba (March).

Chaison, Gary. 1996. *Union Mergers in Hard Times: The View from Five Countries*. Ithaca, NY: Cornell University Press.

Chamberlain, Neil. 1965. *The Labor Sector*. New York: McGraw-Hill.

Choudry, Aziz, and Mark Thomas. 2012. "Organizing Migrant and Immigrant Workers in Canada." In Stephanie Ross and Larry Savage (eds.), *Rethinking the Politics of Labour in Canada*. Winnipeg: Fernwood Publishing.

Christie v. York [1940] S.C.R 139.

CIC (Citizenship and Immigration Canada). 2014. "Work Permit Holders for Work Purposes with a Valid Permit as of December 31st." <cic.gc.ca/english/resources/statistics/facts2013/temporary/1-1.asp>.

CLAC (Christian Labour Association of Canada). 2015. "About Us." <clac.ca/About-us>.

Clark, Dale, and Rosemary Warskett. 2010. "Labour Fragmentation and New Forms of Organizing and Bargaining in the Service Sector." In Norene Pupo and Mark Thomas (eds.), *Interrogating the New Economy: Restructuring Work in the 21st Century*. Toronto: University of Toronto Press.

Clawson, Dan. 2003. *The Next Upsurge: Labor and the New Social Movements*. Ithaca, NY: ILR Press.

CLC (Canadian Labour Congress). 2015. "Supreme Court Affirms Essential Role of the Right to Stike in Collective Bargaining." <canadianlabour.ca/national/news/supreme-court-affirms-essential-role-right-strike-collective-bargaining>.

____. 2014. "Union Advantage 2014." Ottawa: CLC. <canadianlabour.ca/about-clc/union-advantage-2014>.

____. 2013. "How the Conservatives Expanded the Temporary Worker Pipeline." Ottawa: CLC. <canadianlabour.ca/sites/default/files/2013-12-06-finalcomic-en.pdf>.

Clement, Dominique. 2009. *Canada's Rights Revolution: Social Movements and Social Change, 1937–82*. Vancouver: UBC Press.

Compa, Lance. 2001. "NAFTA's Labor Side Agreement and International Labor Solidarity." *Antipode* 33, 3.

Coulter, Kendra. 2014. *Revolutionizing Retail: Workers, Political Action and Social Change*. London: Palgrave Macmillan.

____. 2012. "Anti-Poverty Work: Unions, Poor Workers and Collective Action in Canada." In Stephanie Ross and Larry Savage (eds.), *Rethinking the Politics of Labour in Canada*. Winnipeg: Fernwood Publishing.

Coulter, Rebecca Priegert. 1993. "Alberta Nurses and the 'Illegal' Strike of 1988." In Linda Briskin and Patricia McDermott (eds.), *Women Challenging Unions: Feminism, Democracy and Militancy*. Toronto: University of Toronto Press.

Craig, Alton W.J., and Norman A. Solomon. 1993. *The System of Industrial Relations in Canada*, third edition. Scarborough, ON: Prentice-Hall.

Cranford, Cynthia, Tania Das Gupta, Deena Ladd and Leah Vosko. 2006. "Thinking Through Community Unionism." In Leah Vosko (ed.), *Precarious Employment: Understanding Labour Market Insecurity in Canada*. Montreal: McGill–Queen's University Press.

Cranford, Cynthia, and Deena Ladd. 2003. "Community Unionism: Organising for Fair Employment in Canada." *Just Labour* 3.

Cranford, Cynthia, and Leah Vosko. 2006. "Conceptualizing Precarious Employment: Mapping Wage Work across Social Location and Occupational Context." In Leah Vosko (ed.), *Precarious Employment: Understanding Labour Market Insecurity in Canada*. Montreal: McGill–Queen's University Press.

Creese, Gillian. 1988. "Exclusion or Solidarity? Vancouver Workers Confront the 'Oriental Problem.'" *BC Studies* 80 (Winter).

Cyr, François and Rémi Roy. 1981. *Elément d'Histoire de la FTQ: La FTQ et la Question Nationale*. Laval: Editions coopératives Albert Saint-Martin.

Dart, Chris. 2012. "Librarians, Authors Join Forces at Read-in." *Torontoist,* March 26. <http://torontoist.com/2012/03/librarians-authors-join-forces-at-read-in/>.

Das Gupta, Tania. 1998. "Anti-Racism and the Organized Labour Movement." In Vic Satzewich (ed.), *Racism and Social Inequality in Canada.* Toronto: Thompson Educational Publishing.

Deibert, Ronald J. 2000. "International Plug 'n Play? Citizen Activism, the Internet, and Global Public Policy." *International Studies Perspectives* 1.

Draper, Hal. 1978. *Karl Marx's Theory of Revolution Vol 2: The Politics of Social Classes.* New York and London: Monthly Review.

Drohan, Madeline. 1998. "How the Net killed the MAI." *Globe and Mail,* April 29.

Dunmore v. Ontario (Attorney General), [2001] 3 S.C.R. 1016, 2001 SCC 94.

Eaton, Adrienne, and Jill Kriesky. 2001. "Union Organizing under Neutrality and Card Check Agreements." *Industrial and Labour Relations Review* 55.

Eidelson, Josh. 2013. "Alt-Labor." *The American Prospect,* January 29. <prospect.org/article/alt-labor>.

Endicott, Stephen. 2012. *Raising the Workers' Flag: The Workers' Unity League of Canada, 1930–1936.* Toronto: University of Toronto Press.

Episcopal Commission for Social Affairs. 1983. *Ethical Reflections on the Economic Crisis.* Ottawa: Canadian Conference of Catholic Bishops.

Estreicher, Samuel. 2006. "Disunity Within the House of Labor: Change to Win or to Stay the Course?" *Journal of Labor Research* 27 (Fall).

Evans, Bryan. 2013. "When Your Boss Is the State: The Paradoxes of Public Sector Work." In Stephanie Ross and Larry Savage (eds.), *Public Sector Unions in the Age of Austerity.* Winnipeg: Fernwood Publishing.

Fantasia, Rick. 1988. *Cultures of Solidarity: Consciousness, Action, and Contemporary American Workers.* Berkley: University of California Press.

Ferguson, Rob. 2011. "Tories One-Upped by Working Families." *Toronto Star,* May 31. <thestar.com/news/canada/2011/05/31/tories_oneupped_by_working_families.html>.

Fine, Janice. 2005. "Community Unions and the Revival of the American Labor Movement." *Politics & Society* 33, 1: 153–99.

Fiorito, Jack, and Paul Jarley. 1992. "Associate Membership Programs: Innovation and Diversification in National Unions." *Academy of Management Journal* 35, 5: 1070–85.

Flanagan, Donne. 2003. "Inoculating Traditional NDP Weaknesses Key to Doer's Success." (paper in authors' possession, June).

Fletcher, Bill Jr. 2012. *"They're Bankrupting Us!" And 20 Other Myths about Unions.* Boston: Beacon Press.

Fletcher, Bill Jr., and Richard Hurd. 1998. "Beyond the Organizing Model: The Transformation Process in Local Unions." In Kate Bronfenbrenner et al. (eds.), *Organizing to Win: New Research on Union Strategies.* Ithaca: ILR Press.

Forrest, Anne. 1995. "Securing the Male Breadwinner: A Feminist Interpretation of PC 1003." In Cy Gonick, Paul Phillips and Jesse Vorst (eds.), *Labour Gains, Labour Pains: 50 Years of PC 1003.* Winnipeg/Halifax: Society for Socialist Studies/Fernwood Publishing.

Frager, Ruth. 1983. "Women Workers and the Canadian Labour Movement." In Linda Briskin and Lynda Yanz (eds.), *Union Sisters: Women in the Labour Movement.* Toronto:

Women's Press.

Freeman, R., and J. Medoff. 1984. *What Do Unions Do?* New York: Basic Books.

Fuller, Jerry, and Kim Hester. 2001. "A Closer Look at the Relationship between Justice Perceptions and Union Participation." *Journal of Applied Psychology* 86.

Galabuzi, Grace-Edward. 2006. *Canada's Economic Apartheid: The Social Exclusion of Racialized Groups in the New Century.* Toronto: New Scholars' Press.

Geras, Norman. 1986. *Literature of Revolution: Essays on Marxism.* London: Verso.

Gereluk, Winston. 2001. "Labour Education in Canada Today." Centre for Work & Community Studies, Athabasca University. <labourstudies.athabascau.ca/documents/PLAR_Report.pdf>.

Gibb, Euan. 2005. "International Framework Agreements: Increasing the Effectiveness of Core Labour Standards." Unpublished Master's Thesis, Global Labour University/University of Kassel/Berlin School of Economics.

Gindin, Sam. 1998. "Socialism 'with Sober Senses': Developing Workers' Capacities." In L. Panitch and C. Leys (eds.), *The Socialist Register 1998: The Communist Manifesto Now.* London: Merlin Press.

____. 1995. *The Canadian Auto Workers: The Birth and Transformation of a Union.* Toronto: Lorimer.

Global Unions. n.d. "Who Are Global Unions?" < global-unions.org/-about-us-.html>.

Godard, John. 2011. *Industrial Relations, Economy and Society.* Toronto: McGraw-Hill Ryerson.

____. 1994. *Industrial Relations, Economy and Society.* Toronto: McGraw-Hill Ryerson.

Goldfield, Michael. 1987. *The Decline of Organized Labor in the United States.* Chicago: University of Chicago Press.

Goutor, David. 2007. *Guarding the Gates: The Canadian Labour Movement and Immigration, 1872–1934.* Vancouver: University of British Columbia Press.

Graefe, Peter. 2012. "Quebec Labour: Days of Glory or the Same Old Story?" In Stephanie Ross and Larry Savage (eds.), *Rethinking the Politics of Labour in Canada.* Halifax: Fernwood Publishing.

Gramsci, Antonio. 1971. *Selections from the Prison Notebooks of Antonio Gramsci.* Edited by Quentin Hoare and Geoffrey Nowell Smith. International Publishers.

Greer, Ian. 2006. "Business Union vs. Business Union? Understanding the Split in the US Labour Movement." *Capital and Class* 90, 1-6.

Haiven, Larry. 1995. "PC 1003 and the (Non) Right to Strike: A Sorry Legacy." In Cy Gonick, Paul Phillips and Jesse Vorst (eds.), *Labour Gains, Labour Pains: 50 Years of PC 1003.* Winnipeg/Halifax: Society for Socialist Studies/Fernwood Publishing.

Hanson, S.B. 1974. "Estevan 1931." In Irving Abella (ed.), *On Strike: Six Key Labour Struggles in Canada 1919–1949.* Toronto: James Lorimer.

Harden, Joel. 2013. *Quiet No More: New Political Activism in Canada and Around the Globe.* Toronto: Lorimer.

Hargrove, Basil. 2006. *Laying It on the Line: Driving a Hard Bargain in Challenging Times.* Toronto: Harper Collins.

Harvey, Rowland Hill. 1935. *Samuel Gompers, Champion of the Toiling Masses.* London: Oxford University Press.

Hatfield, Robert. 2005. "Duty to Accommodate." *Just Labour* 5. <http://www.justlabour.

yorku.ca/Hatfield.pdf>.

Health Services and Support—Facilities Subsector Bargaining Assn. v. British Columbia, [2007] 2 S.C.R. 391, 2007 SCC 27.

Henry, Frances, Carol Tator, Winston Mattis and Tim Rees. 2000. *The Colour of Democracy: Racism in Canadian Society*, second edition. Toronto: Harcourt Brace Canada.

Heron, Craig. 2012. *The Canadian Labour Movement: A Short History*, third edition. Toronto: Lorimer.

____. 1998. "National Contours: Solidarity and Fragmentation." In C. Heron (ed.), *The Workers' Revolt in Canada: 1917–1925*. Toronto: University of Toronto Press.

____. 1996. *The Canadian Labour Movement: A Short History*, second edition. Toronto: Lorimer.

____. 1989. *The Canadian Labour Movement: A Short History*. Toronto: Lorimer.

____. 1984. "Labourism and the Canadian Working Class." *Labour/Le Travail* 13.

Holmes, John, and A. Rusonik. "The Break-Up of an International Labour Union: Uneven Development in the North American Auto Industry and the Schism in the UAW." *Environment and Planning* 23.

Horowitz, Gad. 1968. *Canadian Labour and Politics*. Toronto: University of Toronto Press.

Hospital Employees' Union, CUPE. 2011. "BC Federation of Labour Supports 'Occupy Wall Street' Movement's Call for Greater Economic Equality—Will Join October 15 Events." October 12. <heu.org/publications/bc-federation-labour-supports-"occupy-wall-street"-movement-call-greater-economic-equal>.

Hoxie, Robert. 1914. "Trade Unionism in the United States: General Character and Types." *The Journal of Political Economy* 22.

Human Resources and Social Development Canada. 2006. "Union Membership in Canada-2006."

Huot, Christian. 1998. "Unionizing the Impossible." *Canadian Dimension* 32, 5 (September–October).

Hurl, Lorna. 1988. "Restricting Child Factory Labour in Late Nineteenth Century Ontario." *Labour/Le Travail* 21: 87–121.

Iacovetta, Franca, Michael Quinlan and Ian Radforth. 1996. "Immigration and Labour: Australia and Canada Compared." *Labour/Le Travail* 38.

IWW (Industrial Workers of the World). 1905. "Proceedings of the First Annual Convention of the Industrial Workers of the World." New York, 1.

International Trade Union Confederation. 2015. "About Us." <http://www.ituc-csi.org/about-us>.

Isbester, Fraser. 1974. "Asbestos 1949." In Irving Abella (ed.), *On Strike: Six Key Labour Struggles in Canada 1919–1949*. Toronto: Lorimer.

Jackson, Andrew. 2005. *Work and Labour in Canada: Critical Issues*. Toronto: Canadian Scholars' Press.

Jackson, Andrew, and David Robinson. 2000. *Falling Behind: The State of Working Canada, 2000*. Ottawa: Canadian Centre for Policy Alternatives.

Jamieson, Stuart Marshall. 1968. *Times of Trouble: Labour Unrest and Industrial Conflict in Canada, 1900–66*. Ottawa: Supply and Services.

Karabegovic, Amela, Nachum Gabler, and Niels Veldhuis. 2012. "Measuring Labour Markets in Canada and the United States." Vancouver: Fraser Institute.

Kealey, Gregory S. 1993. "The Early Years of State Surveillance of Labour and the Left in Canada: The Institutional Framework of the Royal Canadian Mounted Police and Intelligence Apparatus, 1918–26." *Intelligence and National Security* 8, 3: 129–48.

____. 1984. "1919: The Canadian Labour Revolt." *Labour/Le Travail* 13.

____. 1976. "'The Honest Workingman' and Workers' Control: The Experience of Toronto Skilled Workers, 1860–1892." *Labour/Le Travail* 1: 32–68.

____. 1973. *Canada Investigates Industrialism: The Royal Commission on the Relations of Labor and Capital, 1889*. Toronto: University of Toronto Press.

Kealey, Gregory S., and Bryan D. Palmer. 1982. *Dreaming of What Might Be: The Knights of Labour in Ontario, 1800–1900*. New York: Cambridge University Press.

King, William Lyon Mackenzie. 1918. *Industry and Humanity: A Study in the Principles Underlying Industrial Reconstruction*. Toronto: University of Toronto Press.

Klein, Naomi. 2000. *No Logo: Taking Aim at the Brand Bullies*. Toronto: Alfred A. Knopf.

Kochan, Thomas, David Lipsky, Mary Newhart and Alan Benson. 2009. "The Long-Haul Effects of Interest Arbitration: The Case of New York State's Taylor Law." Working Paper 10-2009, School of Industrial and Labor Relations, Cornell University.

Kumar, Pradeep. 1993. *From Uniformity to Divergence: Industrial Relations in Canada and the United States*. Kingston: IRC Press.

Kumar, Pradeep, and Gregor Murray. 2006. "Innovation in Canadian Unions: Patterns, Causes and Consequences." In Pradeep Kumar and Christopher Schenk (eds.), *Paths to Union Renewal: Canadian Experiences*. Peterborough: Broadview.

Labour Branch, Human Resources and Skills Development Canada. 2005. Minimum Wage Database Introduction. Ottawa: HRSDC. <srv116.services.gc.ca/dimt-wid/sm-mw/intro.aspx?lang=eng>.

Labour Program. 2015. Work Stoppages by Jurisdiction and Year. <labour.gc.ca/eng/resources/info/datas/work_stoppages/work_stoppages_year_sector.shtml>.

Labour Program, Strategic Policy, Analysis, and Workplace Information Directorate. 2015. *Major Wage Settlements by Sector and Year*. Ottawa: Employment and Social Development Canada. <labour.gc.ca/eng/resources/info/datas/wages/wages_year_sector.shtml>.

Labour Program, Workplace Information and Research Division (WIRD). 2014. *Union Coverage in Canada, 2013*. Ottawa: Employment and Social Development Canada. <labour.gc.ca/eng/resources/info/publications/union_coverage/union_cov2013_en.pdf>.

Lambertson, Ross. 2001. "'The Dresden Story': Racism, Human Rights and the Jewish Labour Committee of Canada." *Labour/Le Travail* 47 (Spring).

Lancaster House. 2000. "Legislation in Opposite Directions: Unionization Promoted in Manitoba, Curtailed in Ontario." *Lancaster's Labour Law News* (November–December).

Langille, Brian. 1981. "The Michelin Amendment in Context." *Dalhousie Law Journal* 6.

Lavigne v. Ontario Public Service Employees Union, [1991] 2 S.C.R. 211.

Lenin, Vladimir Ilyich. 1970. *On Trade Unions*. Moscow: Progress Publishers.

Leong, Melissa. 2006. "CUPE Joins Boycott of Israel." *National Post* (May 29).

Lerner, Stephen. 2003. "An Immodest Proposal: A New Architecture for the House of Labor." *New Labor Forum* 12, 2: 8–30.

Lester, Richard. 1958. *As Unions Mature: Analysis of the Evolution of American Unionism*. Princeton: Priceton University Press.

Li, Peter. 1988a. *Ethnic Inequality in a Class Society*. Toronto: Wall and Thompson.

___. 1988b. "Capitalist Expansion and Immigrant Labour: Chinese in Canada." In B.S. Bolaria and P.S. Li (eds.), *Racial Oppression in Canada*, second edition. Toronto: Garamond.

Lipset, Seymour Martin. 1983. "Radicalism or Reformism: The Sources of Working-Class Politics." *American Political Science Review* 77: 1.

Luxton, Meg. 2001. "Feminism as a Class Act: Working-Class Feminism and the Women's Movement in Canada." *Labour/Le Travail* 48.

___. 1983. "From Ladies' Auxiliaries to Wives' Committees." In Linda Briskin and Lynda Yanz (eds.), *Union Sisters: Women in the Labour Movement*. Toronto: Women's Press.

Magna International Inc and CAW. 2007. *Framework of Fairness Agreement* (October 15).

Mansbridge, Jane, and Aldon Morris. 2001. "The Making of Oppositional Consciousness." In Jane Mansbridge and Aldon Morris (eds.), *Oppositional Consciousness: The Subjective Roots of Social Protest*, 1-19. Chicago: University of Chicago Press.

Marks, Lynne. 1991. "The Knights of Labor and the Salvation Army: Religion and Working Class Culture in Ontario, 1882–1890." *Labour/Le Travail* 28.

Marshall, Judith, and Jorge Garcia-Orgales. 2006. "Building Capacity for Global Action: Steelworkers' Humanity Fund." In Pradeep Kumar and Christopher Schenk (eds.), *Paths to Union Renewal*. Toronto: University of Toronto Press.

Martin, Christopher. 2004. *Framed! Labor and the Corporate Media*. Ithaca: Cornell University Press.

Martinello, Felice. 2000. "Mr. Harris, Mr. Rae and Union Activity in Ontario." *Canadian Public Policy* 26, 1.

Marx, Karl. 1955. *The Poverty of Philosophy*. Moscow: Progress Publishers.

___. 1947. *Wages, Price and Profit*. Moscow: Progress Publishers.

___. 1886. "Instructions for the Delegates of the Provisional General Council, The Different Questions." *Der Vorbote* Nos. 10 and 11, October and November.

Mayer, Gerald. 2004. *Union Membership Trends in the United States*. Washington, DC: Congressional Research Service.

McAlevey, Jane. 2012. *Raising Expectations (and Raising Hell): My Decade Fighting for the Labor Movement*. London: Verso.

McBride, Steven, and John Shields. 1997. *Dismantling a Nation: The Transition to Corporate Rule in Canada*, second edition. Halifax: Fernwood Publishing.

McDermott, Patricia. 1993. "The Eaton's Strike: We Wouldn't Have Missed It for the World!" In Linda Briskin and Patricia McDermott (eds.), *Women Challenging Unions*. Toronto: University of Toronto Press.

McNaught, Kenneth. 2001. *A Prophet in Politics: A Biography of J.S. Woodsworth*. Toronto: University of Toronto Press.

McQuaig, Linda. 1995. *Shooting the Hippo: Death by Deficit and Other Canadian Myths*. Toronto: Viking Press.

McQuarrie, Fiona. 2011. *Industrial Relations in Canada*, third edition. Toronto: J. Wiley.

Mehra, Natalie. 2006. "A Community Coalition in Defense of Public Medicare." In Pradeep Kumar and Christopher Schenk (eds.), *Paths to Union Renewal*. Toronto: University of Toronto Press.

Milkman, Ruth. 1987. *Gender at Work: The Dynamics of Job Segregation by Sex during World*

War II. Champaign: University of Illinois Press.

Mills, C. Wright. 1948. *The New Men of Power: America's Labor Leaders*. New York: Harcourt Brace.

Mitchell, Tom, and James Naylor. 1998. "The Prairies: In the Eye of the Storm." In Craig Heron (ed.), *The Workers' Revolt in Canada: 1917–1925*. Toronto: University of Toronto Press.

Monsebraaten, Laurie. 2014. "Ontario's Minimum Wage Jumps to $11 Sunday." *Toronto Star*, May 31. <thestar.com/news/gta/2014/05/31/ontarios_minimum_wage_jumps_to_11_sunday.html>.

Moody, Kim. 1997. *Workers in a Lean World: Unions in the International Economy*. London: Verso.

____. 1988. *An Injury to All: The Decline of American Unionism*. New York/London: Verso.

Morris, Jonathan. 1991. "A Japanization of Canadian Industry?" In Daniel Drache and Meric S. Gertler (eds.), *The New Era of Global Competition: State Policy and Market Power*. Montreal and Kingston: McGill–Queen's University Press.

Mounted Police Association of Ontario v. Canada (Attorney General), 2015 SCC 1.

Murnighan, Bill. 2003. "Organizing at a Crossroads: A Good News, Bad New Story." *Our Times*, July.

Murray, Gregor. 1995. "Unions: Membership, Structures, and Action." In Morley Gunderson and Allen Ponak (eds.), *Union–Management Relations in Canada*, third edition. Don Mills, ON: Addison-Wesley.

Nichols, Leslie. 2012. "Alliance Building to Create Change: The Women's Movement and the 1982 CUPW Strike." *Just Labour: A Canadian Journal of Work and Society* 19 (Autumn).

Noel, Alain, and Keith Gardner. 1990. "The Gainers Strike: Capitalist Offensive, Militancy, and the Politics of Industrial Relations in Canada." *Studies in Political Economy* 31.

OECD (Organisation for Economic Co-operation and Development). 2015. "Trade Union Density." *OECD.StatExtracts*. At <stats.oecd.org/Index.aspx?DataSetCode=UN_DEN#>

____. 2011. *Divided We Stand: Why Inequality Keeps Rising*. Brussels: OECD Publishing.

Ontario (Attorney General) v. Fraser, [2011] 2 S.C.R. 3, 2011 SCC 20.

Palmer, Bryan D. 2009. *Canada's 1960s: The Ironies of Identity in a Rebellious Era*. Toronto: University of Toronto Press.

____. 1992. *Working-Class Experience: Rethinking the History of Canadian Labour, 1880–1991*. Toronto: McClelland and Stewart.

Panitch, Leo. 2009. "What You Need to Know about May Day." *Rabble.ca*. <rabble.ca/news/2009/05/what-you-need-know-about-may-day>.

Panitch, Leo, and Donald Swartz. 2003. *The Assault on Trade Union Freedoms: From Consent to Coercion*, third edition. Toronto: Garamond Press.

Parenti, Michael. 1986. *Inventing Reality: The Politics of Mass Media*. New York: St. Martin's Press.

Parker, Mike, and Martha Gruelle. 1993. *Democracy Is Power: Rebuilding Unions from the Bottom Up*. Detroit: Labor Notes.

Patrias, Carmela. 2011. *Jobs and Justice: Fighting Discrimination in Wartime Canada, 1939–1945*. Toronto: University of Toronto Press.

Patrias, Carmela, and Larry Savage. 2012. *Union Power: Solidarity and Struggle in Niagara*. Edmonton: Athabasca University Press.

Peirce, Jon, and Karen Joy Bentham. 2007. *Industrial Relations*. Toronto: Prentice Hall.

Penner, Norman. 1988. *Canadian Communism: The Stalin Years and Beyond*. Toronto: Methuen.

Perlman, Selig. 1928. *A Theory of the Labor Movement*. New York: Macmiilan Co.

Peters, John. 2010. "Down in the Vale: Corporate Globalization, Unions on the Defensive, and the USW Local 6500 Strike in Sudbury, 2009–2010." *Labour/Le Travail* 66 (Fall).

Petersen, Cynthia. 2009. "Fighting It Out in Canadian Courts." In Gerald Hunt (ed.), *Laboring for Rights: Unions and Sexual Diversity Across Nations*. Philadelphia: Temple University Press.

Piven, Frances Fox, and Richard Cloward. 1977. *Poor People's Movements*. New York: Vintage.

Plourde v. Wal-Mart Canada Corp., [2009] 3 S.C.R. 465, 2009 SCC 54.

Polletta, Francesca. 2004. *Freedom Is an Endless Meeting: Democracy in American Social Movements*. Chicago: University of Chicago Press.

Pope John Paul II. 1981. *Laborem Exercens*. Rome: Papal Encyclical.

Pope Leo XIII. 1891. *Rerum Novarum*. Rome: Papal Encyclical.

Porter, Ann. 2003. *Gendered States: Women, Unemployment Insurance, and the Political Economy of the Welfare State in Canada, 1945–1997*. Toronto: University of Toronto Press.

Pratt, Renate. 1997. *In Good Faith: Canadian Churches Against Apartheid*. Waterloo: Wilfrid Laurier University Press.

PSAC v. Canada, [1987] 1 S.C.R. 424.

R. v. Advance Cutting & Coring Ltd., [2001] 3 S.C.R. 209, 2001 SCC 70.

Reed, L.S. 1966. *The Labor Philosophy of Samuel Gompers*. Port Washington, NY: Kennikat.

Reference re Public Service Employee Relations Act (Alta.) [1987] 1 S.C.R 313.

Riddell, W. Craig. 1993. "Unionization in Canada and the United States: A Tale of Two Countries." In David Card and Richard B. Freeman (eds.), *Small Differences That Matter: Labor Markets and Income Maintenance in Canada and the United States*. Chicago: University of Chicago Press.

Roberts, Wayne. 1994. *Don't Call Me Servant: Government Work and Unions in Ontario, 1911–1984*. Toronto: Ontario Public Service Employees Union.

____. 1980. "Toronto Metal Workers and the Second Industrial Revolution, 1889–1914." *Labour/Le Travailleur* 6 (Autumn).

Robinson, Ian. 1993. "Economistic Unionism in Crisis: The Origins, Consequences and Prospects of Divergence in Labor Movement Characteristics." In Jane Jenson and Rianne Mahon (eds.), *The Challenge of Restructuring: North American Labor Movements Respond*. Philadelphia: Temple University Press.

Roediger, David. 1991. *The Wages of Whiteness: Race and the Making of the American Working Class*, revised edition. London: Verso.

Rose, Joseph. 2007. "Canadian Public Sector Unions at the Crossroads." *Journal of Collective Negotiations* 31, 3.

____. 1983. "Some Notes on the Building Trades-Canadian Labour Congress Dispute." *Industrial Relations* 22, 1.

Ross, Stephanie. 2012a. "Business Unionism and Social Unionism in Theory and Practice." In Stephanie Ross and Larry Savage (eds.), *Rethinking the Politics of Labour in Canada*. Winnipeg: Fernwood Publishing.

____. 2012b. "Review of David Camfield's *Canadian Labour in Crisis: Reinventing the Workers' Movement.*" *Socialist Studies* 8, 1.

____. 2011. "Social Unionism in Hard Times: Union-Community Coalition Politics in the CAW Windsor's *Manufacturing Matters* Campaign." *Labour/Le Travail* 68 (Fall).

Ross, Stephanie, and Larry Savage. 2013a. "Introduction: Public Sector Unions in the Age of Austerity." In Stephanie Ross and Larry Savage (eds.), *Public Sector Unions in the Age of Austerity.* Halifax: Fernwood Publishing.

____. 2013b. "Not Our Dads' Unions Anymore." *Hamilton Spectator,* October 4. <thespec. com/opinion-story/4138009-not-our-dads-unions-anymore/>.

R.W.D.S.U. v. Saskatchewan. 1987. 1 S.C.R. 460.

R.W.D.S.U., Local 558 v. Pepsi-Cola Canada Beverages (West) Ltd., [2002] 1 S.C.R. 156, 2002 SCC 8.

Sack, Jeffrey. 2010. "U.S. and Canadian Labour Law: Significant Distinctions." *ABA Journal of Labor and Employment Law* 25.

Sangster, Joan. 1985. "The Communist Party and the Woman Question, 1922–1929." *Labour/Le Travail* 15.

Saskatchewan Federation of Labour v. Saskatchewan, 2015 SCC 4.

Savage, Larry. 2012. "Organized Labour and the Politics of Strategic Voting." In Stephanie Ross and Larry Savage (eds.), *Rethinking the Politics of Labour in Canada.* Winnipeg: Fernwood Publishing.

____. 2011. "Review of David Camfield, *Canadian Labour in Crisis: Reinventing the Workers' Movement.*" *Labor Studies Journal* 36, 3.

____. 2010. "Contemporary Party–Union Relations in Canada." *Labor Studies Journal* 35, 1.

____. 2009. "Labour Rights as Human Rights: Organized Labor and Rights Discourse in Canada." *Labor Studies Journal* 34, 1.

____. 2008a. "Quebec Labour and the Referendums." *Canadian Journal of Political Science* 41, 4.

____. 2008b "From Centralization to Sovereignty-Association: The Canadian Labour Congress and the Constitutional Question." *Review of Constitutional Studies* 13, 2.

Savage, Larry, and Charles Smith. 2013. "Public Sector Unions and Electoral Politics in Canada." In Stephanie Ross and Larry Savage (eds.), *Public Sector Unions in the Age of Austerity.* Winnipeg: Fernwood Publishing.

Savage, Larry, and Michelle Webber. 2013. "The Paradox of Professionalism: Unions of Professionals in the Public Sector." In Stephanie Ross and Larry Savage (eds.), *Public Sector Unions in the Age of Austerity.* Winnipeg: Fernwood Publishing.

Schiller, Bill. 1998. "Tough Labour Bill Approved Law Will Restrict Rights of Unions." *Toronto Star.* June 24.

Sears, Alan. 1999. "The 'Lean' State and Capitalist Restructuring: Towards a Theoretical Account." *Studies in Political Economy* 59.

Silver, Jim (ed.). 2014. *About Canada: Poverty.* Winnipeg: Fernwood Publishing.

____. 2000. *Solutions That Work: Fighting Poverty in Winnipeg.* Winnipeg/Halifax: Canadian Centre for Policy Alternatives–Manitoba and Fernwood Publishing.

Smith, Charles W. 2012. "Labour, Courts and the Erosion of Workers' Rights in Canada." In Stephanie Ross and Larry Savage (eds.), *Rethinking the Politics of Labour in Canada.* Winnipeg: Fernwood Publishing.

____. 2009. "Fairness and Balance? The Politics of Ontario's Labour Relations Regime, 1949–1963." Unpublished PhD thesis, Toronto: York University.

____. 2008. "The Politics of the Ontario Labour Relations Act: Business, Labour, and Government in the Consolidation of Post-War Industrial Relations, 1949–1961." *Labour/Le Travail* 62 (Fall): 109–51.

Smith, Dennis. 1967. "Prairie Revolt, Federalism and the Party System." In Hugh G. Thorburn (ed.), *Party Politics in Canada,* second edition. Toronto: Prentice Hall

Smith, Doug. 1985. *Let Us Rise: An Illustrated History of the Manitoba Labour Movement.* Vancouver: New Star Books.

Sran, Garry, James Clancy, Derek Fudge and Michael Lynk. 2014. "Why Unions Matter: Unions, Income Inequality, and Regressive Labour Laws." In Matthew Behrens (ed.), *Unions Matter: Advancing Democracy, Economic Equality and Social Justice.* Toronto: Between the Lines.

Stanford, Jim. 2001. "Social Democratic Policy and Economic Reality: The Canadian Experience." In Philip Arestis and Malcolm Sawyer (eds.), *The Economics of the Third Way: Experiences from Around the World.* Cheltenham: Edward Elgar.

____. 1999. *Paper Boom: Why Real Prosperity Requires a New Approach to Canada's Economy.* Toronto: Lorimer and Canadian Centre for Policy Alternatives.

____. 1998. "The Rise and Fall of Deficit-Mania: Public-Sector Finances and the Attack on Social Canada." In Les Samuelson and Wayne Antony (eds.), *Power and Resistance: Critical Thinking about Canadian Social Issues,* second edition. Halifax: Fernwood Publishing.

Statistics Canada. 2015a. "Consumer Price Index, Historical Summary (1995 to 2014)." <statcan.gc.ca/tables-tableaux/sum-som/l01/cst01/econ46a-eng.htm>.

____. 2015b. "Labour Force Survey Estimates (LFS), Employees by Sex and Detailed Age Group, Canada." CANSIM Table 282-0002.

____. 2014a. "Labour Force Survey Estimates (LFS), Employees by Job Permanency, North American Industry Classification System (NAICS), Sex and Age Group." CANSIM Table 282-0080.

____. 2014b. "Labour Force Survey Estimates (LFS), Employees by Union Coverage, North American Industry Classification System (NAICS), Sex and Age Group." CANSIM Table 282-0078.

____. 2014c. Labour Force Survey Estimates (LFS), Employees by Union Coverage, North American Industry Classification System (NAICS), Sex and Age Group, Unadjusted for Seasonality." CANSIM Table 282-0077.

____. 2014d. "Labour Force Survey Estimates (LFS), Employees by Union Status, Establishment Size, Job Tenure, Type of Work and Job Permanency, Canada." CANSIM Table 282-0224.

____. 2014e. "Labour Force Survey Estimates (LFS), Employees by Union Status, Sex and Age Group, Canada and Provinces." CANSIM Table 282-0220.

____. 2011a. *Aboriginal Peoples in Canada: First Nations People, Métis and Inuit.* National Household Survey Analytical Document 99-011-X.

____. 2011b. *Immigration and Ethnocultural Diversity in Canada.* National Household Survey Analytical Document 99-010-X.

____. 2006a. "Unionization." *Perspectives on Labour and Income.* Catalogue No. 75-001-XPE.

____. 2006b. *Canadian Economic Observer.* Catalogue No. 11-010 (November).

____. 2005. "Fact Sheet on Unionization." *Perspectives on Labour and Income.* Catalogue No. 75-001-X.

____. 2001. *Canadian Economic Observer, Historical Supplement 2000/01.* Catalogue No. 11-210-XPB.

____. 2000b. *Women in Canada 2000.* Catalogue No. 89-503-XPE.

____. 1996. *Aboriginal Population as a Proportion of Total Population, Canada, Provinces, Territories and Health Regions.* CANSIM Table 109-0012.

Statistics Canada and Social Science Federation of Canada. 1983. *Historical Statistics of Canada,* second edition. <statcan.gc.ca/pub/11-516-x/11-516-x1983001-eng.htm>.

Steedman, Mercedes. 1997. *Angels of the Workplace: Women and the Construction of Gender Relations in the Canadian Clothing Industry, 1890–1940.* Toronto: Oxford University Press.

Stevens, Andrew, and Doug Nesbitt. 2014. "An Era of Wildcats and Sick-outs in Canada? The Continued Decline of Industrial Pluralism and the Case of Air Canada." *Labor Studies Journal* 39, 2: 118–39.

Storey, Robert. 2005. "Activism and the Making of Occupational Health and Safety Law in Ontario, 1960–1980." *Policy and Practice in Health and Safety* 1.

____. 1983. "Unionization Versus Corporate Welfare: The 'Dofasco Way.'" *Labour/Le Travail* 12 (Fall).

Strong-Boag, Veronica. 1979. "The Girl of the New Day: Canadian Working Women in the 1920s." *Labour/Le Travailleur* 4. Repr. in Michael Cross and Gregory Kealey (eds.), *The Consolidation of Capitalism, 1986–1929: Readings in Canadian Social History* 4. Toronto: McClelland & Stewart, 1983.

Sufrin, Eileen. 1982. *The Eaton Drive: The Campaign to Organize Canada's Largest Department Store 1948 to 1952.* Toronto: Fitzhenry and Whiteside.

Sugiman, Pamela. 1992. "'That Wall's Comin' Down': Gendered Strategies of Worker Resistance in the UAW Canadian Region (1963–1970)." *Canadian Journal of Sociology* 17, 1 (Winter).

Tanguay, Brian. 2002. "Parties, Organized Interests, and Electoral Democracy: The 1999 Ontario Provincial Election." In William Cross (ed.), *Political Parties, Representation, and Electoral Democracy in Canada.* Toronto: Oxford University Press.

Thomas, Mark. 2004. "Setting the Minimum: Ontario's Employment Standards in the Postwar Years, 1944–1968." *Labour/Le Travail* 54: 49–82.

Tillotson, Shirley. 1991. "Human Rights Law as Prism: Women's Organizations, Unions, and Ontario's Female Employees Fair Remuneration Act, 1951." *Canadian Historical Review* 72, 4.

Tremblay, Louis-Marie. 1972. *Ideologies de la CSN et de la FTQ 1940–1970.* Montreal: Les Presses de l'Universite de Montreal.

Tufts, Steven. 2006. "Renewal From Different Directions: The Case of UNITE HERE Local 75." In Pradeep Kumar and Christopher Schenk (eds.), *Paths to Union Renewal: Canadian Experiences.* Toronto: Garamond.

____. 1998. "Community Unionism in Canada and Labor's (Re)Organization of Space." *Antipode* 30, 3: 227–50.

U.F.C.W., Local 1518 v. Kmart Canada, [1999] 2 S.C.R. 1083.

Unifor. 2013. "Unifor Organizing Policy." Toronto: Unifor Founding Convention, August 30–September 1. <newunionconvention.ca/wp-content/uploads/2013/08/675-Organizing-Policy-fin.pdf>.

Uppal, Sharanjit. 2011. "Unionization 2011." *Perspectives on Labour and Income.* Statistics Canada.

Vail, Bruce. 2013. "UNITE HERE and Hyatt Hotels Reach Broad Peace Agreement." *In These Times,* July 2. <inthesetimes.com/working/entry/15214/unite_here_and_hyatt_hotels_reach_broad_peace_agreement>.

Walkom, Thomas. 2010. "The Art of Reverse Class Resentment." *Toronto Star,* February 27. <thestar.com/news/insight/article/771726--walkom-the-art-of-reverse-class-resentment>.

_____. 1994. *Rae Days: The Rise and Follies of the NDP.* Toronto: Key Porter.

Warnock, John. 2005. "The CCF–NDP in Saskatchewan: From Populist Social Democracy to Neo-Liberalism." In William Carroll and Robert Ratner (eds.), *Challenges and Perils: Social Democracy in Neoliberal Times.* Halifax: Fernwood Publishing.

Wells, Donald. 1998. "Labour Solidarity Goes Global." *Canadian Dimension* 13, 2 (March–April).

_____. 1997. "When Push Comes to Shove: Competitiveness, Job Insecurity and Labour–Management Cooperation in Canada." *Economic and Industrial Democracy* 18.

Wesley, Jared. 2005. "Spanning the Spectrum: Political Party Attitudes in Manitoba." Paper presented at the annual meeting of the Canadian Political Science Association, University of Western Ontario.

White, Julie. 1993. *Sisters & Solidarity: Women and Unions in Canada.* Toronto: Thompson Educational Publishers.

Whitehorn, Alan. 1992. *Canadian Socialism: Essays on the CCF–NDP.* Toronto: Oxford University Press.

Wolf, Naomi. 2012. "Hyatt Hurts: Hotel Workers Organise Global Boycott for a Fair Deal." *The Guardian,* October 4. <theguardian.com/commentisfree/2012/oct/04/hyatt-hurts-hotel-workers-boycott>.

Yakabuski, Konrad. 2014. "A Hard Pope for Capitalists to Love." *Globe and Mail,* January 13. <theglobeandmail.com/globe-debate/a-hard-pope-for-capitalists-to-love/article16284293/>.

Yassi, Annalee. 2012. *The Effectiveness of Joint Health and Safety Committees: A Systematic Review.* Vancouver: WorkSafeBC.

Yates, Charlotte. 2006. "Women Are Key to Union Renewal: Lessons from the Canadian Labour Movement." In Pradeep Kumar and Christopher Schenk (eds.), *Paths to Union Renewal: Canadian Experiences.* Toronto: Broadview.

_____. 2004. "Rebuilding the Labour Movement by Organizing the Unorganized: Strategic Considerations." *Studies in Political Economy* 74.

_____. 2000. "Staying the Decline in Union Membership: Union Organizing in Ontario, 1985–1999." *Relations Industrielles/Industrial Relations* 55, 4.

_____. 1998. "Unity and Diversity: Challenges to an Expanding Canadian Autoworkers' Union." *Canadian Review of Sociology and Anthropology* 35, 1.

Yates, Michael. 1998. *Why Unions Matter.* New York: Monthly Review Press.

Yeselson, Rich. 2013. "Fortress Unionism." *Democracy: A Journal of Ideas* 29 (Summer).

Young, Iris Marion. 1990. *Justice and the Politics of Difference.* Princeton: Princeton University Press.

INDEX